D1606283

A Paddler's Guide

to

QUETICO PROVINCIAL PARK

Robert Beymer

Library of Congress Catalog Card Number: 85-80675
International Standard Book Number 0-933287-00-3

Printed in the United States of America

Published by W.A. Fisher Company
123 Chestnut Street — Box 1107
Virginia, Minnesota 55792-1107

To CHERYL

The best canoeing partner a man could ever hope to find!

PREFACE

Back in the spring of 1967, a teenage boy in the rolling farmland of south-central Iowa eagerly made plans for his first North Woods canoe trip. In southern Iowa, the only lakes are man-made reservoirs resulting from public works projects of the Great Depression. The rivers, when running full, are usually brown from the eroded silt of surrounding fields. The few remaining stands of hardwood forests are generally confined to narrow corridors along the meandering streams or to the tops of ridges that farmers found unsuitable for clearing and planting. It is country with its own special qualities and beauty, but hardly a haven for the wilderness canoeist. For that reason, it is understandable why that young man had generated so much excitement over an approaching canoe trip to the North Woods.

That summer he joined fourteen other members of the Indianola Explorer Post on a one-week excursion that skirted the southwest perimeter of Quetico Provincial Park. Never before had he paddled on water that was pure enough to drink, on lakes that were enveloped by a dense forest of conifers that extended without interruption as far as the eyes could see. He was impressed!

To say that that canoe trip was memorable would be a gross understatement. That one-week journey planted a seed in a young man's mind that later sprouted into a way of life. Since 1967, not one summer has passed without at least one visit to "canoe country."

For six summers during the 1970's, I guided canoe trips for Camp Northland, a private camp near Ely, Minnesota. It was my pleasure then to introduce groups of children (as I had been introduced only a few years before) to such "exotic" places as Louisa Falls, Kawnipi and Kahshahpiwi lakes, and the Maligne and Basswood rivers. During that period, my long winters were spent dreaming, scheming, staring at maps for hours on end, and planning future expeditions.

While attending the University of Northern Iowa, I met others who also looked forward to their annual Quetico trips. In Carbondale, Illinois, and Springfield, Missouri, more people revealed their love for the North Woods. Even as far away as Lakewood, Colorado, I heard of a "Quetico Club" that planned annual expeditions to the park.

It was during my employment with the Eddie Bauer Company (an expedition outfitter that "seduces" outdoor sportsmen into its stores by offering them the finest and latest in outdoor gear and clothing) when I confirmed just how MANY others spend their winters also dreaming of trips to the Quetico-Superior region of the Ontario-Minnesota border. Frequent requests were made for a guide book, but none was available. It is for all of the dreamers and planners, whose lives revolve around their annual treks to canoe country, therefore, that this book was written.

Bob Beymer
Ely, Minnesota
January, 1985

ACKNOWLEDGMENTS

Conducting research in a beautiful wilderness park is, indeed, a pleasure. But it is also a great deal of WORK. In order to update my notes (the earliest of which dated back to 1969), my wife and I paddled and portaged our way throughout most of Quetico Park during the summer of 1984. For 2½ months we slept in our Eureka Timberline tent, ate Chuckwagon dehydrated foods, walked our Old Town canoe through countless shallow creeks and carried her over miles and miles of portages, battled hordes of mosquitoes and brisk head winds, and huddled under shelter from violent storms. Throughout any and all adversities, my wife remained cheerful and supportive of the project. Without her help — the physical and moral support she rendered — this project would not have reached fruition. Special thanks and sincere appreciation go to Cheryl.

Other people have also played a role in the completion of this volume. My thanks to them also . . .

A.O. (Nick) Berglund, Jr. — Director of Camp Northland, who first gave me the opportunity to guide in Quetico Park.

A.O. (Skipper) Berglund, Sr. — Founder of Camp Northland, who shared his vast knowledge of the North Woods with me.

My associate guides at Camp Northland, whose notes and post-trip commentaries were most useful: Tim Bloom, Fred Brown, Marty Danekind, Bill Donald, Tim Nichols, and Tom Wilson.

Richard A. Smith — Chuck Wagon Foods (780 N. Clinton Avenue, Trenton, N.J. 08638), who supplied the trail foods at discount for my research trips.

Earl Fisher — W.A. Fisher Company, who supplied all of the maps used for research.

A.M. Harjula, Atikokan District Manager, Ministry of Natural Resources.

Shan Walshe — Quetico Park Naturalist, who supplied me with extensive information about the wildlife, the pictorgraphs and the history of the Park.

The knowledgeable staff of Quetico Park Rangers.

CONTENTS

Fishing on the Malign River

Introduction
to
Quetico Provincial Park

Lower Basswood Falls

"The movement of a canoe is like a reed in the wind. Silence is part of it, and the sounds of lapping water, bird songs, and wind in the trees. It is part of the medium through which it floats, the sky, the water, the shores."

Sigurd F. Olson

THE SINGING WILDERNESS

AN EXTRAORDINARY WILDERNESS

Quetico Provincial Park is among the finest canoe country in the world. Spanning a region of almost eighteen hundred square miles in western Ontario, Quetico is laced with hundreds of miles of interconnected waterways through some of the most beautiful country in the world. Except at the Dawson Trail Campgrounds, it is a roadless wilderness, preserved for those who are willing and physically able to accept the park on its own terms.

Words cannot do justice to Quetico Park. Mention the word "Quetico" to a hundred individuals who have paddled its crystalline waters and you will have conjured up a hundred different images — the eerie wailing of a loon at dusk, the gentle lapping of waves against a granite shore, a fresh breeze against one's face on a warm day in July, a chain of exquisite waterfalls, a majestic bull moose in a quiet cove, a heart-pounding struggle with a scrappy smallmouth bass, a tiny island campsite shrouded by fog in the still dawn of a crisp August morning, white clouds reflecting in a glassy lake that is just too blue to be real, or the tantalizing aroma of a succulent walleye, caught only moments before, now frying to perfection over a hot bed of glowing coals. One Ojibwa legend claims that the word "Quetico" was borrowed from a Cree term describing a benevolent spirit, whose presence was felt strongly in places of great beauty. No meaning could be more appropriate!

If this sounds like Paradise, well, at times, it is. Quetico Park sometimes shows another face, however, and the would-be visitor must also be willing to accept her in that mood. Life there is a constant challenge and not all people are suited for it. To the disgruntled former visitor, the name "Quetico" might conjure up entirely different images: hordes of voracious mosquitos and black flies viciously attacking every inch of exposed skin and even penetrating thin clothing, violent thunderstorms leveling tents and drenching sleeping bags, frustrating winds that barely allow a canoe to inch across a white-capped lake, sinking up to the knees in deep mud that smells like a thousand years of rotting sediment, rugged portages that are difficult to climb without any gear and nearly impossible with it, biting insects that are too small to see but leave welts all over the body, several days of non-stop bone-chilling drizzle that renders the wood supply noncombustible, bog-lined creeks that are too shallow to paddle through and too muddy to walk through, seven days of fishing without a single strike, or the only wildlife witnessed in ten days being the rear end of black bear dragging the only food pack into the darkness. These, too, are accurate images of Quetico Park — at times.

Administered by the Ontario Ministry of Natural Resources, Quetico Provincial Park does not cater to the novice. Indeed, its isolated interior is no place for people who are not well-versed in the ways of wilderness camping and canoeing, unless they are accompanied by an experienced guide. The resourcefulness of park visitors will determine, in large part, the park's images they remember long after their trips have ended.

For those who are ready to accept the park on her own terms, this just may be the paradise they are seeking. Today's visitors may paddle into the past and view the North Woods as it looked to the Sioux and Ojibwa tribes, and as it looked to the first white explorers who penetrated this region. Although your strength and stamina may be tested to the limit, the rewards are many. Accept the challenge of the longest and most rugged portage, and at the other end, you will find the solitude and sense of achievement that few others can experience. Paddle along the shorelines of large lakes, as the Indians did, and you will experience much more than those who charge right down the middle. Take time to explore the back bays, the tiny creeks and the bogs — that is where you will find the magnificent wildlife for which this park is known.

History

Even during the busiest summer months, Quetico Provincial Park now may be the least populated than it has ever been since man first arrived there, approximately 9,000 years ago. The canoe routes used today are the very same ones used once by the Sioux, the Assiniboine, the Ojibwa and the Cree tribes; the same routes that French and English Voyageurs used to transport their fur-laden canoes; the same routes over which settlers struggled to make new lives in the West; and the same routes by which loggers removed thousands of tons of timber. Vastly different cultures have come and gone from this region, but, after all of this, Quetico probably does not look much different now than it did 9,000 years ago.

The first "modern" peoples to inhabit the area were the Sioux, or Dakota, Indians. After possibly three thousand years of occupation, the Sioux were being pushed out of the Quetico region by the Ojibwa Indians during the latter half of the seventeenth century. During this transition of cultures, the first white man to explore the water route west of Lake Superior, Jacques de Noyon, arrived in 1688. By the time the French fur trappers and traders entered the region in the mid-eighteenth century, the Ojibwa tribes were firmly entrenched and the Sioux had been driven onto the plains. The French blended well with their Indian brothers and wholeheartedly adopted many of the Indian ways.

Originally, the French plied the waters of the Kaministikwia River and a route which carried them across Pickerel Lake and Sturgeon Lake, and then down the Maligne River to Lac La Croix. But, the establishment of trading posts by Sieur de la Verendrye between 1730 and 1750 along the (present) border route did much to foster the fur trade in the southern Quetico region. This route ultimately became the primary route used in the shuttle of pelts from the northwest hinterlands to the markets of Montreal and Europe. These wilderness lakes and streams that now symbolize a sanctuary for solitude were, for the last half of the eighteenth century, busy thoroughfares.

In 1763, the Treaty of Paris ended the French and Indian War and ousted the French from its holdings in Canada. English and Scottish fur traders replaced the French men. A fierce rivalry developed between three great fur trading companies: the Hudson's Bay Company, the North West Company and the American Fur Company. Around 1768, John Askin established a trading post at Grand Portage on Lake Superior, and for the next thirty years that site was the hub of trading activity for the North West Company. The old Kaministikwia route was abandoned and nearly forgotten until the end of the century.

In 1803, the Northwest Company moved its station from Grand Portage to Fort William, and the Kaministikwia route again became the customary route to Lac La Croix and beyond, and Grand Portage lost all significance — that is, until the United States and Great Britain signed the Webster-Ashburton Treaty of 1842, following years of disputes. That agreement established the international boundary along the "customary" route of the fur traders. The Americans claimed that the customary Voyageurs' route was up the Kaministikwia River and over the top of Hunter's Island to Lac La Croix. The British claimed the St. Louis River, far to the south, should be the border. Had the Americans won that dispute, much of Quetico Park would fall inside the United States.

In 1821 the Hudson's Bay Company absorbed the Northwest Company and dominated the region from that point on, although the fur trade was already on the decline.

In 1857, Simon J. Dawson was part of an expedition that was commissioned to survey an all-Canadian route from Lake Superior to the Red River Settlement. Dawson's trail began as a 45-mile road from Port Arthur to Shebandowan Lake. At that point, it followed an 80-mile water route to French Lake, joining the old Kaministiquia River route at Baril Portage. At the two-mile French Portage, it entered what is now Quetico Park and began its southwestern course down the Pickerel and Maligne rivers to Lac La Croix.

After the Dominion of Canada was established in 1867, violence erupted along the Red River. To establish control over the area, Lt. Col. Garnet Wolseley led an army of men in 1870 over the trail. For about twelve years after that time the route was used rather extensively by both settlers and the military. Settlers were transported by steam barges across Pickerel and Sturgeon lakes, and then down the Maligne River to Lac La Croix. A small island in Sturgeon Lake is thought to be Dawson's wood yard, where wood was cut to fuel the steam boilers. But the construction of the Canadian Pacific Railroad rendered the Dawson Trail impractical.

With the introduction of the railroad in the 1900's, logging became the dominant activity in this region. A Forest Preserve was established here in 1909, in conjunction with the establishment of Superior National Forest on the United States side of the border. In 1913, Quetico was designated a Provincial Park, but extensive logging operations continued until 1971, when public outcries put a stop to it. In the northwestern part of the park, there are still many dilapidated remnants of the logging era: old dams and sluiceways, rusted cable and long steel spikes, abandoned machinery, clearings where cabins once stood, and even an occasional rusted carcas from an antique automobile.

The Webster-Ashburton Treaty stipulated that ''all the water communications and all the usual portages shall be free and open to the use of the citizens and subjects of both countries.'' Sharing only the boundary lakes and rivers was not enough to some. Sparked by an idea dating back to the 1920's, efforts have been made on both sides of the border throughout much of this century to establish an international park. To be dedicated as a peace memorial, this park would have included much of the Quetico-Superior canoe country on both sides of the border, and it would have been administered by a joint commission. Unfortunately, there were too many political issues at stake, and the disputes were never resolved. The dreams of an international wilderness area faded into the reality of political darkness.

In 1973, Quetico was classified a ''Wilderness Park.'' Aside from an occasional rusted relic at the side of a portage or an occasional crumbling log dam at the top of a small rapids or the sawn stump of a great white pine, Quetico Park, today, looks much as it did when Jacques de Noyon first explored these waters three hundred years ago.

For an indepth examination of this region's colorful history, refer to either of Grace Lee Knute's volumes: **The Voyageur** or **The Voyageur's Highway**, both published by the Minnesota Historical Society. Also published by that Society is the most complete examination of border politics and conservation efforts: **Saving Quetico-Superior: A Land Set Apart**, by Newell Searle.

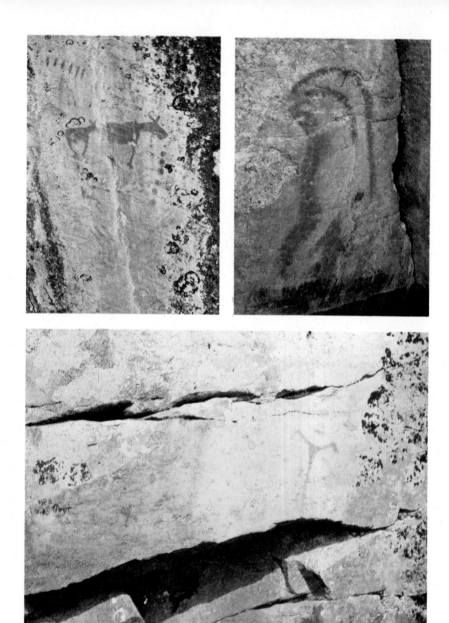

Indian paintings — left, Darky Lake; right, Quetico Lake, bottom, McKenzie Lake.

Pictographs

One of the most fascinating aspects of Quetico Park is the concentration of Indian rock paintings there. Approximately thirty "pictographs" have been discovered to date, located in all but the northeastern corner of the park. The most recent discovery was made by a trapper during the winter of 1983-84, at a remote site north of Montgomery Lake.

The age, the artists and the purpose of these paintings are all subject to speculation. No one knows for certain. Perhaps the only fact upon which everyone can agree is that they are tangible evidence of an ancient woodland culture that once inhabited this region.

The subject matter of these artists included animals that were apparently important in their lives, human figures and man-made objects, hand prints and smears, supernatural beings, and various abstractions and tally marks with no obvious meanings to modern interpreters. Fish, moose, bears, elk, heron, pelicans and a turtle are among the animals represented. A man with a gun on Darky Lake would indicate that the influence of the white man had already been felt when that painting was done. One of the supernatural beings that is represented in several places in the park is the Maymayguishi, the Indian version of an Irish leprechaun. Legends reveal that these mischievous characters would play tricks on the Indians, like stealing their fish. When pursued by the Indians, the Maymayguishi would simply dissolve into the rock. Leaving gifts of tobacco is said to be rewarded by good luck. The Mishipizhiw is another mythological creature that apparently lived underneath the water. It was responsible for whipping up sudden storms that would swamp canoes and drown its occupants. Excellent examples of both of these spirits are found at the south end of Darky Lake. Abstract Thunderbirds are also found throughout the park. This supernatural bird was capable of spawning thunder, lightning and rain.

The pictographs are reddish-brown, colored by iron oxide, and the characters portrayed are seldom more than six inches long. Usually painted just above the water line, they are often found at the base of impressive cliffs. They were probably painted within the last five hundred years, but some are much more vivid than others.

Respect the pictographs as you would an ancient manuscript, whose pages are too fragile to be touched. Study them closely and take your pictures, but please do not touch!

Locations of the pictographs are indicated on the inserted map in the back of this book. Descriptions of each site are included in the text.

Darky Lake

15

Geology

The geologic foundation of Quetico Provincial Park is among the oldest rock in the world. Believed to be as old as three billion years, these Precambrian rocks constitute the southern edge of the Canadian Shield, a massive formation that extends almost two million square miles under eastern Canada and the Lake Superior region of the United States.

Over the millions of years, this region has been subjected to every imaginable force of Mother Nature: vast inland seas where sediments were compressed into sedimentary rocks; volcanic orogenies that transformed the sedimentary rocks into metasedimentary formations; faulting and folding of thick layers of the earth's crust; intrusions of granitic magmas into the cracks and cavities created by the folds. Mountains once existed where Quetico Park now rests. Then, the processes of erosion began and continued for millions of years. Four distinct periods of glaciation occured over the last million years. After the last glacial advance and recession (the Wisconsin Glaciation, lasting from about 100,000 to 11,000 years ago), mounds and ridges of glacial debris were left intermixed with thousands of lakes and interconnecting streams — a bleak version of the same landscape that we see today.

Lakes were formed where glaciers had gouged out basins in the bedrock, or behind natural dams of glacial debris. Sometimes enormous blocks of ice would be buried under glacial debris. When they thawed, lakes formed in the resulting depressions. Meltwater drained in every direction, cascading over glacial debris, filling depressions and forming waterways between the myriad lakes.

Evidence of the Ice Age is everywhere in Quetico Park. Striations (parallel grooves) are sometimes visible on the rock ledges that were scoured by the advancing or receding glaciers. Glacial debris is widespread. Huge boulders, called erratics, are found where glaciers melted and left the rocks standing in seemingly precarious locations.

During the erosion processes, the softer metamorphic rocks of sedimentary and volcanic origin eroded more easily than the harder granite. Of the three basic bedrock types in the park, therefore, granite is, by far, the most predominant. It covers more than 70% of Quetico Park, while the metamorphic rocks cover the remaining 30% of the region. Metasedimentary formations are characteristic of the area southwest of Sturgeon Lake and the area southeast of Cache Lake. Greenstone, an ancient metavolcanic rock, is found in Quetico Park only along the Man Chain lakes and near Cullen and McKenzie lakes. The rest of the park is predominantly granite, often exposed, but usually covered by a thin veneer of glacial deposits.

More than just a pretty face, the type of bedrock that underlies an area determines, in large part, the kinds of flora and fauna that inhabit that area. Granitic soil takes a long time to accumulate and, when it does, it is highly acidic and low in nutrition. Consequently, plants and animals are few in number and diversity. The metamorphic rocks, on the other hand, break down more quickly and, when they do, the soil is less acidic and more rich in nutrients. The result here is a more productive ecosystem supporting larger numbers of animals and plants, as well as a much greater diversity.

One of the greatest distinctions of the Hunter's Island region is the domination of exposed bedrock. When the last glacier receded, a huge body of water, known as Lake Agassiz, covered a vast portion of what later became the North Woods. The bedrock on Hunter's Island was washed clean by the wave action along the shores of Lake Agassiz.

Throughout Quetico Park, faults in the earth's crust have resulted in some of the most impressive topography. Two of the most vivid examples are found along the Man Chain lakes, where the northeast-to-southwest fault line has created bluffs rising more than 150 feet above the shores, and at Agnes Lake, which is also bordered by high cliffs and ridges extending as much as 300 feet above the water.

Born millions of years ago on the floor of an island sea, radically altered by the tremendous forces of volcanic eruption and upheaval of the earth's crust, and finally carved into its present shape by the creeping pressure of the glaciers, Quetico Park has emerged as one of the most extraordinary recreational wilderness areas in the world.

Quetico Cliffs

Wildlife

THE FLORA

After the last glacier receded and the climate warmed, the first forms of life to return to Quetico Park were, most likely, mosses and lichens. Followed by ferns and flowering plants, the stark terrain left by the Ice Age gradually acquired a great variety of plant and animal life.

Lady Slipper (moccasin flower) on Saganaga Lake.

Lichens clinging to exposed bedrock are still common throughout the park. But now the region is almost entirely forested, with jack pines also clinging incredibly to the exposed bedrock, sharing the meager supply of nutrients with the lichens. Black spruce, trembling aspen, white birch, balsam fir and red and white pine are also characteristic of the northern forest. The most impressive stands of huge red and white pine are found in the center of Hunter's Island, in the region just east of McNiece Lake.

Black spruce, white cedar and tamarack are found in the wetter environs. Where the landscape is not forested, countless bogs support a large variety of plants and animals. These bogs were once shallow lakes, which, over the centuries, were slowly filled with various sediments and decayed plants and aquatic animals. Consequently, the bogs are rich in nutrients and able to support a host of plants that are unique to these spongy patches, including orchids, bog laurel, round leaved sundews, and the fascinating pitcher plant.

For a detailed investigation of the many plants that inhabit Quetico Park, refer to **Plants of Quetico and the Ontario Shield,** by Shan Walshe, Quetico Park Naturalist (Quetico Foundation, University of Toronto Press), or **Plants of the Canoe Country,** by W.Q. Loegering and E.P. DuCharme.

THE FAUNA

Perhaps nothing typifies Quetico Provincial Park better than the eerie wail of the loon, a mournful cry that every canoeing visitor expects to hear throughout his journey into the park. Likewise, the sight of a majestic bald eagle soaring above one's path creates the tingle of excitement in the soul of most visitors. In all, over ninety kinds of birds nest here during the summer. Besides the loon and the bald eagle, great blue herons, ospreys, herring gulls, Canadian jays, evening grossbeaks, ravens and red-winged black birds are commonly seen in the park. Barred owls may also be heard on still nights.

The chilling howls of timber wolves are not uncommon sounds in the northeastern part of Quetico, where the greatest concentrations of moose are also found. White-tailed deer, though fairly rare in most of the park, are rather abundant in the greenstone belt of southeastern Quetico, where there are extensive stands of white cedar for food and shelter. Other mammals found in the park include the black bear, red fox, lynx, beaver, otter, mink, fisher, muskrat, marten, weasel and red squirrel. No poisonous snakes inhabit the park — only the harmless garter snake and red-bellied snake.

Moose on Walter Lake

19

BIRDS OF PREY

Perhaps the most misidentified creatures in Canoe Country are three common birds of prey: the Bald Eagle, the Osprey and the Turkey Vulture. Soaring high above the canoe, obscurred by the glaring sun, all three may appear similar — at a glance. By the inexperienced bird-watcher, indeed, it is a temptation to label all large soaring birds as ''Bald Eagles.'' Why not? It is much more impressive to tell the folks back home about the Bald Eagles that were seen than to report sightings of Turkey Vultures! Both are common in Quetico Park, and, to a lesser degree, so is the Osprey.

To help you with positive identifications, here are a few tips.

Identifying Bald Eagles, Osprey and Turkey Vultures Overhead

OSPREY

BALD EAGLE

Soaring high overhead, all of these raptors will appear to be black underneath, and the sizes are deceptive. The quickest, easiest and most dependable identification of these birds is from their silhouettes. The Bald Eagle soars with wings in a straight plane; the wings of a Turkey Vulture are bent at an upward angle; the Osprey's wings are "kinked". Upon closer inspection, of course, you will see the white head and tail of the Bald Eagle and the white belly of the Osprey. The Turkey Vulture is dark all under, but two-toned.

TURKEY VULTURE

Fishing

Although the loon, the bald eagle or the timber wolf may symbolize the wilderness values of Quetico Park to most visitors, it is probably the tremendous fishing opportunities that lure them back to the park, summer after summer. The most sought after game fish are the lake trout, walleyes, northern pike and bass (both smallmouth and largemouth). In addition, black crappies, perch, rock bass, bluegills and sunfish are found in many of the lakes. Sturgeon may be caught in Sturgeon, Russell and Wolseley lakes and in the Maligne River.

Fishing licenses are required for all non-residents of Ontario, available at any of the Ranger Stations where the Camping and Vehicle Permits are issued. The use of live bait-fish is prohibited in Quetico Park.

Walleye from Quetico Lake

As a rule, the opportunity to catch fish is excellent almost anywhere in the park. The best periods, however, are usually in late spring (June) and early autumn (September). Lake trout and walleyes sink to the cooler water during the hot months of July and August (when most canoeists frequent the park!), requiring a bit more expertise. The voracious northern pike, on the other hand, will bite almost anything almost any time of the year.

Pests

Perhaps the only time to visit Quetico Park when there are not pests around is winter (unless you consider a temperature of $-40°$ to be a "pest"). If flying, biting insects make your life miserable, don't even CONSIDER a canoe trip to the North Woods during the months of June and July. Mosquitos are a nuisance throughout most of the summer, but they are generally the worst during the wetter and cooler period from late-May through mid-July. As the temperature rises and the ground dries up, they are not as great a nuisance. BUT that is when the black flies emerge to make the lives of human beings as miserable as possible. Biting gnats (sand flies) and no-see-ums (a tiny flying insect whose entire anatomy must be teeth!) also plague the wilderness camper, particularly during the earlier weeks of the summer.

Needless to say (but I'll say it anyway, in case someone missed the point), INSECT REPELLENT IS A MUST. So is a tent with insect-proof netting (preferably with small enough holes to prevent the attacks of no-see-ums). Wearing long-sleeved shirts (cotton turtlenecks are good) and long pants (with your socks worn over the outside of your pant legs, to seal out critters) will also contribute to the cause. Light-colored clothing may also be effective. Anything is worth a try!

As if these pests aren't enough, there are **larger** pests with which you must also contend: mice, chipmunks, scavenging birds and, yes, black bears. Unlike the insects, these curious critters are not a threat to you, directly. Instead, each and every one of them has a sincere interest in your food supply. Canadian jays will swoop down and pick the food right off your plate, if it is left unattended for a moment. Mice, chipmunks and bears are usually patient enough to wait for you to retire for the night. If your food pack is not suspended above the ground, it is a mighty susceptible target.

Making Your Campsite Bear-able

The careful camper has little, if anything, to fear by a visit from a black bear. The bears that inhabit Quetico Park are NOT the ferocious man-killers that make headlines every now and then in newspapers and on the covers of outdoor magazines. Seldom exceeding six feet in length and 300 pounds in weight, black bears are omnivorous, feeding mostly on plants and berries, but also on insects, fish and some larger animals. They are usually quite timid. Like any wild animal, however, they may be dangerous when wounded, cornered, teased or protecting their young.

In Quetico Provincial Park, bears cause the most problems in the areas that are the most heavily used. Although they wander extensively and may be seen virtually anywhere in the park, the worst areas, traditionally, have been the region around Maria Lake (from Jesse Lake to Mosquito Point on Pickerel Lake), the region surrounding Wet Lake and extending into the middle of the Falls Chain, the Crooked Lake area, and the region between North Bay of Basswood Lake and Isabella Lake. These are NOT the only areas, however, where you must take precautions.

At EVERY campsite, you should assume that bears are in your vicinity and observe the following safety precautions.

• Maintain a clean campsite. Food scraps or garbage scattered about the campsite serves as excellent bait to attract animals, including bears.

• Never take food to your tent.

• Avoid using odoriferous foods, if possible (like fresh bacon). If you can smell the pleasing aroma of bacon cooking twenty feet away, imagine how far away that scent can be detected by animal noses that are infinitely more sensitive than yours.

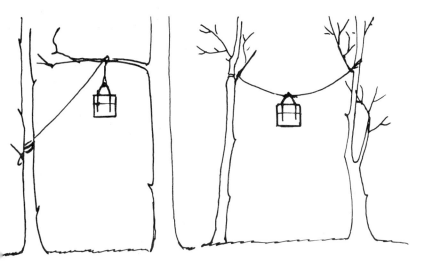

- Store your food in a separate packsack and hang it at least ten feet above the ground at night (or when you are away from camp), away from other trees and large branches. The easiest method is to find a large white pine with a sturdy horizontal branch, toss a rope over it, six or more feet away from the trunk, and suspend the pack ten feet above the ground and at least five or six feet below the branch. (See Sketch A.) If such a tree is not available (which is the case most of the time), and all you can find is a "disgusting" assortment of spruce, birch or aspen trees, none of which has a branch long enough or sturdy enough to support the weight of the pack, don't despair. Use two ropes, or one long rope, and suspend the pack between two trees. (See Sketch B.)

Remember: bears can climb trees very well. Resting your food pack on a branch against the trunk of a tree is no better than leaving it on the ground with a sign reading (in bear-ese) "Take Me."

Also remember: bears can swim, too. Camping on an island is no guarantee that you will be safe from attack.

In the event that a bear does enter your camp, remain calm and observe the following additional safety precautions.

- If cubs are present, stay far away and NEVER allow yourself to come between mom and the kids.
- Never corner the animal.
- Try banging some pots and pans together.
- If the bear is persistent and won't leave, just stay clear and let him roam about. If your food is hung securely and the campsite is clean, there is nothing to fear. On the other hand, if the bear does not leave soon, perhaps you should consider the same alternative.

One final comment: Don't let the many woodland noises keep you awake at night. The biggest noises you hear are the smallest animals: mice, squirrels and chipmunks. One of the most silent animals in the woods is the black bear. If he is out there, you won't hear his steps. Rest assured . . .

Climate

In Quetico Provincial Park, winter occupies half of each year, and the other three seasons are squeezed into a span of only six months. As far as the canoeist is concerned, spring begins when the ice goes out, usually (though not predictably) by the first of May; and autumn ends when ice returns to block the waterways, often by the end of October. Although it is sometimes possible to paddle prior to May or after October, it is not practical to PLAN such a trip.

The best time to plan a canoe trip depends upon your priorities. Early spring (May) and autumn (September-October) are normally almost free of biting insects (at least compared to the summer months), and the fishing is often the best then. But the low temperatures may be chilly, if not downright cold. In June, the temperature is milder and there are relatively few visitors in the park, but the biting insects are horrendous. July is the warmest month, usually, which results in poorer fishing and a preponderance of black flies. August is, perhaps, the most desirable month, because the temperatures are normally comfortably warm during the days and mildly cool during the nights, and the insects are not a serious problem. Consequently, visitors flock to the park at this time, and it may be congested in some areas. Without a doubt, mid-September is the most beautiful time to visit the park, when the vivid deep greens of the conifers are interlaced with the pale yellows and rich golds of the hardwoods and occasionally splashed with reds and rust-browns. Sandwiched between the sky-blue waters and a cloud-studded sky, there is surely no scene any lovelier!

Temperatures and rainfall vary, of course, throughout Quetico Park. The following statistics, based on an eighteen-year study conducted on the southern boundary of the park, were compiled by the Ministry of Natural Resources.

	MAY	JUNE	JULY	AUG.	SEPT.
Average temperature (°F.)	49.0	61.7	66.2	63.5	53.1
Average low each day (°F.)	39.0	50.9	56.0	53.3	44.7
Average high each day (°F.)	60.0	71.7	76.3	72.8	61.5
Precipitation (inches)	2.78	3.85	4.11	3.91	3.10

Loon

Who Needs A Guide Book?

After quotas were established for all of Quetico Park's entry points and a reservation system was adopted, the most popular entry points began to fill up early. Canoeists soon learned that if they didn't reserve a camping permit by the end of May (or earlier!), they might not be able to travel on the popular routes that they had always used before. This is particularly true for those wanting to enter Quetico at Prairie Portage on the U.S. border. The most popular routes through Carp, Agnes and Kashahpiwi lakes were no longer available. This also was true sometimes at the Falls Chain and Knife Lake entry points, accessible from Cache Bay. Dilemma! "Where can I go now?"

The primary purpose of this book is to answer that question. This guide briefly describes eighteen of the twenty entry points for Quetico Park and reveals many of the route options that are available to canoeists, not only in the busy southern part of the park, but also throughout Quetico.

During the four years when I sold canoeing and camping supplies for the Eddie Bauer Company, I fielded countless questions from customers wanting information about canoe routes in the Quetico-Superior region. A fairly typical question might have been: "Where can I go to experience good walleye fishing, see plenty of moose and avoid most other people — with beautiful scenery and not many portages?" That's not an easy order to fill! But I tried . . .

The information contained in this book answers the kinds of questions I heard most often. I found that most people were concerned about four basic elements of a canoe trip: 1) the scenic highlights, 2) the fishing opportunities, 3) the difficulty of portages along the route, and 4) the likelihood of seeing wildlife — particularly big game, like moose, deer and bear.

This book is NOT a complete guide to wilderness canoeing and camping. It does NOT impart all of the information you need to know to ensure a safe and happy trip. This is a "where to" guide, not a "how to" primer, although it does include some useful tips dealing with issues that are bound to affect most visitors to Quetico Park. This guide was written for the canoe camper who already knows how to fend for himself in a wilderness setting, one who knows how to live in harmony with his environment, and one who possesses competence to paddle and portage a canoe. If you cannot build a warming fire from an assortment of rain-soaked wood, if you cannot guide your way across a puzzling lake dotted with a plethora of islands, if you cannot carry your gear and canoe across a portage in two trips or less, if you don't have at least a fundamental knowledge of first aid, and if you cannot leave a campsite with no evidence of your presence there, then you really have no business entering this primitive wilderness park until you have learned those things and more.

If you need "how to" information, I suggest you read one or more of the many books that are available to you. Two, in particular, were written by Minnesotans who are quite familiar with the Quetico-Superior region:

Cary, Bob: THE BIG WILDERNESS CANOE MANUAL. New York: David McKay Company, 1978.

Drabik, Harry: THE SPIRIT OF CANOE CAMPING. Minneapolis: Nodin Press, 1984 (Second Printing).

Jacobson, Cliff: WILDERNESS CAMPING AND CANOEING. New York: E.P. Dutton, 1977.

For basic information about canoeing techniques, two of the better ones are published by the American Red Cross and the Boy Scouts of America:

Schmidt, Ernest F.: CANOEING. North Brunswick, N.J.: The Boy Scouts of America, 1977.

American Red Cross: CANOEING. Garden City, New York: Doubleday, 1977.

No one has captured the emotions of wilderness canoeing better than Sigurd F. Olson in all of his books: REFLECTIONS FROM THE NORTH COUNTRY, THE HIDDEN FOREST, WILDERNESS DAYS, OPEN HORIZONS, RUNES OF THE NORTH, THE LONELY LAND, LISTENING POINT, THE SINGING WILDERNESS.

There are those who will turn up their collective noses at this (and any other) guide book. They have no use for guides. Fine. This book was not written for them.

Others might suggest that a guide book will encourage more people to visit the park and add unwanted stress on the fragile ecology. I doubt that. In the first place, the park's Visitor Distribution Program (quota system) will ensure that too much stress is not applied to any one area within the park. In addition, I sincerely believe that, when an informed public knows the many options that are available to them, they will distribute themselves accordingly. It is for these people that this book was written.

How to Use This Guide

This book is primarily a list of **suggestions.** Thirty-one routes through eighteen entry points are described in detail, and even more alternatives are mentioned. These are, by no means, the only routes available to you. The combinations of lakes and streams and portages in this incredible system of waterways are almost limitless. You may decide to follow only a part of a suggested route. Or you may combine parts of two or more routes into your own unique loop. If this book leaves you with more ideas after you have finished reading it than you had before you picked it up, then it accomplished its purpose.

Most of the suggested routes are complete loops. They begin and end at the same location, thus eliminating the need to shuttle cars or to hire a driver to drop you off. Along the northern boundary of the park, however, Highway 11 enables shuttling without too much difficulty. A few routes were included, therefore, that start and end at different locations. This allows some excellent short trips through the extreme northern part of Quetico Park.

Any party that enters Quetico Provincial Park must have in its possession a Wilderness Camping Pemit, which permits access to the park at only one of the twenty designated entry points. This book includes routes through eighteen of those entry points:

Access to the northern part of the park:
11 Baptism Creek
12 Pickerel Lake
21 Batchewaung Lake
22 Lerome Lake
31 Cirrus Lake
32 Quetico Lake

Access to the western part of the park:
41 Threemile Lake
42 Maligne River
43 McAree Lake
44 Bottle River

Access to the southern part of the park:
51 Basswood River
52 Sarah Lake
53 Kahshahpiwi Lake
61 Agnes Lake
62 Carp Lake

27

Access to the southern part of the park:
71 Knife Lake
72 Man Chain Lakes
73 Falls Chain

Routes through two southeastern entry points were not included in this guide:
23 Mack Lake
74 Boundary Point — Saganagons Lake

Entry at Boundary Point limits one to use only Saganagons Lake. Any loop from here would carry the visitor out of the park entirely. This is not an appropriate entry point, therefore, for canoeists seeking a route into the park's interior. Some very good routes, however, are possible through Mack Lake. Unfortunately, there is no easy access to it, without the use of seaplanes. Indeed, most of the permits issued to people using the Mack Lake entry point go to those who have flown in to Powell Lake. For that reason, it was also eliminated from discussion in this book.

The routes included in this book are grouped according to accessibility: 1) those accessible from Highway 11, 2) those accessible from Lac La Croix, 3) those accessible from Moose Lake (United States), and 4) those accessible from Saganaga Lake (United States side). At the beginning of each of these chapters, general information is presented about each of these four regions, including how to get there, public campgrounds nearby, good places to clean up after the trip, accommodations in nearby communities, and more.

Lunch on Crooked Lake

28

Following this description of the general area, each entry point is briefly discussed. At a glance, the reader is able to see 1) how many groups are allowed to use the entry point each day, and 2) how much overall canoe traffic, relative to others, the entry point receives. Further discussion includes the distance and directions from the closest Ranger Station, the degree of traveling difficulty it requires, and an overview of the scenic and historic attractions that are in its vicinity.

Following the discussion of an entry point are the suggested routes that use that entry point. At a glance, one can quickly see: 1) the minimum number of days to allow, 2) the approximate number of miles to be traveled, 3) the number of different lakes, rivers and creeks to be encountered and the total number of portages required, 4) the difficulty of the route, 5) Fisher maps that cover the route, and 6) the highlights of the trip. The Introduction, then, provides a brief summary of the route, including fishing opportunities. Finally, each route is broken down into suggested days, each listing the sequence of lakes, streams and portages to be traveled. Points of special interest are described, information about the portages is included, and the better campsites are often mentioned, along with the fishing opportunities around them.

Example: **DAY 1 (11 miles): French Lake, French River, Baptism Creek,** p. 40 rods, **creek,** p. 85 rods, **creek,** p. 44 rods, **creek,** p. 53 rods, **creek, rapids, Baptism Lake,** p. 10 rods, **Trousers Lake.**

Explanation: On the first day of this route, you will paddle across French Lake to the French River, and then follow the river to Baptism Creek. Along the creek, you will encounter four portages and a rapids en route to Baptism Lake. A ten-rod portage separates Baptism and Trousers lakes. Discussion will then mention any possible pitfalls to avoid and any portages that require special attention. It will also mention the species of fish that inhabit Trousers Lake, and may direct you to a particular campsite.

How difficult a route is depends on a multitude of factors. The total mileage is not nearly as important as the frequency and length of portages, the water level of creeks or the direction of current in rivers. Other variable factors are the wind direction and how hard the wind is blowing, and even the temperature. Paddling fifteen miles across Basswood Lake on a calm day is no major chore. Replace ''calm'' with ''winds up to twenty-five miles per hour'' and the task may be extremely difficult, if not impossible. Twenty miles of paddling across a calm lake may require only seven or eight hours of mild exertion, while the ten-mile journey between Trousers and McKenzie lakes (with almost five miles of portages) may require ten hours (or more) of exhausting effort. Likewise, traveling ten miles with eight or nine portages will take much longer than traveling the same distance with only one or two carries. By the same token, a route that may seem downright rugged when traversed in five days may seem almost easy when stretched over a span of seven days. Finally, a route that may seem ''rugged'' to one group of novice paddlers might, at the same time, seem ''easy'' to a hearty group of seasoned wilderness trippers.

The recommended number of days for each route should be considered a minimum time for an ''average'' group of paddlers who don't stop and fish in evey lake they cross. If you plan to do a great deal of fishing — certainly if fishing is your primary objective — you should add at least one day for every three days suggested. Even if you don't plan to fish extensively, trips in excess of seven or eight days probably should have ''layover'' days scheduled on the itinerary. Even though you may not need a day of rest in the middle of your trip, it is a good ''safety valve'' for emergencies, such as being wind-bound on a large lake (which happens to almost everyone eventually!). In addition, foul weather, sickness or injury could slow your progress. (For these reasons, it is also a good idea to carry an extra day's supply of food, too.)

Maps

Inside the back cover of this book is a map of Quetico Provincial Park, showing all of the lakes, rivers and creeks that are mentioned in this book. The locations of all entry points, portages, Indian pictographs and points of special interest are indicated on the map. Also included are many campsite locations.

The portage distances are measured in rods. One rod equals 16½ feet. Since this is roughly the length of most canoes, it is the unit of linear measurement used most often in canoe country. Unfortunately, the length of a portage reveals nothing about its difficulty. That information is contained in the text of this book.

The red dots scattered across the map are campsites. They are not ''official'' park campsites. Since camping is permitted at any suitable location throughout the park, the Ministry of Natural Resources has never designated their locations. In fact, to show all of the potential campsites would be impossible. For visitors who carry their own cooking stove, for instance, any clearing large enough to accommodate a tent is a potential campsite. Nevertheless, there are sites throughout the park that have been used, perhaps, for hundreds of years. Most of these are ''obvious'' campsites, often situated on exposed granite outcroppings or behind sandy beaches. After a trip or two through the park, one learns to identify campsites from quite a distance away. Not all lakes have campsites, however — at least not suitable for a comfortable stay. Consequently, as one paddles a route for the first time, he cannot be certain that the lake on which he plans to camp is going to have a site there. The end result may be a long, long day of paddling and an extra portage or two that were not scheduled. That often means exhausted, irritable campers who begin to wonder why they didn't just stay at a resort all week!

To help you avoid that predicament, I have noted all of the campsites with which I am personally familiar. No doubt, there are many more available, but the red dots will help you plan accordingly.

Use the inserted map to plan your routes. Before you depart for the wilderness, however, I recommend that you purchase the F-series maps that are published on waterproof parchment by the W.A. Fisher Company. The maps have excellent detail, and the company strives to make them current and accurate. The maps required for each of the suggested routes are mentioned in the text. These maps should be available at all of the canoe trip outfitters in the vicinity of the park. They are also available at many camping stores located as far away as the Twin Cities in Minnesota. You can also order them directly from the publisher:

W.A. FISHER COMPANY
Box 1107
Virginia, MN 55792 U.S.A.

Obtaining Camping Permits

Anyone who camps overnight in Quetico Provincial Park must first purchase a Wilderness Camping Permit at the Ranger Station that has jurisdiction over the entry point used. The fee is $2.00 per person per day (Canadian funds). The Ranger Stations are located at:

French Lake	for Entry Points 11 and 12
Nym Lake	for Entry Points 21, 22 and 23
Beaverhouse Lake	for Entry Points 31 and 32
Lac La Croix	for Entry Points 41, 42, 43 and 44
Prairie Portage	for Entry Points 51, 52, 53, 61 and 62
Cache Bay	for Entry Points 71, 72, 73 and 74

For each entry point a quota has been established to limit the number of groups entering each day (each with no more than nine people). Seventy-five (75) groups may enter Quetico Park each day through all of its twenty entry points.

All of the Camping Permits may be reserved in advance, beginning March 1, by writing:

> Reservationist
> Quetico Provincial Park
> Ministry of Natural Resources
> Atikokan, Ontario   P0T 1C0

A reservation allows a party to obtain one Camping Permit for entry into Quetico Park on a particular date and at only one specified entry point. Reservations are **not** required, but they are advisable. Many of the entry points will fill up early, and you can avoid disappointment by receiving advance confirmation that a permit is being held for you.

Reservation requests must include a $20.00 reservation deposit ($2.00 is an administrative fee; $18.00 will be applied to the cost of Camping Permit) and the following information:

1) The party leader's name, address and phone number,
2) The name of at least one alternate leader,
3) The desired entry point and an alternate choice,
4) The desired starting date an an alternate choice, and
5) The number of people in your group.

The request must be received at park headquarters at least two days prior to the starting date. The Camping Permit will be held only through 5:00 p.m. (local time) on the date requested.

CROWN LAND CAMPING PERMITS

As part of a "trial program" that was initiated in 1984, non-residents visiting northwest Ontario (including the Atikokan district) are required to buy a permit to camp on Crown Land (public land outside of Quetico Provincial Park). This new regulation may affect those who wish to paddle to Lac La Croix Ranger Station. Paddling from Crane Lake or from the Namakan River bridge, it is virtually impossible to enter Quetico Park in one day. Unless you camp in the Boundary Waters Canoe Area Wilderness (which also requires a permit), you must secure a Crown Land Camping Permit prior to your departure. Along the routes included in this book, the permit will be required to camp on the Canadian side of Little Vermilion Lake, Loon Lake, Lac La Croix, Namakan Lake and Sand Point Lake, as well as along the entire course of the Namakan River and the lakes that constitute part of its course.

The permits are available at many of the fish and wildlife license issuers near the park, including outfitters. The fees for individuals and families are comparable to those charged at commercially operated campgrounds. Consult an outfitter or Park Ranger prior to departure.

ENTERING FROM THE UNITED STATES

Americans who wish to enter Quetico Provincial Park must first report to Canada Customs. A food duty is assessed on the retail value of the foods that you possess, but the first two days are duty free. If you do not know the value of your food, Customs officials will estimate the cost to be equivalent to that of food supplied by outfitters. In 1984, the duty was 17.5%; but that rate will vary. In other words, if your food is valued at $100.00, the duty will be $17.50 (Canadian funds). If your food is purchased at a grocery store, or if you are traveling light and hoping to catch most of your meals, bring receipts to prove the food's value. It is bound to be much lower than the outfitters' rates for food.

When you complete your trip and return to the United States, you must also report to U.S. Customs to be cleared for re-entry. Failure to do so may result in a federal penalty. U.S. Customs offices are located at Crane Lake, Ely and Grand Marais.

THE BOUNDARY WATERS CANOE AREA WILDERNESS

Americans who enter Quetico Park from Moose Lake or Saganaga Lake must first pass through the Boundary Waters Canoe Area Wilderness. Similar to Quetico, this park is also governed by regulations with which you must be familiar. All visitors must carry a valid Travel Permit. Those who do not plan to camp in the BWCAW, but will be passing through it en route to Quetico Park, must have a Day Use Permit. Those who plan to camp in the BWCAW are required to possess an Overnight Travel Permit. Since quotas limit the number of people who enter both of these entry points (overnight use only), it is advisable to reserve your permit in advance, to coordinate with your reservation for a Quetico Park Camping Permit. For further information about the BWCAW contact:

Forest Supervisor
Superior National Forest
Box 338
Duluth, Minnesota 55801

Louisa Lake

32

Outfitting Your Trip

For those who are embarking on their first North Country canoe trip — people with little or no gear of their own — it is a good idea to employ the services of a professional canoe trip outfitter. A good outfitter can supply EVERYTHING but your clothing and personal items. If you are inexperienced in the ways of wilderness camping, you should probably also employ an experienced guide. A remote canoe trip through a wilderness park without a guide by a group with little or no camping experience is foolish. Period.

Professional outfitters are located near all of the park's entry points. For a list of the outfitters near the entry point that you have selected, write or call one of the agencies listed below. Information pertaining to the outfitters' services and rates will be sent to you promptly.

For the northern entry points:
— Atikokan Chamber of Commerce
Box 997B
Atikokan, Ontario, Canada P0T 1C0

For the western entry points:
— Crane Lake Commercial Club
Crane Lake, Minnesota 55725
U.S.A.

For the sourthern entry points:
— Ely Chamber of Commerce
1600 E. Sheridan Street
Ely, Minnesota 55731
U.S.A.
Phone: (218) 365-6123

For the southeastern entry points:
— Tip of the Arrowhead Association
Grand Marais, Minnesota 55604
U.S.A.
Phone: (218) 387-1330 or (218) 387-2524

Park Regulations

In this day of more and more, often complicated, government laws and regulations, one may seek refuge from rules in the wilderness parks. Because of the ever-increasing human pressure on the parks, however, rules are necessary even in the wilderness. They are for the long-range benefit of all who use the parks. The following regulations apply to all visitors of Quetico Provincial Park.

1. Group size may not exceed nine (9) persons.
2. One member of each group must have in his or her possession a valid Wilderness Camping Permit, designating a specific entry point that must be used.
3. Non-burnable, disposable food and beverage containers (including returnable beverage containers for which a deposit was paid) are not permitted in the park's interior.
4. Separate groups may not camp together.
5. Use of outboard motors in the park is not allowed, except by approved members of the Lac La Croix Guides Association, who are limited to motors that don't exceed 10 h.p. used only on Beaverhouse, McAree, Minn, Quetico, Tanner and Wolseley lakes, and on the Maligne River between Lac La Croix and Tanner Lake.

6. Hunting, molesting wildlife or possessing a firearm of any kind is prohibited.

7. The use or possession of live bait-fish is not allowed.

8. Fires must be built on bare rock or mineral soil, at least three feet from any flammable materials and with no low-hanging branches overhead, as close as possible to the water's edge. Be CERTAIN that the fire is dead out before abandoning it.

9. Latrines should be dug on a flat surface in sufficiently deep soil, at least 100 feet from the water and away from the campsite. Cover it with topsoil before departure.

10. Campsites must be kept in a clean and sanitary condition at all times. Any garbage that has not been burned to ashes must be carried out of the park. After cleaning fish, place the entrails on an exposed rock away from any campsite and above the waterline, where seagulls and other scavengers can devour them.

11. Removal or damage of ANY vegetation, facility, building or monument of any kind is prohibited. Removal of artifacts is against the law. Touching the sensitive Indian pictographs is prohibited. Removing moss or birch bark from living trees is also not allowed.

12. No person is allowed to store or leave unattended any watercraft, motor, mechanical device or equipment except in a place designated for such a purpose and authorized by the superintendent.

Grave on McKenzie island

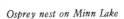

Osprey nest on Minn Lake

34

Safety

People sometimes die in wilderness parks. They die by drowning. They are killed by lightning. They die more slowly from the fatal effects of hypothermia, or "exposure." Others are more fortunate, suffering "only" from wounds that necessitate their immediate removal from the wilderness. They swing axes into their legs, and infection results. They severely sprain their ankles while traversing slippery portage trails. Their legs may be broken, pinned under the crushing weight of trees that were felled during severe thunderstorms with straight-line winds exceeding 50 mph. Yes, all of these accidents have happened in wilderness parks, like Quetico, and, unfortunately, they will continue to happen in the future. Nevertheless, statistically, you are safer in the wilderness than you are in your own home!

Most accidents probably could have been avoided by exercising more caution and using more common sense. Because of isolation and the lack of rapid communication, a wilderness park is NO PLACE TO TAKE CHANCES. Help is a long way off!

Not all of the risks associated with a wilderness canoe trip could be eliminated; nor should they be! Risks from tough physical challenges, adverse weather conditions and isolation are, very simply, part of your itinerary. To many, eliminating the risks would also be eliminating the excitement of a wilderness expedition. This is not necessary. What IS imperative is that all park visitors observe a few basic "laws" of common sense, and consider the following tips:

1. Never go ANYWHERE without a compass on your person. If it isn't in your pocket or suspended on a cord around your neck or pinned to your shirt, the chances are good that you will not have it when you need it most.
2. Always follow the map to know exactly where you are.
3. Observe and heed Mother Nature's warnings! Approaching thunderheads are a clear indication that it is time to seek shelter. Never attempt travel during a lightning storm.
4. Stay off large lakes when the waves are running high. There is no disgrace to being wind-bound. Relax and enjoy your respite from flying insects.
5. On large lakes, even when the wind is not a problem, paddle close to the shoreline as the Indians always did. Not only is it safer, but there is also much more to see.
6. Shooting rapids without first scouting them is extremely foolish! The condition of the same whitewater may vary from season to season and year to year. A rapids that was safe during a prior trip may be dangerous next time. Whenever there is ANY doubt in your mind, use the portages. When there is only one canoe for your party, it would be wise to not attempt any whitewater. Instead use ropes to "line" your canoe up or down a rapids, or use the portage.
7. On portages beware of gusty winds, both while carrying a canoe and after it is placed at either end of the trail. An empty canoe is a wind-catcher. When it is on your shoulders, a gusty wind may throw you off balance, resulting in a damaged craft and possibly an injured back or neck. A more common misfortune occurs at the ends of portage trails. When the canoe is set down at the edge of the water and the portager returns to the other end of the trail, a gusty wind may catch the canoe and toss it into the water. If this is at the top of a rapids or falls, the result may be disastrous.
8. Keep the weight low and centered in the canoe, and never stand.
9. When unaccustomed to rigorous exercise, don't push yourself to extremes. You may not be as young as you used to be!?!
10. A good first aid kit must accompany every group, and every member of the group should be familiar with it and know how to use it. Every member should know how to administer CPR.

11. If your canoe does capsize, stay with it. It floats.

12. Quetico Park is not a safe place to climb steep cliffs. There may not be a doctor at the next campsite!

13. If you must use a wood-splitting device, make it a small hatchet, and keep the blade SHARP.

14. Before departure into the wilderness, leave your itinerary with someone — relative, friend, outfitter or Park Ranger — with instructions to contact authorities if you are overdue.

15. Boil or treat your drinking water. It is the only SURE way to avoid sickness.

16. Always carry an extra paddle in each canoe. Without a spare, someday you might literally find yourself ''up a creek without a paddle!''

17. See to it that every canoeist in your group knows how to swim.

18. In the event that a serious accident does occur, send one canoe for help, if possible, or use a **heavy smoke** signal to attract attention. In all wilderness areas, the standard distress signal is a series of **three signals,** either audible or visual.

''3rd Falls'' on Falls Chain

Tips On Portaging

To many who travel in this wilderness preserve, portages can "make or break" a canoe trip. Routes are often planned to avoid the longer carries and the chains of lakes with frequent portages. In so doing, though, they may be eliminating from consideration the best routes in the Park.

It is because of this concern that I have included so much text pertaining to portage conditions in Quetico. Portages need not be a cause for great concern, however, if two fundamental rules are obeyed: 1) Know your limitations, and 2) Be prepared. Here are a few tips to consider . . .

Locating the portages: Most maps of Quetico Provincial Park attempt to show the locations of portages. Some do better jobs than others. And on any map there is always a chance that errors will exist. Until you find one, however, trust your map and compass.

In the first place, you should always know where you are — precisely. Keep your map in a plastic case, tied to the thwart in front of you (if possible) and use it to pinpoint your exact location, inch by inch, as you pick your way through the often complicated mazes of islands, bays and peninsulas that were put there for no other reason than to confuse you.

Before you cross an expanse of water en route to a portage, use your compass to translate what you see on the map to what you see in front of you. If the lake is dotted with islands, you may not be able to discern the islands from the mainland beyond. From a mile or two away, it all appears to be one solid shoreline. Confusing? Perhaps. Complicated? No. Not if you rely on your map and compass.

It is best to pinpoint where you believe the portage should be. Then "aim off" to one side of that point, to allow for error. In this manner, when you reach the opposite shoreline, you will know that you must follow it a short distance to the right, for instance, until you find the portage. If you were to aim directly for the suspected portage, and if it were not there when you arrived, you wouldn't know whether to paddle to the left or to the right in search of the illusive footpath. This results in a time delay and frustration if you search in the wrong direction.

Normally, this method will get you to the portage. Common sense and observation of the terrain is helpful, too. As you look across a lake toward where the map indicates a portage should be, watch for two things: 1) a low point on the horizon, and 2) a small clearing or "worn spot" along the shoreline. The portage is often (though, by all means, not always) over the lowest terrain. And, because others have surely used the path before you, there is always some evidence of wear on the shoreline.

When your common sense tells you (from two miles away) that a large brown spot on the distant shoreline must be the portage, but your map indicates that the trail should be 20° to the left of that point, I suggest you believe the map first. Bare rocks and slopes covered with pine needles appear much like the beginnings of trails, so don't let them fool you. If the location on the map is wrong, you can always head for the place you thought it should be in the first place.

Use your common sense when the map is wrong. I once spent the better part of an hour searching for the portage between Nest and Point Lakes. My group was paddling north, and the map indicated that the portage should be on the right side of the large peninsula forming the north shore of Nest Lake. Upon arriving at that point, however, we found no portage. We searched and searched, but there was no portage to be found. "So, now what do we do?" One suggestion was to get out our compasses (which should have already been out!) and "bushwhack" our way straight north to Point Lake. I had another idea. The two closest points between the two lakes are at the northernmost tip of the east bay and at the northernmost tip of the west bay. If the portage could not be found in the east bay (right side of the peninsula) as the map indicated, then it might just be in the west bay. Sure enough. And the trip continued after an hour's delay.

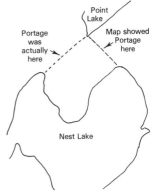

Once you have found what you believe is the beginning of a portage, how can you be sure? There are no signs in Quetico Park (as there often are in the Boundary Waters Canoe Area Wilderness across the border). If the path is so inconspicuous that it appears to be nothing more than a moose path, then it is probably just that. Remember that these portage trails have been used for hundreds of years, first by Indians, then by trappers and Voyageurs, and for the past fifty years or so, by people just like you. Even some of the most isolated and least-used portages in the Park are still obvious footpaths (though some are much more obvious than others!). If you arrive at a moose path, keep looking. There is probably a better trail nearby.

Crossing the portage: Now that you have found the trail, what is the best (least exhausting) way to get your gear across it?

Before you depart each morning from your campsite, make portage assignments. Each person in your group must have specific items that he or she is reponsible for transporting across the portages. The assignment will depend, of course, on each person's strength and stamina. How much is not so important. What is important is that every bit of gear gets carried across the portage and placed back into the canoe(s), so that nothing is lost along the way. Never assume that "if you don't carry it, someone else will." Bad habits can result in delays, if not catastrophes.

Some groups prefer to "double pack." All gear is carried across a portage trail in just one trip. If a canoe contains three packs, therefore, one person must carry a pack and the canoe. The other person carries two packs, usually one on the front and one on the back, with a paddle in each hand, and perhaps a camera bag on one side. The fishing pole(s) and spare paddle(s) can be tied under the thwarts. Life jackets will stuff into the bow and stern, not affecting the balance of the canoe (which is extremely important). I find that a "fanny pack" works best to carry the miscellaneous items that might otherwise clutter the bottom of the canoe: sun screen, mosquito repellent, sun glasses, emergency matches, trail snacks, and a handy roll of toilet paper.

If you're not excited about the idea of double packing, you are certainly not alone. There is no wilderness ethic dictating that one must strain to the maximum while on a canoe trip. If you want to carry your gear in two trips, usually the heavier packs are carried on the first trip across, and the lighter ones on the second. If the trail is long, split it up into 5-minute segments. Carry the first load for approximately five minutes. Then stop, and set your gear along the side of the trail (not right in the middle, where someone might trip over it; and not too far off the trail, where it might be overlooked later). Your shoulders and back can rest while you walk back for the next load. With the second load, walk past the first discarded load for an additional five minutes. Lay that load beside the trail, and return to the spot where the first load is waiting. Continue this "hopscotch" procedure until all gear has been transported across the portage. This is the most efficient method to make two trips and enjoy many rests along the way.

If it is possible, when making two trips, try to have someone always keep an eye on the food pack. In some of the more well-traveled parts of the Park, a bear may wait to ambush a portaging group. When the food pack is left unattended at one end of the portage, the bear will move in and grab it before the party returns. If the group hasn't assigned that pack to one individual, the group may not even notice the loss — until meal time, that is.

Comfort Tips: Canoe rests are not found along portage trails in Quetico Provincial Park, as they are on the U.S. side of the border. If you need to rest your aching shoulders along the way, look for two trees growing twelve to eighteen inches apart. Tilt your canoe back, aim the bow between the trees, and simply walk forward until the bow is wedged tight enough to hold the canoe steady. Lower the stern to the ground and walk out from under it.

Some people with slight, or outright bony, shoulders prefer to wear their life jackets while carrying the canoe. This provides an extra couple of inches of padding between your bones and yoke.

If you have arrived at a portage, and it is time for lunch, I recommend completing the portage first. A strenuous portage is much easier on an empty stomach. Besides, you will probably want to rest a spell after the trek, anyway.

When undertaking a long portage on a hot day, be sure to carry water with you. Yes, it's a little extra weight. But you will need to replenish the water that is lost from your system by sweating.

On any portage, always carry your map and compass on your person. If trails intersect, as they sometimes do, your map and compass won't do you a bit of good if they are back at the landing.

Canoe Routes of Quetico Park

The eighteen entry points that are discussed in this book are presented in the order in which they were numbered by Park authorities. Entry points numbered 11 through 32 (the northernmost) are presented first, therefore, and those numbered 41 through 73 (the southernmost) follow.

On fairly frequent occasions, my canoeing acquaintances have asked me "What is your favorite entry point?" or "What is your favorite route?" or "Which is your favorite lake?" To all of those questions I can, and do, honestly respond: "I have no favorites." Every entry point, every route, and every lake in Quetico Park is unique. Each has something special to offer its visitors. And, quite frankly, each has its trade-offs.

First, there is nothing mystical about the far-northern environs of Quetico Provincial Park. Many American paddlers seem to equate "northernmost" with "best." But what is "best" for one may not be "best" for another.

In particular, these Americans seem to believe that the farther north one paddles, the fewer people that will be encountered. Well, yes and no. Generally, the northern half of the Park does indeed receive less use than the southern half. But one reaches a "point of diminishing returns" as he paddles north (assuming that solitude and isolation are the "returns"). During the peak summer season, because of three busy entry points along the northern perimeter, there is a good deal of canoe traffic along the routes connecting French, Batchewaung and Beaverhouse lakes.

At the same time, however, it is even busier along the southern perimeter of the Park, as well as on all of the major arteries between the north and the south: Agnes Lake, the Kahshahpiwi chain, and the entire Hunter's Island Route, to name a few of the busiest routes.

The best way (indeed the ONLY way) to escape from most other canoeists is to 1) avoid the major canoe routes, and 2) cross at least one long portage. To say more would be telling . . .

Some of the most spectacular scenery in the Park is found along the American border, from the lovely southeast end of Lac La Croix to the dazzling Silver Falls. But, then, there is splendid scenery to be found throughout the Park.

Regarding wildlife, the quiet and patient observer will always see plenty, anywhere in the Park. The best section in which to see moose, however, is in the northeast. Deer, on the other hand, are most numerous in the southeast, along the Man Chain. But I have seen both throughout the park. Without a doubt, the best place in the Park to hear the haunting howl of the timber wolf is in the same northeast section where the moose are found. Between howls, however, the eerie silence is often interrupted by the menacing low roar of diesel engines on the Canadian National Railroad. The epitome of wildness is thus blended with a constant reminder of the not-too-distant civilization to which you must soon return.

What area is "best" for your trip? Only you can decide!

A Final Word

Believe it or not, these ageless waterways do change. They change from season to season, and they change from year to year. What is normally a gently flowing stream may have a dangerous swift current following a heavy rainfall. A shallow riffle that necessitates a portage in the middle of summer might have been a deep and navigable channel after the spring melt. A portage indicated as 25 rods on your map may be, in reality, 75 rods long when a beaver dam has broken and a creek becomes too dry for navigation. Occasionally, a new portage trail is cut to replace one that has become eroded from over-use or one that has become too swampy from natural changes in the environment.

In addition, sometimes an author's memory and notes fail him and a mistake is made — in spite of his constant striving for accuracy. If you have suggestions, corrections or questions pertaining to this guide book, please write the author (in care of the publisher). Thank you. Have a GREAT TRIP!

CHAPTER 3: Entry From Highway 11 — The Northern Region

Six entry points are accessible from Highway 11, which passes east-west, just north of Quetico Provincial Park. All are served by the small community of Atikokan, Ontario, and several outfitters located throughout the area.

Atikokan, which claims to be the "canoeing capital of Canada," is located at the end of Highway 11B, three miles north of Highway 11. It is approximately 130 miles west of Thunder Bay, Ontario and 90 miles east of Fort Frances, Ontario. It is a modern town with supermarkets, service stations, hotels and motels, restaurants, a laundromat, various specialty and department stores, and a municipal airport. Canadian Customs service is available at both the airport and a seaplane base located ¾ mile west of the airport. A Tourist Information Centre is located at the junction of Highways 11 and 11B. It is from this Centre that all directions lead to the six entry points in this region.

For canoeists who wish to camp in the vicinity the night prior to their scheduled trips, Dawson Trail Campgrounds are located at French Lake, 24 miles east of Tourist Information Centre. The two adjacent campgrounds contain a total of 133 campsites. The campsite fee is $6.50 per night. There is also an area in which large groups may camp. To reserve a group site, contact the Campground Superintendent at least 24 hours in advance at the park office.

There are no shower facilities at Dawson Trail Campgrounds. There are showers, however, at the Nym Lake Ranger Station. The road to Nym Lake intersects Highway 11 eighteen miles west of the French Lake road, six miles east of the Tourist Information Centre. (See "Directions" for the Batchewaung Lake Entry Point.) Any visitors may use the facility at no charge.

Camping Permits for both the Baptism Creek (#11) and Pickerel Lake (#12) entry points are issued at the French Lake Ranger Station, at the entrance to the Dawson Trail Campgrounds. Permits for the Batchewaung Lake (#21) and Lerome Lake (#22) entry points must be picked up at the Nym Lake Ranger Station. (See "Directions" for the Batchewaung Lake Entry Point.) Canoeists using either the Cirrus Lake (#31) or Quetico Lake (#32) entry points will have to stop at the Beaverhouse Lake Ranger Station (See "Directions" for the Cirrus Lake Entry Point).

Atikokan Tourist Bureau

Entry Point 11 — Baptism Creek

Daily Quota: 2

Use Level: Low

LOCATION: Baptism Creek is accessible from French Lake, in the northeast corner of Quetico Provincial Park. From the Atikokan Tourist Bureau, drive east on Highway 11, 23.8 miles to the well-marked turn-off on the right. This good road will lead you 1/10 mile south to the French Lake Ranger Station. The ranger will direct you to the best boat launching area and large parking lot, 1 ½ miles south of Highway 11.

DESCRIPTION: Dawson Trail Campground is located on the northeast shore of French Lake. In addition to the administrative offices, a museum, two large camping areas, and a public beach, a fairly large staff of Provincial employees are there to accommodate the heavy use of this site.

In spite of potential crowds in the immediate vicinity of French Lake, few visitors venture southeast of the lake, up the French River to Baptism Creek and the peaceful wilderness beyond. This is due, in part, to the restrictive quota for this entry point. Even if the quota were raised, however, it is doubtful that many voyagers would seriously consider a route from this entry point.

Route #1 is a dead-end that requires backtracking. Route #2 is recommended only for seasoned trippers who are physically able to surmount two of the Park's most formidable obstacles — the Cache Lake portages. Nevertheless, for those who don't mind backtracking or rugged portages, this entry point offers canoeists the quick escape into wilderness solitude and isolation that is not found at many other entry points.

Route #1: The Trousers Lake Trip

3 Days, 22 Miles, 3 Lakes, 1 River, 1 Creek, 10 Portages

DIFFICULTY: Challenging

FISHER MAP: F-30

HIGHLIGHTS: Solitude, Scenery

Introduction: This short route offers canoeists one of the best introductions to wilderness canoeing in Quetico Provincial Park: shallow, meandering streams, steep and rocky portages, medium-sized lakes with scenic appeal, and few (if any) other people. Allow one day each for travel to and from your campsite on Trousers Lake, and enjoy the day between by exploring the far-eastern reaches of Trousers Lake. Northern Pike are found in both Baptism and Trousers lakes.

DAY 1 (11 miles): **French Lake, French River, Baptism Creek,** p. 40 rods, **creek,** p. 85 rods, **creek,** p. 44 rods, **creek,** p. 53 rods, **creek, rapids, Baptism Lake,** p. 10 rods, **Trousers Lake.** Get an early start and allow plenty of time for this first challenging day. Although the route extends only eleven miles, you'll be paddling against the current much of the way. In addition, the portages, though relatively short, are steep in places, and generally uphill all of the way.

Though it is extremely difficult to get lost on a river, there are two good opportunities this day. The first chance to "go wrong" will come when you paddle out of French Lake. The only obvious channel draining the lake is at the southwest end of that shallow body of water. Indeed, most of the traffic leaving the canoe landing will be pointed in that direction. Bear in mind, however, that most of the expeditions departing from French Lake are heading for Pickerel Lake via the Pickerel River. The mouth of the French River is very well camouflaged and, therefore, easy to miss. To avoid this frustrating (and somewhat embarrassing!) error, stay close to the south shore and bear left as soon as you pass the sand bars that will grab at the bottom of your canoe. The river enters the lake immediately adjacent to the campground.

The second opportunity for an error that will cause even greater frustration, though less embarrassment (since there will likely be no one else around to see you; unless, of course, you are the seasoned, omniscient leader of a nervous group of neophytes), is at the junction of the French River and Baptism Creek. About three miles upstream, you will paddle past the gravel embankment of an abandoned road once used by loggers in the region. Soon thereafter, you will encounter the rivers junction. Baptism Creek continues straight ahead, while the French River enters from the left (east).

From that point on, Baptism Creek will direct you to Baptism Lake, but only after four portages and a small rapids are negotiated. All of your carries, of course, are generally uphill as you continue moving upstream. The third one, in particular (44 rods), follows a treacherous, rocky path, first uphill and then steeply down, as it bypasses a scenic waterfall on the creek. The fourth portage (53 rods), also, climbs uphill most of the way, but then drops steeply at the end. The final obstacle before Baptism Lake, a small rapids draining the lake, should not necessitate a portage. If your feet are still dry, and you want to keep them that way, you should have no difficulty lining your canoe up through the current. Otherwise, jump right in and walk your craft to the lake beyond.

Besides the designated portages, you are likely to encounter beaver dams on any part of the French River or Baptism Creek. These may require quick liftovers or the pulling of your canoe through swift channels of constricted water.

On a peninsula along the west shore of Baptism Lake, you will notice an old, dilapidated log structure. It was once used as a "way station" by park rangers who patrolled Quetico Park routinely in search of poachers.

You will find a couple of nice campsites on Trousers Lake, in the vicinity of the Cache Lake portage.

DAY 2 (Layover): Trousers Lake is known as a good lake for northerns. Good luck!

DAY 3 (11 miles): **Trousers Lake,** p. 10 rods, **Baptism Lake, rapids, Baptism Creek,** p. 53 rods, **creek,** p. 44 rods, **creek,** p. 85 rods, **creek,** p. 40 rods, **creek, French River, French Lake.** With the current going in your direction and the portages generally downhill, you will find the going to be much easier than your first day. Allow about three-fourths as much time for your return trip as you took on the first day.

Route #2: The Cache Lake Loop

6 Days, 77 Miles, 18 Lakes, 3 Rivers, 1 Creek, 20 Portages

DIFFICULTY: Rugged

FISHER MAPS: F-30, F-26, F-25, F-29

HIGHLIGHTS: Solitude, rough portages, falls and rapids, pictographs, moose sightings likely

Introduction: This varied route contains only three long portages, but they alone qualify the route for its "rugged" rating. Unfortunately, the worst part of the route comes at the beginning. The Voyageur who survives the Cache Lake portages will surely find the rest of the loop "no problem." Don't even THINK about following this route unless you are in the best of shape and you are mentally prepared for one totally exhausting day. Frankly, I recommend reversing the route, so that you will end with the Cache Lake portages, instead of starting with them. But that, of course, means that you will be entering Quetico Park via the Pickerel Lake entry point (#12), instead of through #11.

The rewards, however, may make the effort worthwhile. Whenever you enter a lake or a region of lakes that is buffered on both ends by long portages, you can be confident that few, if any, other people will be seen on that lake or in that region. Such is the case with Cache Lake, which is accessible from the north only after bog-trotting 2½ miles from Trousers Lake, and is "protected" on the south end by a portage of similar extent. Consequently, your group is likely to be alone during the first 2½ days of this expedition, all the way from the French River through the northeast end of Kawnipi's McKenzie Bay. As you paddle down into the main part of Kawnipi Lake, however, and follow a portion of the popular Hunter's Island Route, your feeling of wilderness isolation may abruptly disappear as you encounter more and more canoeists. But soon you will encounter the most spectacular scenery of the entire route as you paddle and portage your way through the scenic chain of lakes, rapids and falls that constitute the Maligne River flowage, including Snake, Splitrock and Chatterton falls. After paddling across Russell and the northeast end of Sturgeon lakes, you will once again leave much of the traffic behind as you follow the Pickerel River flowage northeast through a chain of small lakes. Continuing northeast you will follow the south shoreline of gigantic Pickerel Lake back to your origin at French Lake.

There will be plenty of opportunities for wildlife sightings throughout the route. This northeast part of the park contains more moose than anywhere else. The flat, swampy bog that characterizes much of the area between French Lake and Kawnipi Lake is ideal habitat for these majestic animals. And, wherever the moose are found, you can be sure the wolves are close by. These shy critters are seldom seen by park visitors, but they may be heard howling in their moonlit kingdom. Bald eagles and ospreys are also seen along this route. According to Shan Walshe, Park Naturalist, French, Kawnipi and Russell lakes are especially good locations to view the soaring bald eagle. On our most recent excursion, my wife and I witnessed moose, deer, otter, bald eagles, seven herons and two ospreys along the route, during the busiest time of the year for human visitation. Walleye and northern pike are found in nearly all of the lakes along the route (only northern in Baptism and Trousers lakes). Trout may also be caught in Cache, McKenzie, Olifaunt and Pickerel lakes.

DAY 1 (11 miles): **French Lake, French River, Baptism Creek,** p. 40 rods, **creek,** p. 85 rods, **creek,** p. 44 rods, **creek,** p. 53 rods, **creek, rapids, Baptism Lake,** p. 10 rods, **Trousers Lake.** (See comments for DAY 1, Route #1)

DAY 2 (10 miles): **Trousers Lake**, p. 795 rods, **Cache Lake**, p. 766 rods, **Lindsay Lake**, p. 6 rods, **McKenzie Lake.** For most people, portaging 2½ miles with canoe and packs would be a formidable task, even if it were along a highway shoulder in Kansas. And, then, to turn around and do it again after an hour's rest would be bordering on a suicidal tendency. But, add to that the fact that these two portages cross marshy terrain characterized by mud holes and bogs on paths seldom used by the human animal, and you've got a full-fledged challenge ahead of you!

The first portage, connecting Trousers and Cache lakes, has only three bad sections: the beginning, the middle, and the end! The trail first climbs over a steep, though small, hill, before settling along the edge of a swamp. A muddy and/or boggy path leads most of the way to the Cache River, which intersects the portage about a third of the way across. Unfortunately, the river is just barely deep enough and wide enough to necessitate using a canoe to ford it. The trail gains elevation and improves markedly as it nears an intersection with an old abandoned logging road, which has become overgrown with brush and saplings. At this point you will be about ⅔ of the way across. The path then continues on higher ground, crossing over a rocky ridge, before descending into another swamp for the final one hundred rods. Much of the portage is muddy or boggy, even during the drier period of late summer. Pick your path carefully to avoid sinking up to your knee. (Expletives deleted!)

The second long portage, leading to Lindsay Lake, is only slightly shorter than the first and a bit drier. The trail is relatively level most of the way, but it does pass over two small hills. Much of the trail is over bog and through mud, and dense underbrush often makes it difficult to see the path. Soon after passing a small pond on your right, the trail simply ends on the edge of a large, open bog. If you splash your way straight across it for about ten rods, however, you will pick up the trail on the other side. Another overgrown logging road will intersect the portage at about the midpoint. East of that point is a stand of elegant virgin white pines.

When following this route in this direction (clockwise), it is not difficult to find these two portages. **NOTE,** however, that two trails lead north from Lindsay Lake. The correct portage begins near the west end of the lake, straight across from the McKenzie Lake portage. Another trail begins near the northernmost tip of the lake. This trail appears to be well-enough used at the beginning, but it soon disappears. Then, the only means to find your way is by watching carefully for old blaze marks on trees or blue ribbons attached to bushes. Don't be tempted to follow this path! (Trust me. I know, because I followed the ribbons and blaze marks in August of 1984. It took me five hours to complete the portage from Lindsay Lake to Cache Lake.)

Upon reaching Lindsay Lake, don't cast your caution to the wind — not yet. That one last, little 6-rod portage to McKenzie Lake is treacherous. Large boulders make walking very difficult. So be careful!

In spite of its immensity, McKenzie Lake offers weary trippers few good campsites. There is a nice, large island site, however, about three miles south of Lindsay Lake, at the point where McKenzie bends toward the southwest.

If you have any energy left, cast a line. McKenzie Lake harbors northern, walleye and trout.

DAY 3 (16 miles): **McKenzie Lake**, p. 160 rods, **McKenzie Bay** (Kawnipi Lake), **Kawnipi Lake** (vicinity of Rose Island). Although the mileage this day is greater than that of either DAY 1 or DAY 2, don't be alarmed. Only one portage separates your departure from your destination, and that one will seem easy compared to what you have already experienced.

Before leaving McKenzie Lake, be sure to paddle past the two displays of Indian rock paintings near the center of the lake. The pictographs include representations of a canoe carrying seven men, a cross, an abstract Thunderbird symbol, and two canoes, each with three paddlers.

The 160-rod portage follows a good path that is fairly level most of the way. At the beginning, however, the trail climbs for about ten rods, and at the end it drops abruptly over a large hill.

The last time I paddled across Kawnipi Lake, it was a gloomy day indeed. A northwest wind swept across my bow. Rain squalls frequently emerged from the overcast sky. It was the kind of day in which no one really enjoys paddling. But, for some strange reason, a ''trade-off'' usually occurs on that kind of day. Those gloomy days bring out the wildlife; or, at least, I notice more wildlife. On that August day in 1984, near the north end of McKenzie Bay, I first observed a bald eagle soaring gracefully above my humble path. Further down the bay (within sight of four occupied campsites), a young deer strolled along the

Portage to Cache Lake

shoreline as I drifted silently past. Near the mouth of McKenzie Bay were seven Great Blue Herons flying in loose formation at an altitude much lower than that of the bald eagle. From my island campsite I watched a moose swim from Rose Island to Kasie Island. These were some of the rewards that made paddling in the rain thoroughly worthwhile.

DAY 4 (12 miles): **Kawnipi Lake,** p. 10 rods, **Maligne River, Rapids, river,** p. 11 rods, **Shelley Lake,** p. 60 rods, **Keats Lake,** p. 72 rods, **Chatterton Lake,** p. 76 rods, **Russell Lake.** This could be the most delightful day of the whole trip, as you carefully glide your way through the winding maze of islands, bays and peninsulas that constitute the Maligne River flowage from Kawnipi Lake to Russell Lake. Keep your compass handy, particularly on a cloudy day, because the narrow channels of Shelley Lake and northwestern Kawnipi Lake may, indeed, be confusing.

If you have time for a diversion, you might enjoy a side-trip through Montgomery Lake to the most recently discovered Indian pictographs. During the winter of 1983-84, a trapper noticed them along the westernmost creek feeding the northeast end of Montgomery Lake, a couple miles up the creek.

As you paddle down the Maligne River toward Shelley Lake you may be able to avoid the first two short portages by running or lining down the gentle rapids, depending on the water conditions and your ability and confidence to negotiate whitewater.

''Have a Smoke Portage'' drops twenty-four feet from Shelley Lake to Keats Lake, to bypass Snake Falls. Here the river splits around an island. You have a choice of the 60-rod portage on the north side, or two shorter carries on the south side. From this point on, you will notice that the trails are much more worn (hence well-traveled) than those north of Kawnipi Lake.

Split Rock Falls drops only eleven feet from Keats to Chatterton Lake, but it offers the visitor a more dramatic view of the cascade and a pleasant lunch spot besides. The portage is fairly steep and rocky in places, as the trail climbs first to a ridge high above the falls. The carry can be shortened at times to 50 rods by putting in at the base of a steep granite face and entering the river in the swift current just below the final rapids. Because this option is rather treacherous, however, the recommended portage extends an additional 22 rods to a more level (and safer) place to put in.

The portage around Chatterton Falls is located a half mile south of the cascade. Although the 76-rod trail passes over a steep hill, the path is much better than the one adjacent to the falls — and much shorter. Take the portage first, and then paddle to the base of the falls. The view is much better there than at the top. Throughout its long, tumultuous descent, Chatterton Falls drops a total of thirty-three feet en route to Russell Lake.

Several nice campsites await you on Russell. Anglers will find walleye and northern in this lake, as well as in all of the lakes paddled this day.

DAY 5 (14 miles): **Russell Lake, Maligne River,** p. 6 rods, **River, Sturgeon Lake,** p. 80 rods, **Olifaunt Lake, Pickerel River,** Rapids, **River,** p. 320 rods, **River, Fern Lake, Rapids, Pickerel River,** p. 36 rods. **Bud Lake.** Depending on the water level, that first short portage on the Maligne River will probably not be necessary. The swift current drops no more than a foot from Russell to Sturgeon Lake. Beyond Sturgeon, you will be paddling and portaging up the Pickerel River flowage all the way back to your origin at French Lake, climbing a net total of 112 feet. Most of the traffic in this area does not follow this route, most likely because of the mile-long carry that is required. (An easier route back to Pickerel Lake leads north through Twin Lakes and Dore' Lake.)

The first overland trek climbs for 25 rods, but then follows a virtually flat course for the remaining 55 rods. In early spring or after heavy rains, much of the trail will be muddy, especially just after the midpoint of the trail.

Soon after exiting Olifaunt Lake, you will encounter a small rapids in the Pickerel River around which no portage has been designated. It should pose no problem to pull your canoe up over the rock ridge causing the riffle.

The mile-long portage provides a stark contrast to the two-mile "bog trotters" you have already conquered. The path won't carry you over bogs or through muddy swamps. On the contrary, you will hike along a steep, rocky ridge high above the river much of the way. At the beginning, however, the trail follows closely along the north shore of the roaring rapids. There are access points to small pools separating the intermittent rapids, enabling one to break up the long carry into two or three shorter segments. The paddling segments are so short, however, I recommend struggling all the way on the footpath to beat the challenge more quickly. Don't be tempted to take one of the side paths leading away from the main trail. There are no shortcuts!

At the north end of Fern Lake is another small rapids around which no good portage exists. The shallower right (east) side of the river offers the best course through which to pull your canoe up the swift current. The 36-rod portage follows a good path up to Bud Lake, where you will find a couple of small campsites at its north end.

An astute angler may hook walleyes and northern in Fern, Bud or Beg lakes. Smallmouth bass, too, inhabit Fern.

DAY 6 (14 miles): **Bud Lake, Pickerel River,** p. 4 rods, **Beg Lake,** p. 33 rods, **Bisk Lake,** p. 90 rods, **Pickerel Lake, Pickerel River, French Lake.** The portage out of Beg Lake may be shortened to 28 rods by paddling against some swift current at the base of a rapids draining into Beg Lake. The good trail bypasses a scenic 10' cascade. The same is true at your final portage, around the Pickerel Dam. Because of swift water below the last set of rapids, voyagers paddling upstream may begin their portage at a smooth rock outcropping 18 rods south of the regular put-in for those heading in the opposite direction.

The Pickerel Dam was originally constructed around 1870, to raise the level of

Pickerel Lake, to enable steamboats carrying soldiers, settlers and others to pass through the river between French Lake and Pickerel Lake. In the 1920's, the dam was rebuilt by loggers, but it washed out in 1941. It was not replaced until 1956, when the concrete dam was built to allow motor boats to pass from French Lake to Pickerel Lake. In 1978, Park employees began removing stop logs from the dam, very gradually, and by 1983 all of the stop logs had been removed. This dropped the water level on Pickerel and French lakes about 4½ feet below the dammed level. As a result, you will now see numerous sand beaches along the shores of Pickerel Lake, the Pickerel River and French Lake. As a further result, you may also notice some striking discrepancies between what your map indicates and what you actually witness. What were once islands may now be the ends of peninsulas. Channels that were once navigable to canoeists may now be dead-ends. Accordingly, as you paddle through the southwest end of Pickerel Lake, it is best to chart your course through the wider channels separating the many islands in that part of the lake.

Rest stop on the Cach River

Entry Point 12 — Pickerel Lake

Daily Quota: 14

Use Level: Moderate

LOCATION: Pickerel Lake is accessible from French Lake, in the northeast corner of Quetico Provincial Park. From the Atikokan Tourist Bureau, drive east on Highway 11 23.8 miles to the well-marked turn-off on the right. This good road will lead you 1/10th mile south to the French Lake Ranger Station. The ranger will direct you to the best boat launching area and large parking lot, 1 ½ miles south of Highway 11.

To avoid paddling across French Lake and the expansive eastern half of Pickerel Lake, which is subject to the hinderance of strong west winds, expeditioners may eliminate those ten miles by starting their trips at Stanton Bay, at the north-central part of Pickerel Lake. To get there, however, one must drive over a very rough road that is not recommended for most cars. Only vehicles with high clearance are suitable, such as pickups or four-wheel-drive vehicles. After picking up your permit at the French Lake Ranger Station, drive west on Highway 11 for 6 ½ miles. One half mile after the intersection of Highway 11 with Highway 633 (to Kawene), there is a gravel road (#18) leading south (left) from the highway. From there it is a 45-minute drive over rough roads to the Stanton Bay portage, a short trail down to the bay.

DESCRIPTION: Because the Dawson Trail Campgrounds are located on French Lake, and because sixteen groups are allowed to enter Quetico Park each day by way of French Lake (14 to Pickerel, 2 to Baptism Creek) — the second greatest number for any single Ranger Station — you are likely to encounter a fair number of other parties in the vicinity of French and Pickerel lakes, especially during July and August. Nevertheless, Pickerel Lake is certainly large enough to accommodate an influx of canoeists. And, since routes lead in three different directions from the west end of Pickerel, groups are dispersed somewhat before the end of the first day.

Beware of potentially strong winds whipping up hazardous waves on Pickerel Lake. Even a moderate west wind could slow your progress enough to prevent you from reaching your scheduled destination. Finding yourself half a day behind schedule on the first day of your trip might require rerouting your entire journey. If strong west winds appear likely, you may want to consider starting your trip at Stanton Bay. Leave your car at the French Lake parking lot and have a local outfitter drop you off to start the journey.

Route #3: The Deux Riviéres Route

4 Days, 44 miles, 10 Lakes, 2 Rivers, 8 Portages

DIFFICULTY: Challenging to Easy

FISHER MAPS: F-30, F-29

HIGHLIGHTS: Rapids, 1 falls, 1-mile portage, pictographs, historic logging relics, nice scenery

Introduction: This short loop will introduce you to a good variety of Northwoods wilderness scenery. Across lakes of all sizes, you will follow the Pickerel River flowage southwest to Sturgeon Lake. Then you will return to Pickerel Lake via the Deux Riviéres system. Along the way, you will have the opportunity to view many charming rapids and a ten-foot waterfall, a fading Indian rock painting, and a sunken barge and other relics from logging operations of years gone by. If wind isn't a problem, the first and last days will be quite easy. The second day, however, could prove to be a challenge to almost any group.

Your opportunities for wildlife sightings may depend somewhat on the season and how many visitors are in this part of the Park. Don't forget to look skyward, though. Five eagle nests and four osprey nests have been sighted along this route over the past few years. Your chances of seeing either of these raptors is excellent in Quetico Park. The Deux Riviéres region, in particular, is a place that you are most likely to view wildlife. According to Shan Walshe, Park Naturalist, that is one of the best areas in the park to view moose, wolves, bald eagles and osprey.

DAY 1 (14 miles): **French Lake, Pickerel River, Pickerel Lake,** p. 72 rods, **Bisk Lake,** p. 28 rods, **Beg Lake.** Get an early start this day, so that you will make it across the wide-open expanse of Pickerel Lake before the winds pick up.

Don't be alarmed when you see a modern concrete dam at your first portage. Upon closer inspection, you will see that it is no longer in use. Originally built around 1870 by Simon Dawson to raise the level of Pickerel Lake and thus allow steamboats carrying soldiers and settlers to pass through the Pickerel River between French and Pickerel lakes, it was rebuilt by loggers during the 1920's. After it washed out in 1941, the dam was not replaced until the concrete dam was constructed in 1956. Between 1978 and 1983, the stop logs were gradually removed from the dam to allow the water to return to its natural level, 4½ feet below the dammed level. That is why you saw so many sand beaches along the shores of both French and Pickerel lakes. Now those beaches offer an almost unlimited potential for campsites along the shores of Pickerel Lake.

On a busy day in August,1984, I observed thirty-five other canoes between French Lake and the Pickerel Dam. Ours, though, was the only one to follow the route of the Pickerel River.

The first portage bypasses Pickerel Dam and the rapids below it. If you find the current to be too swift at the end of your 72-rod carry, you may want to continue your trek an additional 18 rods to a smooth rock outcropping further downstream. A similar condition exists at the 28-rod portage around a 10′ cascade, where there is a 5-rod extension at the end of the regular portage.

An osprey nest has been sighted near the narrows at the east end of Beg Lake. Although I have not witnessed it, I have observed two osprey soaring over the south shore of Beg Lake.

DAY 2 (9 miles): **Beg Lake,** p. 4 rods, **Pickerel River, Bud Lake,** p. 36 rods, **Pickerel River, Rapids, Fern Lake, Pickerel River,** p. 320 rods, **River, Rapids, River, Olifaunt Lake,** p. 80 rods, **Sturgeon Lake.** You may wish to run or line your canoe down the first short rapids, eliminating the 4-rod "liftover." After the 36-rod portage out of Bud Lake, there is another short rapids flowing into Fern Lake. Under normal conditions, it can be easily run by following the main channel on the west (right) side of the river. Watch carefully, however, for submerged boulders that may grab your canoe.

The biggest challenge of the trip is the mile-long portage that follows. This rugged, rocky trail first climbs steeply from the river's edge. It follows a high ridge for half a mile, but then it drops down and follows closely the north shore of the turbulent river. There are access points to pools separating several rapids that enable canoeists to break up the long hike into two or three shorter carries. The paddling segments are so brief, however, that I find it easier to simply portage the entire 320 rods without a break. Keep on the main path, which is easy to discern. Occassional side trails are not shortcuts, but frustrating diversions.

Soon after putting in, there is another short rapids over a rock ledge where no portage exists. Run or line your canoe right down the middle of the current, watching carefully for hidden rocks.

The final portage is a "piece of cake" compared to what you have already experienced. It is level most of the way, before dropping seventeen feet over the last 25 rods. In early spring and after heavy rains, though, count on mud! The worst stretch is a 10-rod mud puddle just before the midpoint of the trail.

Sturgeon Lake serves as an intersection for several good routes. Consequently, you may want to find a campsite as early as possible. There are several near the north end of the lake.

DAY 3 (10 miles): **Sturgeon Lake, Deux Rivières, Twin Lakes,** p. 142 rods, **Doré Lake,** p. 97 rods, **Pine Portage Bay** (Pickerel Lake), **Pickerel Lake.** Deux Rivières is a rather shallow stream that may be blocked by beaver dams along its winding course. Deux Rivières portage, connecting Twin and Doré lakes, has been renovated in recent years. The old trail, which began on the east (right) side of the river, has been replaced by a newer trail that begins on the west (left) side of the river. About midway across, it joins the old trail. Keep to the left, or you may end up back on Twin Lakes. The portage is well-maintained and well-traveled. But there are three major mud holes, with some cordurory scattered about (to cling to when you sink up to your neck!?!).

As soon as you push away from the portage, begin to watch for a sunken barge along the south shoreline of Doré Lake. This craft was used by settlers moving west over the Dawson Route. Surveyed in 1857 by Simon Dawson, this route followed part of the Kaministikwia fur trade route which passed through the center of present Quetico Park. It was used primarily in the 1870's to carry settlers and soldiers between Prince Arthur's Landing, Ontario and Fort Garry, Manitoba.

Further east on the south shore, across from a small island, is a faded Indian pictograph. There appears to be the representation of a canoe among the indistinct figures. The rock painting is difficult to locate, however, and not one of the better displays in Quetico Park.

Pine Portage begins and ends at sandy beaches, and it follows a good path over a small hill in between. Laying on the beach at the east end of the portage are more rusted relics from Dawson's operations: parts of a metal steam engine and a saw mill. This was called Steamboat Bay, and is believed to be where Dawson built some of his barges.

There are a couple of island campsites southeast of Emerald Island, in the main part of Pickerel Lake.

DAY 4 (11 miles): **Pickerel Lake, Pickerel River, French Lake.** With a prevailing southwest breeze, you can sail most of the way back to the French Lake landing.

Relics on Pine Portage

Route #4: The Sturgeon Lake Loop

7 Days, 82 Miles, 16 Lakes, 1 River, 2 Creeks, 19 Portages

DIFFICULTY: Challenging to Easy

FISHER MAPS: F-30, F-29, F-24, F-25

HIGHLIGHTS: Outstanding variety of scenery, 1-mile portage, lovely Jean Creek, 3 huge lakes

Northern caught in Sturgeon Lake

Introduction: Were it not for the second day, this route would have to be classified as a fairly easy trip. On two days, you will have no portages at all. And, over the entire loop, only three carries are longer than 100 rods. Not even a seasoned Voyageur, though, should get bored on this multifaceted trip.

From French Lake, you will paddle across big Pickerel Lake and down the Pickerel River flowage to Sturgeon Lake. A full, uninterrupted day of paddling will push you most of the way across this enormous, awesome lake. Abruptly, then, you will find yourself on tiny Jean Creek, leading you north through Burntside Lake to Jean Lake. At Quetico Lake, you will steer an easterly course through Oriana, Jesse and Maria lakes and back to sprawling Pickerel Lake. Hopefully, a southwest breeze will gently nudge your canoe all the way back to your origin at French Lake.

The variety of lakes and streams along the route provides a perfect change of pace throughout the scenic journey. Just when you become weary from uninterrupted paddling on a long lake, you find yourself in a region of small lakes, meandering streams and moderate portages on which to stretch your legs.

Breakfast on Sturgeon Lake

Anglers will also find a variety of fishing opportunities. Trout dwell in the depths of Pickerel, Olifaunt, Burntside, Jean and Oriana lakes. Smallmouth bass inhabit Pickerel, Fern, Olifaunt, Sturgeon, Burntside and Jean lakes. And, in all of the lakes along the route, you can cast your line for walleyes and northern pike.

DAY 1 (14 miles): French Lake, Pickerel River, Pickerel Lake, p. 72 rods, Bisk Lake, p. 28 rods, Beg Lake. (See comments for DAY 1, Route #3.)

DAY 2 (9 miles): Beg Lake, p. 4 rods, Pickerel River, Bud Lake, p. 36 rods, Pickerel River, Rapids, Fern Lake, Pickerel River, p. 320 rods, River, Rapids, River, Olifaunt Lake, p. 80 rods, Sturgeon Lake. (See comments for DAY 2, Route #3.)

DAY 3 (14 miles): Sturgeon Lake, Sturgeon Narrows, Sturgeon Lake. You need not put on your boots this morning.

Ranger cabin on Burntside Lake

There won't be a single portage all day. You will be paddling on an historic route, the northernmost stretch of the Hunter's Island Route. Legends say that, on a quiet night, you may still hear the laughter and songs of the French-Canadian Voyageurs who made this lake part of their fur trading highway.

Sturgeon Lake was a veritable highway during the 1800's. The Dawson Trail extended across the lake, and the steam barges plied the waters then. The long island southwest of Scripture Island was the reputed site of Dawson's wood yard. It is likely that wood was cut there to power the steam engines on his barges. At the southwest end of the lake, close to the portage, a boiler was discovered submerged in the water. It can be mistaken for a large, flat rock. But, when the light is right, the door gives it away. It was one of Dawson's boilers that burned the wood to generate steam in a barge on Sturgeon Lake.

Beach on Jean Lake

The island west of Dawson's wood yard is said to be the site of McLaren's Post, an old Northwest Company trading post. All that remains now is a low, but discernible, mound where the trading post once stood.

Impressive sand beaches along the shores are testimony to the pulverizing action of waves against the Precambrian rock, caused by prevailing southwest winds whipping across this enormous expanse of water. If you awake to the roar of a strong southwest wind, you might as well go back to sleep. You won't be the first to wind-bound on Sturgeon Lake. As on any lake of this magnitude, it is wise to arise with the sun (or before) and get an early start on the day.

Plan to camp near the west end of the lake and save Jean Creek for the next day. There are no campsites on the creek.

Anglers will find a large assortment of fish in Sturgeon Lake. Walleyes, northern, sturgeon, smallmouth bass, suckers, saugers, whitefish and herring have all been reported.

DAY 4 (10 miles): **Sturgeon Lake**, p. 40 rods, **Jean Creek**, p. 21 rods, **Creek**, p. 18 rods, **Creek**, p. 9 rods, **Creek**, p. 22 rods, **Rouge Lake, Jean Creek, Burntside Lake**, p. 80 rods, **Jean Lake.** You will be paddling upstream on Jean Creek, but there is virtually no current with which to contend. Although the portages are frequent, none is difficult. Beaver dams and the level of the creek may pose more serious problems. If the water level is high enough, you may be able to eliminate the 21-rod carry, by paddling or walking your canoe through the rock-strewn stream. In 1984 there was a broken beaver dam just upstream from here, and the water level was quite low between it and the next 18-rod portage. Nevertheless, you are sure to find this to be a very pretty and serene part of the route.

At the north end of Burntside Lake, next to the 80-rod portage, is an old cabin. This was used by Park Rangers early in the history of the Park, as they patrolled throughout the winter for possible poachers. Cabins were once distributed throughout the Park, a day's journey apart, so that Rangers could travel lighter and not worry about a shelter for the evening.

There are a few very nice campsites on Jean Lake, located on peninuslas in the northern part of the lake. This is a converging point for routes from several entry points. So, during the busier weeks of late summer, it is wise to claim your campsite early. Then cast your line for one of the trout, walleyes, northern or bass that inhabit this beautiful lake. Jean's bottom is deceiving. At one point, near a peninsular campsite in the north part of the lake, the lake is so shallow that one can walk 20 or 30 rods out into the lake and still be only knee deep. On the other hand, parts of the lake are deep enough to satisfy lake trout.

DAY 5 (12 miles): **Jean Lake**, p. 30 rods, **Conk Lake**, p. 19 rods, **Quetico Lake**, p. 32 rods, **Oriana Creek**, p. 20 rods, **Oriana Lake**, p. 133 rods, **Jesse Creek, Rapids, Jesse Lake.** On this day, you will continue paddling on long, lovely lakes. From Conk Lake the water cascades a scenic thirty feet down to Quetico Lake, where hills rise nearly 200 feet from its shores — an inspirational first look at Quetico Park for those who enter from Beaverhouse Lake, bordering Quetico on the west.

On Oriana Creek you'll see the broken remains of an old log dam at the top of the first rapids. Beaver dams spring up along this creek, so be prepared for a short liftover, in addition to the two easy portages mentioned.

In July of 1984, I was fortunate to view three bald eagles soaring above Oriana Lake. At first they were low enough to receive a positive identification with the naked eye. As I watch with admiration, they soared higher and higher until they were but three minute specs on a blue canopy. Finally they were engulfed by fluffy white clouds.

Cedar Portage, connecting Oriana and Jesse lakes, is uphill most of the way, climbing 130 feet before dropping slightly to Jesse Lake. The trail follows a good, dry path, however.

No sooner do you put in and begin paddling than another small rapids obstructs your course. It appears that most people pull their canoes up through it. Depending on the water level, a portage here would extend only one to five rods.

Most of the campsites on Jesse Lake are in the eastern half. Walleyes and northern pike lurk beneath its surface. Listen on a silent night for timber wolves in the area.

DAY 6 (12 miles): **Jesse Lake, p.** 145 rods, **Maria Lake, p.** 43 rods, **Pickerel Lake.** Your next-to-the-last portage of the trip is also the second longest. It is fairly level and well maintained, but in early spring or after heavy rains the trail will be muddy. The worst mud holes are at 30, 60 and 100 rods down the path. Board walks and corduroy, however, have been constructed to make fording easier.

Your last portage follows an excellent path downhill to Pickerel Lake. In 1984, Park Rangers warned campers to be wary of a bear and her two cubs who were ''working the portages'' around Maria Lake. Visitors were advised to not camp on the lake. Canoeists passing through, likewise, should not leave their food packs unattended.

If you camp in the vicinity of the east end of Long Island, you will have about eleven miles left to complete this route.

DAY 7 (11 miles): **Pickerel Lake, Pickerel River, French Lake.** If gentle west winds prevail, this should be an easy conclusion to an outstanding canoe trip. Watch for an eagle's nest that has been reported on Lookout Island.

Another Route Suggestion

6-Day Loop: Begin Route #2 at the Pickerel Lake Entry Point, and take the loop counter-clockwise, concluding down the French River. In this direction, canoeists will be able to challenge the Cache Lake portages near the end of the route, when food packs are lighter and participants a bit stronger.

Entry Point 21 —
Batchewaung Lake

Daily Quota: 10
Use Level: Heavy

LOCATION: Batchewaung Lake is located a scant eight miles (by air) from Atikokan. From the Atikokan Tourist Bureau, drive east on Highway 11 5.8 miles to its intersection with the Nym Lake road. A good sign is located across from the turn-off; but there is no advance warning, so be alert. Turn right and follow this paved road ¾ mile. Just prior to reaching a marked "Y" intersection in the paved road, a gravel road appears on the left (east side of the road). Turn left there and drive ½ mile on this good gravel road to the Nym Lake Ranger Station. A large parking lot beyond the Ranger Station accommodates the heavy use received by Batchewaung Lake entrants to the Park. Access to the lake is at a long dock 15 rods downhill from the southeast corner of the parking lot. Batchewaung Lake is one portage south of Nym.

DESCRIPTION: At the far end (south) of the parking area is a "courtesy house" with modern toilets, sinks and shower facilities. This is available at no charge to canoeists tripping in Quetico Park.

Perhaps because of its proximity to Atikokan, or maybe because of its central location on the north side of Quetico Provincial Park, Batchewaung Lake is the most popular entry point for those entering the Park from the north. Its popularity is more likely attributed to the fact that so many excellent routes may begin there. Without much difficulty, canoeists may travel southwest toward Beaverhouse Lake, south toward Sturgeon Lake, or southeast to Pickerel Lake.

Nym Lake provides a beautiful starting point for a trip. It is located entirely outside the boundaries of the Park, however. Cabins sit on many of the islands, and motor boats may be seen and heard across the lake. Near the Ranger Station is a Ministry of Natural Resources heliport that is the hub of air traffic over the Park.

Nym Lake Ranger Station

Route #5: The Nym-French Route

3 Days, 28 Miles, 4 Lakes, 1 River, 1 Portage

DIFFICULTY: Easy

FISHER MAPS: F-29, F-30

HIGHLIGHTS: Beautiful scenery, Only one portage

Introduction: This short, scenic route offers canoeists an excellent, easy opportunity to experience Quetico for the first time. After only one, well-maintained half-mile portage into the Park, it is then clear sailing all the way to French Lake. Upon entering Pickerel Lake from Batchewaung Lake, you will steer an easterly course across the entire length of this expansive, attractive body of water. From the east end of Pickerel, a short paddle up the Pickerel River will take you to your conclusion near the Dawson Trail Campgrounds on French Lake.

Although most of the route is across Pickerel Lake, there are so many bays, channels and islands forming the western half of this huge lake, you will feel like you are paddling on several interconnected smaller lakes instead of just one. This creates a much more interesting paddling environment for a Quetico neophyte.

The fishing opportunities are numerous. Trout, walleye, northern and perch are found in all of these Quetico lakes. Smallmouth bass and sauger are also known to exist in Pickerel Lake.

DAY 1 (7 miles): **Nym Lake,** p. 168 rods, **Batchewaung Lake, Little Batchewaung Bay** (Pickerel Lake). Your trip's only portage is long enough, but it is very well-traveled and equally well-maintained. It crosses over mildly rolling terrain for the first 120 rods, then drops rather steeply for 30 rods, before leveling off at a potentially muddy part of the trail, and then terminating at a large gravel beach. (Don't be tempted to take the two shorter portages to and from Jump Lake. The trails are poor, and very steep in places!)

Batchewaung Lake is every bit as beautiful as Nym, and without civilization to detract from its natural splendor. If the wind is a prevailing westerly, you will certainly want to hug the northwest shore.

You will find numerous campsites along Little Batchewaung Bay and, a bit further, at the north end of Batchewaung Bay.

DAY 2 (11 miles): **Little Batchewaung Bay** (Pickerel Lake), **Batchewaung Bay** (Pickerel Lake), **2 Rapids, Pickerel Narrows, Pickerel Lake.** There are two small rapids draining Batchewaung Bay into Pickerel Narrows. When the water level is up, you should have no problem gliding down the narrow channels. During low-water periods, however, you may have to step out of your canoe and walk your craft between the cluster of boulders. Beyond that point, you may notice discrepancies between the map's information and your own observations. Between 1978 and 1983, the Pickerel Dam, located at the south end of Pickerel Lake, was dismantled. This action reduced the water level to its original state, four to five feet lower than it had been for most of the previous century, when information was gathered for most of the maps. The result is that maps may indicate islands which are now peninsulas. What were once open channels are now blocked. These errors surely won't result in life-threatening adventures for you, but it is a frustrating nuissance to paddle into a dead-end bay when you think you are taking a shortcut. Steer a course through the widest channels, and don't consider yourself lost if an island turns out to be a peninsula.

Another result of the dam dismantling project (that's d-a-m) is the "clean" rocky shoreline and frequent sand or gravel beaches all the way from Nym-Batchewaung portage to the public swimming beach at French Lake. Many good campsites now exist

Putting in at Nym Lake

Batchewaung Lake

where there was none before. Plan to camp in the vicinity of Long Island to Lookout Island.

DAY 3 (10 miles): **Pickerel Lake, Pickerel River, French Lake.** If there is a wind this day, it will, most likely, be at your back. That is why this route is planned from west to east. If a gale is pushing at your back, however, don't cast caution aside and sail off into the fury. A strong tail wind across a long stretch of water may be more treacherous, and more deceiving than a strong head wind. Stay close to shore and get off the lake if giant rollers are more than you can comfortably handle.

Obviously, this route ends many miles from its origin. There are three good parking areas at French Lake, at which to leave your car(s).

On One-Way Routes

Most of the routes recommended in this Guide begin and end at the same point. This eliminates the need to shuttle cars between two different beginning and ending points.

If this Guide were limited to only round-trip loops, however, some excellent one-way routes would be omitted. One-way trips are no problem, if you remember these two tips:

Shuttling cars: If your group does its own shuttling, don't forget to leave your canoe carrier(s) with the car(s) being left off at the ending point. If your group consists of four people, two cars and two canoes, for instance, you may save a great deal of time at the end of your trip by having a two-canoe carrier on the car left at the end of the route. If that car is not too small, you may be able to load up all of your gear, with both canoes, and drive back for your other car.

Being dropped off: If you pay an outfitter to deliver you and your gear, have the outfitter drop you at the beginning of the route and leave your car(s) at the end. In this manner, you won't be obligated to a deadline. Instead of planning to meet an outfitter at an access point after a trip, at a pre-designated time, you will have the freedom of knowing that your car(s) will be waiting there regardless of when you pull in.

Both of these subtle points are obvious to a seasoned canoe tripper. They are points that a novice should consider.

Route #6: The Lonely-Maria Loop
5 Days, 51 Miles, 11 Lakes, 1 River, 1 Creek, 13 Portages

DIFFICULTY: Challenging
FISHER MAPS: F-29, F-25, F-24
HIGHLIGHTS: Good variety, Wildlife potential, pictograph, historic relics

Introduction: For strong trippers, this scenic loop could easily be completed in four days, at thirteen miles per day. Five days, however, will allow sufficient time for fishing, exploring the back bays for wildlife, and simply absorbing the pleasing scenery along the course. The loop begins the same as Route #5. Just east of Pickerel Narrows, however, you will steer toward the south and then portage into Pickerel's Pine Portage Bay. From there, you will follow a southwesterly course, through Doré and Twin Lakes, to big Sturgeon Lake. After half a day's paddling across the narrow northeast part of this historic lake, you will veer north. Between Lonely and Maria lakes you'll have a good opportunity to witness big game, including moose and bear, or hear timber wolves howling on a still, moonlit night. Portaging north from Maria Lake, you will again be paddling on Pickerel Lake, and the last day will be a reverse of the first.

During the peak season, in July and August, you are not likely to escape from all other people — anywhere along this loop. In the vicinities of Batchewaung Bay and Sturgeon lakes, in particular, Park visitors tend to congregate at night. It is wise to get early starts each day and find your campsites before late afternoon.

Anglers will have opportunities to catch virtually any species of game fish known to Quetico Park. Trout lurk in the depths of Batchewaung, Pickerel, Doré and Walter lakes. Walleyes and northern pike are found anywhere along the route (except no walleyes in Doré). Smallmouth bass, perch, sturgeon, herring and other species are also living in various waters along the way.

On still evenings, it is not unsual to hear timber wolves howling in the vicinity of Maria, Jesse and Elizabeth lakes. If you are fortunate enough to hear them, as I have, this spine-chilling occasion will not soon be forgotten!

Merganzers on Pickerel Lake

DAY 1 (11 miles): **Nym Lake,** p. 168 rods, **Batchewaung Lake, Little Batchewaung Bay** (Pickerel Lake), **Batchewaung Bay** (Pickerel Lake), **2 Rapids, Pickerel Narrows.** (See comments for DAY 1, Route #5.) Plan to camp just after the two small rapids, north of Mosquito Point, where there are several sites from which to choose.

DAY 2 (11 miles): **Pickerel Narrows, Pickerel Lake,** p. 28 rods, **Pine Portage Bay** (Pickerel Lake), p. 97 rods, **Doré Lake,** p. 142 rods, **Twin Lakes, Deux Rivieŕes, Sturgeon Lake.** If you prefer paddling to portaging, that first easy portage (28 rods) may be bypassed by paddling an additional three miles through the mouth of Pine Portage Bay. Pine Portage (97 rods) begins and ends at sand beaches, and follows a very good path over a low hill en route to Doré Lake. On the east side of the portage you will see antique relics of Simon Dawson's steamboat industry; parts of a metal steam engine and a saw mill. This was called Steamboat Bay, and is believed to be where Dawson built some of his barges.

Likewise, at the southwest end of Doré Lake, just east of Deux Rivieŕes Portage, you may see an old barge submerged just below the surface of the lake. This craft was used by settlers and soldiers moving west over the Dawson Route in the 1870's. Before reaching that point, however, you may enjoy looking for a faint display of Indian rock paintings located on the south shore of the lake, across from a small island. The pictograph appears to be the likeness of a canoe, among a small group of indistinct figures.

Deux Rivières portage offers the first real challenge of the day. Although it is well-maintained and quite well-traveled, there are three bad mud holes on the trail. Corduroy has been placed over the mud to keep you from sinking up to your eye brows, so watch your step! The old, original portage trail has been replaced by a better trail that does not cross over the river. Whenever the trail splits, take the right path leading to higher and drier ground.

The north and south parts of Twin Lakes are separated by a narrow, shallow channel. No portage should be necessary there. Along the course of the river, however, you may find it necessary to pull over a beaver dam or two.

The Deux Rivières region is teeming with wildlife. According to Shan Walshe, Park Naturalist, this is one of the best areas in the park to encounter moose, wolves, bald eagles and osprey.

There are several campsites on Sturgeon Lake, in the vicinity of just west of the Olifaunt Lake portage. If you are ahead of schedule, stop anyway. There aren't many good sites in Sturgeon Narrows. But, then, if you can make it all the way to the north end of Scripture Island, there is a truly outstanding campsite on the northeast shore of the lake. It can accommodate several tents.

DAY 3 (12 miles): **Sturgeon Lake, Sturgeon Narrows, Sturgeon Lake,** p. 20 rods, **Lonely Creek,** p. 24 rods, **Lonely Lake.** This will prove to be one of the easiest days of the whole trip. After a long stretch of paddling over the narrowest part of Sturgeon Lake, you will encounter two very easy portages leading into and then out of Lonely Creek. It is a very pretty scene along the creek. The bottom is sand, and the creek is filled with ''angel hair'' bending gracefully with the current.

If you have arrived at Lonely Lake in late July, when blueberries are ripe, look for a large patch along the north shore of the lake.

There aren't many campsites on Lonely Lake. One at the north end of the lake is large enough for a couple tents. If it is still early in the afternoon, you might want to continue on to Walter Lake, where a beautiful site is located on an island in the middle of the lake.

DAY 4 (11 miles): **Lonely Lake, Lonely Creek,** p. 24 rods, **Creek,** p. 7 rods, **Walter Lake,** p. 48 rods, **Elizabeth Lake,** p. 165 rods, **Jesse Lake,** p. 145 rods, **Maria Lake,** p. 43 rods, **Pickerel Lake, 2 Rapids, Batchewaung Bay** (Pickerel Lake), **Little Batchewaung Bay** (Pickerel Lake). Almost half of the portages for this entire 5-day route are contained in this 11-mile stretch. Only two present much of a challenge, though. The first one (24 rods) climbs steeply on a rocky path for the first 5 rods, before leveling off and then descending to Lonely Creek. The 48-rod trail also climbs uphill for the first 40 rods, but it is not too steep. The half-mile portage to Jesse lake is the worst. It is quite rocky and generally uphill at the beginning. There are several mud holes in the path (the worst near the midpoint of the trail), but sufficient corduroy has been placed over the mud to keep you from sinking — too far. The slightly shorter portage to Maria Lake is fairly level, but it also has potential to be quite muddy at times. Fortunately, the trail is well-maintained, with board walks and corduroy over most of the mud holes. In contrast, your final portage of the day follows an excellent path, and it is also downhill most of the way.

On our last visit to this area in 1984, my wife and I enjoyed several wildlife sightings along the route. Blueberries were ripe, and the animals were enjoying them more than we were. At the north end of Lonely Lake a young black bear was seen browsing on a sun-drenched patch of berries, not more than twenty rods from an occupied campsite. At the south end of Walter Lake, a family of merganzers was also dining on those juicy blueberries — a sight I had never witnessed before. Our presence caused great commotion, since the birds were several yards up from the shore, away from their aquatic security blanket. Still chuckling from the sight of their flustered behavior, we paddled quietly around the bend, steering northward to our next portage. While passing a small bay on the left, we were delighted to see a large — very large -bull moose browsing (no, not on blueberries) on the succulent aquatic vegetation on the shallow bottom of the calm bay. Regardless of how often we see moose in the North Country, we always look on with awe. The moose embodies the true spirit of wilderness for which Quetico Park has earned so much esteem. That night, we both awakened from deep sleeps to the chilling sounds of timber wolves howling in their distant kingdom. It was the perfect conclusion to a memorable day in the wilderness.

DAY 5 (6 miles): **Little Batchewaung Bay** (Pickerel Lake), **Batchewaung Lake,** p. 168 rods, **Nym Lake.** This, of course, should look familiar. You'll be reversing the route you followed on the first day. With only six miles to travel, you should get back to the Nym landing in plenty of time to take advantage of the "courtesy house" there. Enjoy your hot shower!

Jean Lake

Route #7: The Twin-Jean-Jesse Loop

6 Days, 70 Miles, 14 Lakes, 1 River, 3 Creek, 18 Portages

DIFFICULTY: Challenging

FISHER MAPS: F-29, F-25, F-24

HIGHLIGHTS: Good variety, pictograph, historic relics, 3 serene streams, 2 huge lakes

Introduction: This popular route combines the first two days from Route #6 and the last four days of Route #4 to create an interesting combination of large and small lakes, lovely creeks and portages of little consequence. Upon reaching Pickerel Lake from Batchewaung, you will steer an easterly course through Pickerel Narrows. Then you will head south and southwest, through Doré and Twin Lakes, to gigantic Sturgeon Lake. Near its west end, you will leave the windy world of Sturgeon Lake and enter the winding wilderness of Jean Creek. After paddling north through Burntside and Jean lakes, you will bear to the east on Quetico Lake and continue through Oriana, Jesse and Maria lakes. From there you will portage back to Pickerel Lake and return to Nym Lake by reversing the same route that you followed on the first day.

Avid anglers should probably allow an extra day to adequately explore the waters along the route. On the other hand, an experienced crew of strong paddlers could easily complete the journey in five days (some in four).

DAY 1 (11 miles): **Nym Lake,** p. 168 rods, **Batchewaung Lake, Little Batchewaung Bay** (Pickerel Lake), **Batchewaung Bay** (Pickerel Lake), **2 Rapids, Pickerel Narrows.** (See comments for DAY 1, Route #5.) Plan to camp just after the two small rapids, north of Mosquito Point, where there are several sites from which to choose.

DAY 2 (11 miles): **Pickerel Narrows, Pickerel Lake,** p. 28 rods, **Pine Portage Bay** (Pickerel Lake), p. 97 rods, **Doré Lake,** p. 142 rods, **Twin Lakes, Deux Riviéres, Sturgeon Lake.** (See comments for DAY 2, Route #6.)

DAY 3 (14 miles): **Sturgeon Lake, Sturgeon Narrows, Sturgeon Lake.** (See comments for DAY 3, Route #4.)

DAY 4 (10 miles): **Sturgeon Lake,** p. 40 rods, **Jean Creek,** p. 21 rods, **Creek,** p. 18 rods, **Creek,** p. 9 rods, **Creek,** p. 22 rods, **Rouge Lake, Jean Creek, Burntside Lake,** p. 80 rods, **Jean Lake.** (See comments for DAY 4, Route #4.)

DAY 5 (12 miles): **Jean Lake,** p. 30 rods, **Conk Lake,** p. 19 rods, **Quetico Lake,** p. 32 rods, **Oriana Creek,** p. 20 rods, **Oriana Lake,** p. 133 rods, **Jesse Creek, Rapids, Jesse Lake.** (See comments for DAY 5, Route #4.)

DAY 6 (12 miles): **Jesse Lake,** p. 145 rods, **Maria Lake,** p. 43 rods, **Pickerel Lake, 2 Rapids, Batchewaung Bay** (Pickerel Lake), **Little Batchewaung Bay** (Pickerel Lake), **Batchewaung Lake,** p. 168 rods, **Nym Lake.** (See comments for DAY 6, Route #4.)

Entry Point 22 — Lerome Lake

Daily Quota: 3
Use Level: Low

LOCATION: Lerome Lake is the closest canoe access to the town of Atikokan. From Atikokan Tourist Bureau, drive west on Highway 11 for 5½ miles to an unmarked intersection on the left (south) side of the highway. Watch carefully, since there is no sign to warn you of the upcoming turn-off. By the time you see Lerome Lake, you will have already driven too far. The dirt access winds its way for a quarter mile down to the edge of the lake. Although there is no clearly designated parking area near the landing, you will see a few scattered clearings that will accommodate the few people who park at this point of entry.

DESCRIPTION: In spite of its close proximity to Highway 11 and to Atikokan, Lerome Lake is used by relatively few canoeists en route to Quetico Park. The Park boundaries are actually nine miles south of this canoe access point, but you certainly won't be sacrificing any "sense" of wilderness as you paddle south over these lovely lakes and scenic streams. In fact, I rate this route as one of the more interesting ways to reach Quetico Park, characterized by smaller lakes, meandering creeks, three short portages and a couple of longer carries. After one short day, you will have an excellent idea of what tripping in Quetico Park is all about. You will see a few cabins on Lerome Lake, and one on Cole Lake, but the wild scene is unspoiled everywhere else.

Route #8: The Lerome-to-Nym Route

3 Days, 30 Miles, 11 Lakes, 3 Creeks, 9 Portages

DIFFICULTY: Challenging
FISHER MAPS: F-28, F-29
HIGHLIGHTS: Good variety, Sue Falls, pictograph, 1-way trip

Introduction: This short route is an excellent introduction to canoeing in Quetico Provincial Park. After paddling down the Lerome chain of lakes and creeks to Cirrus Lake, you will portage south to Kasakokwog Lake and then steer easterly. From Kasakokwog, you will continue eastbound, across McAlpine Lake and the east end of Pickerel Lake to Batchewaung Bay. From there, you will paddle northeasterly through Little Batchewaung Bay and Batchewaung Lake to your destination at Nym Lake. Since this is not a round-trip loop, of course, you will have to make arrangements before departure to have your car(s) waiting at the Nym Lake Ranger Station, 12½ miles by road from your origin. See "On One-Way Routes."

If this is your first trip into the Park, you may want to stretch it over four days, or even five. Cirrus Lake has a reputation as a good walleye lake. In fact, anglers will find that species in all of the Quetico lakes along this route. In addition, trout may be caught in Cirrus, McAlpine and Batchewaung lakes. Northern pike and perch also inhabit Cirrus, Kasakokwog and Batchewaung lakes.

DAY 1 (10 miles): Lerome Lake, p. 6 rods, (Unnamed lake), p. 19 or 134 rods, Jackfish Creek, Bewag Lake, p. 26 rods, Lark Lake, p. 22 rods, Cirrus Creek, Cole Lake, Cirrus Creek, p. 175 rods, Cirrus Lake. That 6-rod portage isn't as easy as it might seem. The path climbs steeply to the lake above Lerome. The next carry could be very easy, or a real challenge, depending on the water level of Jackfish Creek. If the beavers have been cooperating, you'll have an easy carry of only

Cirrus River above Sioux Falls

19 rods. Late in the summer, however, you probably should plan to "bog trot" an additional 115 rods. When this is necessary, after the good path ends, continue hiking along the left (southeast) side of the creek for 43 rods. At that point, if you see a trail in the tall grasses continue to bear left (heading nearly due south), ignore it! Instead, plot a course straight west and cautiously pick your way across the bog for about 72 more rods, where the creek should be deep enough to float a loaded canoe. Be on the look for water pockets hidden underneath thin layers of matted grass. A 175-pound man carrying 100 pounds of gear will sink quickly up to his thighs if he steps into such a hole. How do I know? First, I saw it happen right here in August of 1984. Second, it has happened to me elsewhere. One tip: Tie your boot laces tightly before crossing the bog. In the unfortunate event that you sink up to your knees (or higher!), you will surely want your boot to stay on your foot when the extraction process begins.

After completion of that carry, you should have little trouble the rest of the way, although the 22-rod trail may be hard to locate. It starts near the west end of a long beaver dam, and may be muddy near the beginning.

In 1984 a small beaver dam blocked Cirrus Creek, in a narrow channel between two rock bluffs. It merely requires a quick "liftover," if you are unable to "run" it.

The final portage is nearly level for the first 132 rods. Then it drops steeply down to Cirrus Lake. After the first 11 rods (an extension to the original portage trail, caused by a beaver dam), the portage follows an excellent path.

After completing the portage, load up and paddle a quarter mile west to view Sue Falls, where Cirrus Creek plunges over 100 feet to Cirrus Lake.

There are several campsites in the vicinity of Sue Falls.

DAY 2 (12 miles): **Cirrus Lake,** p. 190 rods, **Kasakokwog Lake, McAlpine Creek,** p. 4 rods, **Creek, McAlpine Lake,** p. 260 rods, **Batchewaung Bay** (Pickerel Lake). That first long portage will get your blood circulating in a hurry. It passes over a large hill that requires climbing nearly 150 feet, before steeply descending to Kasakokwog. The trail follows a good path much of the way, however. Just watch out

65

for slippery rocks on a wet day and a potentially muddy stretch about midway across the portage.

After paddling up McAlpine Creek, you will come to a small rapids where there was once an old log dam. Some remnants still remain there from the logging operations of Shelvin Clark back in 1921 and 1922.

McAlpine Lake is very shallow and littered with large tree stumps at its west end. Paddle along the north shoreline on your way to the next portage. Before reaching the portage, you will pass a small rock cliff on which an Indian pictograph has been painted, including a spiral abstraction.

McAlpine Portage, though over ¾ of a mile long, is a "highway." Park Rangers refer to it as "the garden walk." Over the path of an old logging road, the trail crosses gently rolling terrain, ascending gradually a total elevation of 80 feet from McAlpine Lake to Batchewaung Bay.

There are several campsites at the north end of the Bay. During the busiest times of the summer, however, this area receives many visitors from popular Nym Lake. So you may want to find your campsite early then.

DAY 3 (8 miles): **Batchewaung Bay** (Pickerel Lake), **Little Batchewaung Bay** (Pickerel Lake), **Batchewaung Lake,** p. 168 rods, **Nym Lake.** You'll find your last portage of the trip to be another "heart-pumper." The trail climbs abruptly to 115 feet above Batchewaung Lake, before dropping 35 feet down to Nym. The portage begins at a wide gravel beach. A short distance inland, there is a low part of the trail just before the steep ascent that has potential to be very muddy after rains or in early spring.

Nym Lake is populated with summer cabins. To the west of the canoe landing (a large dock below the Ranger Station), the Ministry of Natural Resources operates an active heleport. After you have concluded your trip, you may want to take advantage of the "courtesy house" located at the south end of the parking area. Hot showers are yours for the taking, compliments of the Park.

Pictos on Quetico Lake

Route #9: The Lerome-Hamburg-Quetico Loop
7 Days, 71 Miles, 13 Lakes, 4 Creeks, 21 Portages

DIFFICULTY: Challenging to Easy

FISHER MAPS: F-29, F-28

HIGHLIGHTS: Sue Falls, many pictographs, good fishing, variety of beautiful terrain

Introduction: This delightful round-trip loop begins the same as Route #8. At Batchewaung Bay, instead of turning north, however, you will portage south, into Maria Lake. From there, you will follow a southwesterly course, through Hamburg and Oriana lakes to picturesque big Quetico Lake. After a long day of paddling across the narrow southeastern channel of Quetico Lake, you'll pass by Eden Island en route to a campsite near four displays of ancient Indian rock paintings. The next morning you will portage into Cirrus Lake and follow this long lake back to Sue Falls and then north to your origin at Lerome Lake.

You are not likely to see many other people during the beginning and end of this route. However, the vicinity of Pickerel Lake receives a good deal of traffic from the Batchewaung Lake entry point. Likewise, Quetico Lake offers a popular route for those who begin their trips at Beaverhouse Lake. The region between Quetico and Pickerel lakes is a converging point for routes originating at both points of entry.

Persistent anglers will have an opportunity to catch trout in McAlpine, Oriana, Quetico and Cirrus lakes. Walleyes and northern pike are living in nearly all of these Quetico Park lakes (except no northern in McAlpine). Cirrus Lake, in particular, is considered to be an excellent walleye lake. For the bass fishermen, Quetico Lake contains both largemouth and smallmouth bass.

Historians will see several good examples of ancient Indian rock paintings along the north shore of Quetico Lake, as well as remnants of old-time logging operations along Oriana and McAlpine creeks and at a few other locations.

DAY 1 (10 miles): **Lerome Lake,** p. 6 rods, **(Unnamed lake),** p. 19 rods or 134 rods, **Jackfish Creek, Bewag Lake,** p. 26 rods, **Lark Lake,** p. 22 rods, **Cirrus Creek, Cole Lake, Cirrus Creek,** p. 175 rods, **Cirrus Lake.** (See comments for DAY 1, Route #8.)

DAY 2 (10 miles): **Cirrus Lake,** p. 190 rods, **Kasakokwog Lake, McAlpine Creek,** p. 4 rods, **Creek, McAlpine Lake,** p. 260 rods, **Batchewaung Bay** (Pickerel Lake). (See comments for DAY 2, Route #8.) Plan to camp just after completing the "garden walk."

DAY 3 (10 miles): **Batchewaung Bay** (Pickerel Lake), **2 Rapids, Pickerel Lake,** p. 43 rods, **Maria Lake,** p. 27 rods, **Oriana Creek,** p. 24 rods, **Creek,** p. 8 rods, **Hamburg Lake.** If the water level is high, you should have no problem running your canoe down those two small rapids between Batchewaung Bay and Pickerel Lake. If the level is low, take time to walk your canoe down the current.

The first easy portage follows an excellent path, though uphill, to Maria Lake. All three portages along Oriana Creek are generally downhill, following closely beside the creek. When the creek is low, the first carry may stretch to five rods longer, or more. In fact, if the creek appears to be very dry, you may want to take an alternate route south of Maria to Jesse Lake. That route requires two longer portages, but it bypasses most of Oriana Creek. During a dry year, consult a Ranger about the condition of Oriana Creek before departure.

In 1984, Park Rangers warned travelers heading for Maria Lake about a bear and her two cubs that were "working the portages" around Maria. The cunning bears are wise enough to ambush canoeists when they leave their food packs sitting at one end of a portage unattended. Don't let this happen to you!

There is a very nice campsite on the northwest shore of Hamburg Lake, about a mile after your last portage. Take precautions, though, to avoid bear troubles.

DAY 4 (10 miles): **Hamburg Lake,** p. 68 rods, **Oriana Creek, Oriana Lake,** p. 20 rods, **Oriana Creek,** p. 32 rods, **Quetico Lake.** The stretch of Oriana Creek between Hamburg and Oriana lakes may be plagued with beaver dams. During a dry year, this could be a real problem area. The same is true on the creek draining into Quetico Lake.

There are several campsites near the east end of Quetico Lake, but not many further on. Since this is a fairly high traffic route from Beaverhouse Lake, you will want to find your site early in the day — at least during late July or in August. Get your chores over with early, and then concentrate on catching one or two of the trout, walleyes, northern, largemouth or smallmouth bass that dwell nearby.

DAY 5 (10 miles): **Quetico Lake.** Pack away your boots this morning and prepare to enjoy a leisurely day of paddling across this long and lovely lake. At the south end of Eden Island, veer northeast and follow the east shore of this large island to the north shore of Quetico Lake. Four displays of Indian rock paintings are located on the rocky north shore. (See the map for precise locations.) The locations of most are relatively easy to spot from a distance as they are situated at the base of steep cliffs. The best display of all, however, was inconspicuously painted under a low rock overhang. It is the eastern-most exhibit of the Quetico Lake ''gallery.'' The painted figures include a caribou head, a moose, a canoe, three human figures and abstractions.

DAY 6 (12 miles): **Quetico Lake,** p. 14 rods, **Cirrus Lake.** This will prove to be almost as easy a day as the one before it. Except, if the wind was against you yesterday, it will likely be at your back today. Cirrus receives less use than most of the lakes along this route. Plan to camp at its east end, perhaps at the site where you camped your first night.

The most luck I have ever experienced while fishing for walleyes was on Cirrus Lake. Anglers will also find northern pike, trout, crappies and sunfish inhabiting the depths below you.

DAY 7 (10 miles): **Cirrus Lake,** p. 175 rods, **Cirrus Creek, Cole Lake, Cirrus Creek,** p. 22 rods, **Lark Lake,** p. 26 rods, **Bewag Lake, Jackfish Creek,** p. 19 or 134 rods, **(Unnamed Lake),** p. 6 rods, **Lerome Lake.** This is all familiar country to you, the reverse of the first day. Eat a hearty breakfast, though, because this time you will be climbing that steep portage around Sue Falls.

Oriana Creek

68

Entry Point 31 — Cirrus Lake

Daily Quota: 2
Use Level: Low

LOCATION: Cirrus is a 14-mile long lake located in the far northwestern corner of Quetico Provincial Park. At its closest point, Atikokan is only twelve miles northeast of the lake. The entry point, however, is at the west end of Cirrus, requiring one of the longest drives from Atikokan.

From the Atikokan Tourist Bureau, drive west on Highway 11 for 23.8 miles. A sign there calls attention to "Flanders Road" coming in from the north (right) side of the highway. Turn left onto a gravel road and proceed on this wide, but rough, road for 4.9 miles to a "Y" intersection with road #7-3. Bear left and continue for another 5.2 miles to an unmarked intersection with road #7-4. Turn left here and drive on this narrower gravel road, past Dinner Lake and a large gravel pit, 4.3 miles to the road's end. The road gets rougher and narrower after passing the gravel pit. Keep left at an intersection just prior to the road's end.

DESCRIPTION: There are parking spaces for 20-25 cars along the side of the road. At the road's end, a portage trail continues for 75 rods along the path of what was once an extension of the same road you drove in on. The trail is level and wide — an easy portage to Beaverhouse Lake. Beaverhouse is one of only two fly-in access lakes in Quetico Park. Most people prefer to drive there, however.

Cirrus Lake is two portages and a short paddle northeast of Beaverhouse Lake. "As the crow flies" (or should we say "raven?"), Cirrus is scarcely more than a mile from the end of the road. Unfortunately, though, you must first paddle five miles out of your way (round-trip) to the Ranger Station on the south side of Beaverhouse, in order to pick up your travel permit. While there, be sure to ask the friendly Ranger if you may fill up your water bottle with the ice-cold spring water oozing from the shaded ground behind his cabin. That will help make this five-mile side-trip seem worthwhile.

Cirrus Lake composes the northwest perimeter of Quetico Provincial Park. Its enormous volume is concealed somewhat by its elongated contour. The low, sometimes marshy, terrain surrounding the lake's west end yields to a more prominent relief further east, with hills rising abruptly from the water's edge to more than 150 feet above the lake.

Although it is a relatively easy journey from both Beaverhouse and Lerome lakes, and a mere "hop" from popular Quetico Lake to the south, Cirrus receives light traffic most of the time.

If walleye fishing is your "game," you'll surely enjoy cruising over this often overlooked lake. It is prized for its prestigious pickerel population.

Route #10: The Sue Falls Loop
4 Days, 40 Miles, 5 Lakes, 1 River, 1 Creek, 7 Portages

DIFFICULTY: Easy (but with a couple ½-mile portages!)
FISHER MAPS: F-28, (F-29 optional)
HIGHLIGHTS: Sue Falls, pictographs, long lakes, few portages

Introduction: This attractive loop is ideal for those who prefer long, uninterrupted stretches of paddling, with only an occasional portage for leg-stretching. After a brief visit to the Beaverhouse Ranger Station, you will paddle back to the northeast corner of Beaverhouse Lake and then portage east, first to an unnamed lake and then to Cirrus Lake. With nearly ½ of the route's portages behind you now, you will follow Cirrus all the way to its east end. After viewing scenic Sue Falls, you will steer south to surmount the longest and most difficult portage of your trip. Upon reaching Kasakokwog Lake, then, you will plot a westerly course, down McAlpine Creek to another enormous lake. Paddling close to the north shore of Quetico Lake, you will have an opportunity to view several exhibits of ancient Indian rock paintings (pictographs) on its sheer granite cliffs. From the west end of Quetico Lake, the Quetico River will carry you back to Beaverhouse Lake. And, from there, it is a short hike back to your car.

Most of this route consists of two long lakes: east on Cirrus and west on Quetico. You are more likely to feel a sense of wilderness isolation while on Cirrus Lake. After your portage on Kasakokwog Lake, however, you will be back on a route that receives more use. As many as twelve (12) groups per day are allowed to enter Quetico Lake from Beaverhouse Lake. This rarely occurs. But on a "busy" day in late July or in August, canoe traffic will be noticeably heavier from Kasakokwog through Quetico Lake to Beaverhouse.

Ardent anglers will surely find walleyes, northern, trout and perch along most of the route. Smallmouth bass inhabit Quetico and Beaverhouse lakes, and there are also largemouth and rock bass in Quetico Lake.

DAY 1 (9 miles): P. 75 rods, **Beaverhouse Lake,** p. 160 rods, **(Unnamed Lake)**, p. 38 rods, **Cirrus Lake.** Resist the temptation to ''postpone'' your stop at the Beaverhouse Ranger Station, located 2½ miles south of your portages. Even with a reservation, you must have a Camping Permit in your possession throughout your trip. Besides, you'll enjoy visiting with the friendly folks who operate the station. They can inform you about the current condition of portages, where the fish are hiding and where the bears are causing a ruckus.

Sunset on Kasakowag Lake

The dilapidated remains of an old bridge mark the location of the half-mile portage out of Beaverhouse Lake. Both the bridge and the portage trail were once part of the same road on which you drove in. Consequently, the path is very smooth and level most of the way. It ends at the edge of a creek flowing out of an unnamed lake. A beaver dam there keeps the course navigable.

The next portage is short, but it winds considerably and may be overgrown during the summer months.

During my first visit to Cirrus Lake, I quickly confirmed that which I had already been told: it's a good lake for catching walleyes. From the small rock outcropping below my campsite, I cast my slightly-weighted artificial lure. Allowing it to sink to a five-count, I then slowly reeled it in. Strike! A nice, little walleye looked me in the eye. Six more casts produced six more fish. One was just the right size to feed my wife and me for breakfast. The others will be forever grateful to me.

There is a nice, large campsite almost three miles east of the portage into Cirrus Lake.

DAY 2 (12 miles): **Cirrus Lake.** Portage boots don't need to be a part of your wardrobe today. The whole day will be devoted to paddling, exploring the shoreline and isolated bays of this sprawling lake. Near the east end of the lake is an Indian pictograph site. There you will see an abstraction that has four small discs inside an oblong-shaped outline, and a large disc. There are several campsites in the vicinity of Sue Falls, at the far eastern end of Cirrus.

DAY 3 (10 miles): **Cirrus Lake.** p. 190 rods, **Kasakokwog Lake,** p. 76 rods, **McAlpine Creek, Quetico Lake.** The first portage is the only exhausting challenge of the whole trip. It ascend nearly 150 feet before dropping steeply down to Kasakokwog Lake. Watch out for slippery rocks on a wet day and a stretch about midway across the trail that could be muddy.

The next portage bypasses a quarter-mile length of rapids in McAlpine Creek. Above the rapids is a well-preserved log dam and lumbering sluice, probably constructed by Shelvin Clark in the 1920's. The portage access is at a shallow, rocky landing. The trail is also rocky and treacherous at the beginning, but it follows a good path most of the way.

Four Indian pictographs have been identified along the rugged north shore of Quetico Lake (See the map for precise locations). The most interesting, perhaps, is the easternmost exhibit. But it is also the most difficult to find. Instead of paintings at the base of impressive rock cliffs, where most of the pictographs are located, these fascinating figures are nearly covered by a low rock overhang. If you are not watching carefully, you could easily paddle right past.

Plan to camp in the vicinity of the north end of Eden Island.

DAY 4 (9 miles): **Quetico Lake, Quetico River,** p. 24 rods, **River, Beaverhouse Lake,** p. 75 rods. The 24-rod carry around a set of rapids in the Quetico River follows an excellent, well-beaten path across a grassy meadow that was once the headquarters of a logging operation that worked Quetico and Jean lakes. Beside the trail are the rusted remains of an old automobile. The trail splits into two paths about midway across. Either branch will lead you to the river, but the right branch is a bit shorter.

Before returning to your car, you might consider stopping at the Ranger Station again to report the highlights of your trip. You'll be helping the Rangers keep abreast of the latest wildlife sightings, fishing reports, and campsite and portage conditions.

Route #11: The McAlpine-Oriana Creeks Loop

6 Days, 65 Miles, 10 Lakes, 1 River, 2 Creeks, 15 Portages

DIFFICULTY: Easy (but with three portages in excess of ½ mile)
FISHER MAPS: F-28, F-29
HIGHLIGHTS: Sue Falls, pictograph(s), logging relics, long lakes and few portages, some creek paddling

Introduction: This excellent route offers the same long, uninterrupted stretches of paddling as does Route #10. But good variety is found at the east end of the loop, where smaller lakes and tiny creeks contribute to a more well-rounded experience in Quetico Park. As in route #10, you will first paddle the entire length of Cirrus Lake to view Sue Falls at its eastern end. From there you will portage south to Kasakokwog Lake, and then you will continue on an east-bound course through McAlpine Lake to Pickerel Lake. At Mosquito Point you will begin your return trip, traversing a chain of lovely lakes connected by tiny Oriana Creek, which eventually feeds into the east end of Quetico Lake. Before leaving this beautiful lake, you may wish to paddle to its rocky north shore to view one or more of the four pictograph exhibits located there. Continuing a westward course, then, you will portage back to Beaverhouse Lake where this route began.

Anglers will have ample opportunity to try their skills catching walleyes, northern, trout, smallmouth and largemouth bass and some varieties of panfish along this route. Walleyes and northern, in particular, inhabit nearly all of the waters. Trout may be caught in all but Kasakokwog and Maria lakes. Largemouth bass live in Quetico and Oriana lakes. And Quetico Lake is also popular with smallmouth bass fishermen.

Historians will see evidence of 60-year-old logging operations at many of the portages. Log dams held together by foot-long spikes, coils of rusted cable and

Hamburg Lake

72

remnants of abandoned machinery all leave clues about another, much older, reason for the popularity of this region. How different it must have looked back then . . . .

DAY 1 (9 miles): P. 75 rods, **Beaverhouse Lake**, p. 160 rods, **(Unnamed Lake)**, p. 38 rods, **Cirrus Lake**. (See comments for DAY 1, Route #10.)

DAY 2 (12 miles): **Cirrus Lake**. (See comments for DAY 2, Route #10.)

DAY 3 (10 miles): **Cirrus Lake**, p. 190 rods, **Kasakokwog Lake, McAlpine Creek**, p. 4 rods, **Creek, McAlpine Lake**, p. 260 rods, **Batchewaung Bay** (Pickerel Lake). (See comments for DAY 2, Route #8.) Plan to camp just after completing the "garden walk."

DAY 4 (10 miles): **Batchewaung Bay** (Pickerel Lake), **2 Rapids, Pickerel Lake**, p. 43 rods, **Maria Lake**, p. 27 rods, **Oriana Creek**, p. 24 rods, **Creek**, p. 8 rods, **Hamburg Lake**. (See comments for DAY 3, Route #9.)

DAY 5 (12 miles): **Hamburg Lake**, p. 68 rods, **Oriana Creek, Oriana Lake**, p. 20 rods, **Oriana Creek**, p. 32 rods, **Quetico Lake**. (See comments for DAY 4, Route #9.)

DAY 6 (12 miles): **Quetico Lake, Quetico River**, p. 24 rods, **River, Beaverhouse Lake**, p. 75 rods. If time and weather permit, you may want to paddle an extra four miles to the north shore of Quetico Lake before heading west. There you will find four fascinating displays of ancient Indian rock paintings, called pictographs. One of the more interesting exhibits is the one furthest east (see map for locations). There you will see an assortment of symbolic figures just above the water level, sheltered by a low rock overhang, including a caribou head, a moose, a canoe and three human figures. Watch carefully, or you might paddle past it. As you follow the north shoreline to the west, you will come across three more displays, these located near the bases of impressive bare cliffs.

At the 24-rod portage, you'll see the rusted remains of an antique automobile, sitting beside the path. The good, smooth trail crosses a grassy meadow that was once part of a logging operation. The trail splits into two paths about midway across. Either branch will lead you to the river, but the right fork is slightly shorter.

Suggestion For Extended Route

8-Day Loop: This rigorous route will carry you through much of Quetico's northwestern region. It begins the same as Route #11, from Beaverhouse east to Pickerel Lake. You will continue paddling east, through Pickerel Narrows. Then you will begin a southwesterly course, crossing Doré and Twin Lakes en route to big Sturgeon Lake. After one full day on Sturgeon Lake, you will veer north and navigate scenic Jean Creek to Rouge and Burntside lakes. After a memorable night with Jean (lake), you will continue traveling north through Conk Lake to Quetico Lake. From there, you will complete this route by following the Quetico River back to Beaverhouse Lake.

Along the way, you will enjoy a good variety of scenery and navigable water. To complete the journey in eight days, I suggest that you camp in the Pickerel Narrows (DAY 3), at the northeast end of Sturgeon Lake (DAY 4), near the southwest end of Sturgeon Lake (DAY 5), on Jean Lake (DAY 6), and in the east-central part of Quetico Lake (DAY 7).

For details of this extended route, see the comments for DAY 2, Route #6, and for DAYS 3-5, Route #4, in addition to the comments for DAYS 1-3 and 6, Route #11.

Entry Point 32 — Quetico Lake

Daily Quota: 12
Use Level: Moderate

   LOCATION: From its closest shore, Quetico is fifteen miles southwest of Atikokan. Like Cirrus Lake, however, the entry point is at the opposite end, by way of Beaverhouse Lake. (Refer to the directions to Entry Point 31 — Cirrus Lake.)

   DESCRIPTION: Beaverhouse Lake has long been a popular drop-off point for sea planes delivering visitors to Quetico Park. It is still one of only two fly-in access lakes in the Park (the other is Lac La Croix). Now, however, most people prefer to drive to Beaverhouse. There are parking spaces for 20-25 cars along the side of the road. At the end of the road, a 75-rod portage trail connects the parking lot with the lake. The trail follows an easy, level path to the lake.

   Quetico Lake is straight east of Beaverhouse. Entry requires only a short portage and a brief paddle up the Quetico River, after stopping at the Beaverhouse Ranger Station to pick up your Camping Permit. The station is in a small bay along the south shore of Beaverhouse Lake.

   Although twelve groups are allowed to enter Quetico Lake each day, seldom does such a crowd appear. Nevertheless, there is enough canoe traffic through Quetico Lake to warrant concern for campsites while it is still early in the day, especially during the busy season of late July and the month of August.

   Anglers need not travel far. Quetico Lake harbors trout, walleyes, northern and perch. It is also considered a good source for bass, both smallmouth and largemouth, as well as rock bass. Beaverhouse, too, contains most of the same species.

Route #12: The Northern Lakes Route

4 Days, 49 Miles, 6 Lakes, 2 Rivers, 1 Creek, 5 Portages

DIFFICULTY: Easy
FISHER MAPS: F-28, F-29, F-30
HIGHLIGHTS: 1-way, Pictographs, Only 1 long portage, well-traveled, good fishing opportunities

   Introduction: This route skims the entire northern perimeter of Quetico Provincial Park, from Beaverhouse Lake east to French Lake. With only five portages (totalling a mere 439 rods), it is one of the easiest four-day trips available in the Park, without spending all three nights at the same campsite. From Beaverhouse you will enter the west end of Quetico Lake and then follow its slendor north arm northeast to Kasakokwog Lake. Continuing on an east-bound course, you will paddle up McAlpine Creek to McAlpine Lake. From the middle of this long and narrow lake, you will cross the only long portage of the route — the ¾-mile "garden walk." From the west end of Pickerel Lake, you will navigate the entire length of that 21-mile aquatic expanse. Then it will be a short journey up the Pickerel River to your destination at French Lake.

   If the winds prevail from the west, which is normal, you should have an easy time paddling, drifting or sailing along this scenic course. For newcomers to Quetico Park, it offers an easy opportunity to experience the wilderness preserve without contending with the kind of crowds that often clutter the southern perimeter of the Park. At the same time, though, you will never be completely isolated from the rest of the world, since there is moderate canoe traffic along this northern route.

In addition to the excellent fishing in Quetico Lake, you may also catch walleyes and trout in McAlpine Lake, walleyes and northern in Kasakokwog Lake, and most species in Pickerel Lake. On a trip like this one, there is plenty of time for trolling or diverting your course to explore some of the many tempting bays along the route.

DAY 1 (12 miles): P. 75 rods, **Beaverhouse Lake, Quetico River,** p. 24 rods, **River, Quetico Lake.** Before paddling up the Quetico River, you will have to stop at the Beaverhouse Ranger Station, located in a small bay on the south side of the lake. After the bureaucratic paperwork is tended to, ask the Ranger if you may fill your water bottle with the ice-cold water oozing from the spring located behind the cabin. On a hot summer's day, you can't beat this treat!

Your only portage this day climbs up around a set of rapids in the Quetico River. At the top of the portage, you will be hiking through a grassy meadow that was once the headquarters of a logging operation sixty years ago that worked Quetico and Jean lakes. Beside the trail is the rusted carcass of an antique automobile.

When you reach Quetico Lake, bear left and paddle to the north shore of this beautiful lake. Along that rocky, rugged north coast are four separate displays of ancient Indian rock paintings (pictographs). Watch closely to find the reddish symbols that were likely painted hundreds of years ago. They are normally just a few feet above the water level, at the base of prominent cliffs. The fourth exhibit, however, is an exception. This one is nearly hidden under a low rock overhang, inconspicuous from a distance. Plan to camp near the east end of the Quetico Lake ''gallery.''

DAY 2 (12 miles): **Quetico Lake, McAlpine Creek,** p. 76 rods, **Kasakokwog Lake, McAlpine Creek,** p. 4 rods, **McAlpine Lake.** McAlpine Creek provides the only variation from the big-lake paddling that typifies this trip. At both portages are more reminders of the logging era. The quarter-mile portage follows a good path most of the way, but it becomes rocky and a bit treacherous toward the end, as you climb 32 feet up to Kasakokwog Lake. At the top of the rapids is an old log dam and lumbering sluice, one of the few in the Park that hasn't nearly deteriorated. It is a much better specimen than the dam located at the next (4-rod) portage.

The far-west end of McAlpine Lake is very shallow and cluttered with stumps of large trees that were cut by loggers. Plan to camp at one of the sites along the western half of the lake.

DAY 3 (12 miles): **McAlpine Lake,** p. 260 rods. **Batchewaung Bay** (Pickerel Lake), 2 Rapids, **Pickerel Narrows.** Your longest overland trek of this entire route, McAlpine Portage, is a ''highway.'' Because it crosses gently rolling terrain and follows the good path of an old logging road, Park Rangers refer to it as ''the garden walk.'' Walking ¾ of a mile with pack and canoe, even on a ''highway,'' however, may generate a good deal of sweat!

While paddling toward the long portage, follow closely the north shore of McAlpine Lake. A half-mile west of the portage is another Indian pictograph, this one showing a spiral abstraction.

Two small rapids separate Batchewaung Bay from Pickerel Narrows. If the water level is high enough, you should have no difficulty running your canoe down them. On the other hand, if the water level is low, you should take the time to walk or line your canoe between the boulders.

There are numerous campsites in Pickerel Narrows. But don't wait too late to claim one. This is a convenient camping location for the many trippers who begin and end their expeditions at Nym Lake, to the north.

DAY 4 (13 miles): **Pickerel Narrows, Pickerel Lake, Pickerel River, French Lake.** Although the wind is usually from the west (though, by all means, not always!), avoid getting caught out in the middle of this huge lake during a gale. You will always be safer if you follow closely the shoreline. Besides, there is much more to see there; and that makes paddling across vast expanses of open water much more interesting. You are much more likely to view a moose along the shoreline than out in the middle of a big lake (although the latter may occur at times).

French Lake is the hub of activity in Quetico Park. Administrative offices, a museum, public beach and Dawson Trail Campgrounds are all located along the northeast shoreline.

Since this is a one-way route, you should have made prior arrangements to have your vehicle waiting here (See "On One-Way Trips.").

Route #13: Jean's Bentpine Trail
5 Days, 56 Miles, 15 Lakes, 1 River, 4 Creeks, 22 Portages

DIFFICULTY: Challenging

FISHER MAPS: F-28, F-29, F-24, F-23

HIGHLIGHTS: Excellent variety, lovely Jean Creek, historic Bentpine Creek, 1-mile portage

CAUTION: During low-water periods, the creeks along this route may be too low for navigation of a loaded canoe! Consult a Ranger before departure.

Introduction: When the water level isn't too low, I consider this loop to be one of the best routes available to canoeists with a week's vacation. There will be days on long lakes with uninterrupted paddling, days on tiny, twisting creeks, and days when you will hop from small lake to small lake. Most portages are generally not difficult. Although, near the end of this route is a one-mile trail that will challenge a seasoned Voyageur.

From Beaverhouse Lake, you will paddle up the Quetico River to Quetico Lake. Traveling across its long, south arm, you will follow Quetico Lake nearly to its east end. Turning south there, you will traverse a series of pretty lakes en route to scenic Jean Creek, which will carry you further south to the west end of Sturgeon Lake. At that southern-most point of the route, you will steer a northwesterly course and follow Bentpine and Trail creeks to Little Pine Lake. Following a more northerly course, you will paddle across a chain of smaller lakes to Badwater Lake and then portage a mile back to Quetico Lake's southwest corner. From there it is an easy journey back to your origin at Beaverhouse Lake.

Anglers will have ample opportunity along the way to catch trout, walleyes, northern, perch and bass, as well as sturgeon and herring in big Sturgeon Lake. Distributing 56 miles over a 5-day period should allow for plenty of time to fish, or to explore the many logging relics that exist along Bentpine Creek.

DAY 1 (11 miles): P. 75 rods, **Beaverhouse Lake, Quetico River,** p. 24 rods, **River, Quetico Lake.** (See comments for DAY 1, Route #12.) Instead of paddling up to the north shore of Quetico Lake, however, steer south of Eden Island and follow the south arm of this enormous lake. There is a nice campsite on the left shore, about midway down this long channel.

DAY 2 (10 miles): Quetico Lake, p. 19 rods, Conk Lake, p. 30 rods, Jean Lake. The picturesque east end of Quetico Lake is lined with hills that rise abruptly from the water's edge to nearly 200 feet above the lake. The first short portage is around a small, scenic waterfall that cascades 34 feet from Conk Lake down to Quetico. The portage is over a rocky path that climbs steeply in places.

A 200-foot sand beach accommodates two very nice campsites on a peninsula along the south shore of the north part of Jean Lake. The water nearby is amazingly shallow. A hundred yards out from the peninsula, one can stand on a sandy bottom in crystal-clear water and not be more than waist deep. In other parts of the lake, however, the depth is great enough to satisfy lake trout. Jean is a unique and beautiful lake.

There is a cluster of campsites at the narrows, between the north and south parts of Jean Lake. It was there, one sunny morning in July, 1984, that my wife and I were attacked by an army (or should I say navy?) of otters. Well, it wasn't exactly an "army," and I guess we weren't actually "attacked." As we paddled leisurely through that narrow channel, three feisty otters "greeted" us with vicious, agressive hissing sounds. They bobbed their heads in and out of the water as they swam uncomfortably close to our canoe. I had encounterd otters on close terms before, but never had I witnessed such a display of apparent trepidation.

Astute anglers should have no problem providing fish for breakfast. Jean Lake is home for trout, walleye, northern pike, rock bass, bluegill, largemouth and smallmouth bass, and perch.

DAY 3 (10 miles): Jean Lake, p. 80 rods, Burntside Lake, Jean Creek, Rouge Lake, p. 22 rods, Jean Creek, p. 9 rods, Creek, p. 18 rods, Creek, p. 21 rods, Creek, p. 40 rods, Sturgeon Lake. The quarter-mile portage is an easy one, passing over a small hill, with only one potentially muddy section about midway across. There is an old cabin at the south end of the trail, a run-down structure that once was a trapper's cabin.

The five portages along the lower part of Jean Creek are well traveled, but the first three are in better condition than the final two. All, of course, are generally downhill, bypassing their respective rapids; but the third (18 rods) surmounts a fairly steep, though small, hill en route. When the water level is sufficient, one can paddle or pull his canoe through the shallow, rocky creek to eliminate the 21-rod carry. During a dry year, Jean Creek could be a problem — especially after the 18- rod portage.

There are several campsites at the west end of Sturgeon Lake. If you are ahead of schedule, it is best to resist the temptation to continue along the route, unless you have several hours of traveling time to spare. There are few campsites of any merit along Bentpine Creek. Stop early and test your luck at catching some of the fish that inhabit Sturgeon Lake: walleyes, northern, sturgeon, smallmouth bass, suckers, saugers, whitefish, herring and red horse.

Sturgeon Lake is part of the popular Hunter's Island Route, as well as a destination in itself for many others.

DAY 4 (10 miles): Sturgeon Lake, Bentpine Creek, p. 17 rods, Creek, p. 35 rods, Creek, p. 25 rods, March Lake, p. 60 rods, Trail Lake, Trail Creek, Little Pine Lake, Rapids, Snow Lake, p. 167 rods, Your Lake. This morning you will depart from one of the most traveled routes and enter one of the least traveled routes in Quetico Provincial Park. The scenery is not spectacular along this route, but historians will see many locations worthy of investigations. Evidence of early 20th century logging operations is seen at nearly every portage. In fact, before the first portage, you will paddle past the dilapidated remains of an old barge run aground along the north shore of Bentpine Creek. It was likely used in 1936 and 1937. At each of the three small portages east of March Lake are remnants of log dams with sluiceways for transporting logs over the shallow rapids. At the 60-rod portage to Trail Lake is a succession of rusty steel rollers that were used to roll logs overland. The winter haul went this way, and then down Trail Creek to the Maligne River. The summer haul, on the other hand, followed Bentpine Creek to the Maligne River.

There will probably be a beaver dam or two blocking Trail Creek. It is a very shallow and narrow stream, and may be nearly choked with pondweeds. Another beaver dam and short rapids between Little Pine and Snow lakes will require a "liftover."

The only difficult portage of the day is the last one, and it more than makes up for all the easy ones. It follows a wet path over a muskeg bog much of the way. At first, the swampy places are intermittent. But, later, you find yourself walking through the middle of a marsh. Fortunately, a new, drier bypass has been cleared on the right side of the bog. But it is easy to miss when there is a canoe over your head, obscuring your vision. Watch for blaze marks on the trees.

Nearly all of the waters along this route lack an interesting shoreline. The terrain is low, and forest is typically cedar and spruce. Campsites are few and far between. The only nice, large one is the island site near the west end of Your Lake.

DAY 5 (15 miles): **Your Lake,** p. 30 rods, **Creek, Fair Lake,** p. 30 rods, (**Unnamed Lake**), p. 30 rods, **Badwater Lake,** p. 320 rods, **West Bay** (Quetico Lake), p. 5 rods, **Quetico Lake, Quetico River,** p. 24 rods, **River, Beaverhouse Lake,** p. 75 rods. That first little portage is a dandy — in the negative sense! It has potential to be a very muddy trail — the kind with deep, smelly swamp ooze that grabs your foot and climbs quickly up to your knee. I sank so deep on one occasion, I had to drop my canoe to pull my foot free. If the water level is low, you might have to extend the portage more than 30 rods — perhaps all the way to Fair Lake.

Between Fair and Badwater lakes there are two options. Near the center of Fair Lake there is a 167-rod portage extending north to Badwater Lake. There is also a route extending from the east end of Fair Lake across two short portages and a small, unnamed lake to Badwater. The latter option offers an easier route, but not without obstacles. The first 30-rod trail passes over a small hill and then drops steeply down to the nameless lake. The next 30-rod path starts just above and to the right (east) of a beaver dam, crosses a creek, drops steeply downhill, and then crosses the creek again — over a crude log bridge that requires a balancing act to remain upright!

The worst was saved for the last part of the trip. The mile-long trail connecting Badwater and Quetico lakes isn't all that bad when it is dry. But, after heavy rains or in early spring, look out! The portage follows a general uphill course for the first 195 rods. It is in the occasional valleys, not on the hills, however, where the challenges wait. You will cross over two spongy spruce bogs during your gradual ascent. Then, after 250 rods into the portage, you will encounter the first of two mud holes. The final 40 rods are dry, but extremely rocky, with a path that is difficult to walk on. The landing may be muddy. Fortunately, in 1984, young portage crews worked extensively to upgrade the portage. "Corduroy" covers most of the trail over the bogs now.

If you have had enough portaging for one day, you can bypass the 5-rod carry by paddling around the long peninsula over which it passes. From there on, you will be back in what should be familiar country.

Lily pads on Jean Creek

Logger's houseboat

Logging structure on Bentpine Creek

Beaver House on Bentpine Creek

Route #14: The Quetico River - Bearpelt Creek Loop

5 Days, 53 Miles, 9 Lakes, 2 Rivers, 1 Creek, 17 Portages

DIFFICULTY: Challenging
FISHER MAPS: F-28, F-23
HIGHLIGHTS: Ivy Falls, historic Bearpelt Creek, pictographs
WARNING: During dry years or late in the summer, when the water level is low, Bearpelt Creek may be too low for the navigation of a canoe. Consult an outfitter or Park Ranger prior to departure.

Introduction: Although the designated entry point for this loop is #32-Quetico Lake, you will not see Quetico Lake until the fourth day of this river-running trip. From the Beaverhouse Ranger Station, you will paddle WEST to the far western end of big Beaverhouse Lake. From there, you will journey down the Quetico River to its confluence with the Namakan River, and then follow the Namakan upstream to Ivy Falls. From the east side of Threemile Lake, then, you will begin your trek up historic Bearpelt Creek, along which you will view many dilapidated remnants of the logging era. At Badwater Lake, you will veer toward the northwest and portage an exhausting mile to Quetico Lake. From West Bay of Quetico, you will then paddle northeast all of the way to the rugged north shore of this sprawling lake, where there are four fascinating exhibits of Indian rock paintings. After carefully scrutinizing the pictographs, you will portage from Quetico to Cirrus Lake and then follow this long lake to its west end. After crossing two more portages, you will find yourself back on Beaverhouse Lake, and your final portage will return you to the parking lot north of the lake.

This is an excellent route for early summer expeditions, when the water level is likely to be high in Bearpelt Creek. During dry years and late in the summer, the creek is usually too low to carry a loaded canoe. Even during a "good" year, you may have to get out and walk through part of the Bearpelt. The rewards, though, are well worth the effort. Even during the busiest part of the summer, you are not likely to encounter many — if any — other people between Wolseley and Quetico lakes. But throughout the length of the creek, you may see fascinating evidence of the bygone logging era — time-worn log dams and sluiceways, rusted cable and enormous spikes. It is truly amazing how quickly the northern forests recuperate from the devastations of man.

DAY 1 (9 miles): P. 75 rods, **Beaverhouse Lake.** This is, by far, the easiest day of your trip; so relax and enjoy it! After that first, easy portage, don't forget to paddle to the small bay in the southeastern corner of the lake to pick up your Camping Permit at the Beaverhouse Ranger Station. If it's a hot day, ask the Ranger if you may help yourself to some of the ice-cold spring water that oozes from the forest floor behind the Ranger's cabin. When you have had your fill, paddle to the far western end of Beaverhouse and find your campsite near the headwaters of the Quetico River. Along the way, you'll pass a display of Indian rock paintings along the southern shore of the lake. Hand smears, a small moose and various abstractions were painted there hundreds of years ago by an unknown artist who belonged to a woodland culture that once thrived in this region.

Trout, walleye, northern pike, smallmouth bass and perch all dwell in the depths of Beaverhouse Lake. Anglers should enjoy this leisurely day.

DAY 2 (11 miles): **Beaverhouse Lake, Quetico River,** p. 64 rods, **River,** p. 60 rods, **River,** p. 60 rods, **River, Namakan River,** p. 4 rods, **Threemile Lake** to **Ivy Falls.** Regardless of the water level, it should not be a problem on either of these two rivers. They offer a delightful change of pace from the big lake that was just crossed. At the last portage on the Quetico River, stay to the left (east) side of Wawa Island. You will have paddled DOWNstream on the Quetico River, but it will be an UPstream paddle on the Namakan. There may be some swift current in constricted parts of the river, but the only bona fide rapids is at the 4-rod portage.

There are several nice island campsites on Threemile Lake, but the loveliest of locations is the campsite on the small island at the base of Ivy Falls. Threemile Lake is not within the boundary of Quetico Provincial Park. Consequently, you must have a Crown Land Camping Permit to legally camp on any of the island campsites. See that it is secured PRIOR to the start of the trip, since vendors are "scarce" in the wilderness.

DAY 3 (13 miles): **Threemile Lake, Bearpelt Creek,** p. 15 rods, **Creek, Wolseley Lake, Bearpelt Creek,** p. 12 rods, **Creek,** p. 57 rods, **Creek,** p. 25 rods, **Creek, Cub Lake, Omeme Lake.** (See comments for DAY 2, Route #15.)

DAY 4 (10 miles): **Omeme Lake,** p. 10 rods, **Bearpelt Creek,** p. 40 rods, **Creek,** beaver dam, **Creek,** p. 7 rods, **Creek, Badwater Lake,** p. 320 rods, **West Bay** (Quetico Lake), **Quetico Lake.** If you had problems with low water on the lower part of Bearpelt Creek, it's likely to be worse this day. The shallowest part of the creek may be between the first two portages. In fact, that 10-rod carry may stretch out to 30 or 40 rods, depending on the depth of the creek. Fortunately, there is a grassy bank on which to extend the portage.

At the end of the 40-rod portage is a meadow filled with grasses and wild flowers that was the site of Shelvin Clarke's 1937 logging camp. Beyond that point, the creek should be deeper, but there may be a couple of beaver dams obstructing your path.

The biggest challenge of this route awaits you at the west end of Badwater Lake. Even when it is dry, that mile-long trail is exhausting. If it's wet, though, you're in for a real "treat." The portage generally follows a gentle uphill grade for the first 195 rods; but it is the valleys, not the hills, that create the problems. The trail passes through two muddy spruce bogs. Fortunately, though, portage crews have deposited a good deal of "corduroy" to help you avoid sinking up to your waist. But those logs may be treacherous, too. Be careful! On the downhill side of the portage there are a couple more mud holes, but the final 40 rods of the trail is normally dry — extremely rocky and difficult to walk over, but dry.

From the muddy put-in at this portage, paddle to the north end of Quetico Lake and find your campsite. Anglers may want to try their luck for the trout, walleyes, northern, smallmouth bass, largemouth bass, perch or rock bass that inhabit this spectacular lake.

DAY 5 (10 miles): **Quetico Lake,** p. 14 rods, **Cirrus Lake,** p. 38 rods, **(Unnamed Lake),** p. 160 rods, **Beaverhouse Lake,** p. 75 rods. Before leaving Quetico Lake, be sure to paddle along the north shoreline to inspect the mysterious pictographs. There are four separate exhibits. The most interesting one is located the furthest east. Unlike the others, which are found at the bases of impressive granite cliffs, the easternmost display is nearly hidden under a low rock overhang. Among the reddish-brown figures that you will see there are three human figures, a canoe, a moose and a caribou head, along with other abstractions. (See the map for precise locations.)

Cirrus is known as a good walleye lake. Anglers may want to prolong their journey to its west end.

The half-mile portage to Beaverhouse Lake follows an old road bed — the extension of the same road on which you drove, five days prior. It follows a very easy, level path most of the way.

Suggestion for Extended Route

7-Day Loop: For the first four days this interesting loop follows the same route as that of Route #13. From Badwater Lake, however, instead of heading north toward Beaverhouse Lake, you will veer to the southwest and follow the flowage of Bearpelt Creek through Wolseley Lake to the Namakan River. Turning toward the northwest, you will paddle down the Namakan River to its confluence with the Quetico River. There you will leave the Namakan and paddle up the Quetico to your origin at Beaverhouse Lake.

To complete this loop in seven days, I suggest that you plan to camp on Bearpelt Lake (DAY 5) and on Threemile Lake (DAY 6). Your seventh day will require 14 miles of paddling, much of that against the Quetico River current.

For details of this extension, see the comments for DAYS 4 and 5 of Route #15, and DAY 4 of Route #14.

CHAPTER 4: Entering From Lac La Croix — The Western Region

Welcome sign at Sand Point Customs

Four Quetico Entry Points are controlled by the Lac La Croix Ranger Station: 41 — Threemile Lake, 42 — Maligne River, 43 — McAree Lake, and 44 — Bottle River. The Ranger Station is located in a small bay at the north end of Irving Island, near the southwest end of Lac La Croix.

Since there are no roads leading to this gigantic lake, paddlers considering a trip through any of these entry points must first consider how they are going to arrive there. And since Lac La Croix is part of the international boundary, your first question should be: Will I begin my trip on the Canadian side of the border, or will I originate my trip in the United States?

For Canadians entering from the north, the primary choices are: 1) Fly in from the Atikokan area, or 2) Drive to the Namakan River and then paddle 2 days to the Ranger Station.

For Americans entering from the south, there are three plausible choices: 1) Fly in from Ely or Crane Lake, 2) Have an outfitter tow you in from Crane Lake, or 3) Paddle in along the border from Crane Lake to the east end of Lac La Croix, a journey that will take most people three full days.

If your primary motivation for this camping vacation is to see Quetico Park and/or your time is limited, by all means fly in or have your canoe(s) towed. If, however, you simply desire a good Northwoods canoe trip, and it matters not that half of the trip is outside the boundaries of Quetico Park, then why not paddle all the way?

Now then, some pawky paddler is bound to study his map and come to the canny conclusion that one could most easily reach Lac La Croix from the south, not from the west. Americans, in particular, may be tempted to begin on the Moose River and paddle north, across the Boundary Waters Canoe Area Wilderness, by way of Moose and Nina-Moose rivers. Why not? Only one reason that I know of: American citizens must first be cleared by Canada Customs before they may lawfully enter Quetico Provincial Park. Unfortunately, for them, there is no Customs Office at the east end of Lac La Croix. In fact, the only Customs anywhere near the west side of Quetico Park is the one on Sand Point Lake, straight north of Crane Lake. There are no ''shortcuts'' through the BWCAW!

For those who would rather paddle to the Ranger Station, the descriptions of two access routes follow. The first is for Canadians who begin at the Namakan River. The second is for Americans who begin at Crane Lake. **Don't Forget** to acquire Crown Land Camping Permits if you plan to camp on public land outside of Quetico Park!

Sand Point Customs

The Namakan River Access

LOCATION: The Namakan River drains the north-central part of Lac La Croix and carries its waters north and west eighteen miles to Namakan Lake. The only road access to the river is 45 miles southwest of Atikokan. From the Atikokan Tourist Bureau, drive west on Highway 11 for 23.8 miles. A sign there points to "Flanders Road" on the right. Turn left onto a gravel road and proceed 4.9 miles to a "Y" intersection with road #7-3. Bear left and continue driving sixteen miles on this rough road to the Namakan River bridge.

DESCRIPTION: The bridge crosses the Namakan River at Lady Rapids. A boat launch and parking area are located just east of the bridge, above the rapids.

Because the Namakan is outside of any designated wilderness area, motors are permitted along its entire course, as

Rainbow over Little Vermilion River

well as on the Canadian side of Lac La Croix. Consequently, it is not unusual to see and hear motorized canoes on the Namakan and larger motor boats on Lac La Croix.

DAY 1 (12 miles): **Namakan River,** p. 146 rods, **Little Eva Lake, Namakan River,** p. 18 rods. **Bill Lake, Namakan River,** p. 10 rods, **River,** p. 4 rods, **River, Threemile Lake.** Since you will be paddling upstream, there will be times when the swift current is a drag (so to speak). Most of the time, however, a strong west wind would more than compensate for the opposing current. The long portage around Hay Rapids (146 rods) follows a nearly level, good path, although it will be muddy after rains. The following 18-rod trail climbs up the southwest edge of High Falls, a dazzling 20' cascade. About midway across the portage, a small path branches off to the left (east). After you have deposited your gear at the other end of the trail, be sure to hike back to that path with your camera. It leads to a breathtaking overlook.

While portaging around the next two small sets of rapids, inspect them closely. If the water level is suitable, you may be able to eliminate these two portages on your return trip by skillfully running the tempting whitewater.

After you pass the mouth of the Quetico River, you will be paddling on the western perimeter of Quetico Park. As long as you camp on an island or along the west shore of Threemile Lake, you will be outside of the Park, where Crown Land Camping Permits are required. Camping on the east shore would require a Quetico Camping Permit.

DAY 2 (18 miles): **Threemile Lake, Namakan River,** p. 25 rods, **River,** p. 48 rods, **River, Lac La Croix.** You'll paddle up another lovely stretch of the Namakan River, portaging around Ivy Falls and Snake Falls, before venturing out onto the vast, windswept northern part of Lac La Croix. At the source of the Namakan is a village of the Neguaguon Lake Indian Reserve. Indians who are members of the Lac La Croix Guides Association are the only people permitted to use motors (10 h.p. or less) on certain lakes in the western part of Quetico Park.

It is a long afternoon of paddling across Lac La Croix; if the wind isn't a menacing force, you should be able to camp in the vicinity of Hilly Island, 1 mile northeast of the Ranger Station. Plan to pick up your Quetico Camping Permit the following morning and get an early start toward your designated entry point.

Fawn on Loon Lake.

Crane Lake Access

LOCATION: From its East Bay, Crane Lake is scarcely more than a mile west of the Canadian border through Little Vermilion Lake. To drive there from the town of Orr, Minnesota, follow County Road 23 seventeen miles to its junction with County Road 24 at Buyck. Crane Lake is twelve miles north of Buyck on Co. 24. From Ely, Minnesota, drive the entire length of the Echo Trail (49 miles) to its junction with County Road 24. Turn right and follow Co. 24 north for eight miles to the public access at the south end of Crane Lake.

DESCRIPTION: There are several parking areas near the boat landing, but none is public. You will have to pay a daily fee in order to park there.

Crane Lake is a busy, little lake port, serving visitors to three large government preserves: Voyageurs National Park and the Boundary Waters Canoe Area Wilderness in America, and Quetico Provincial Park. The lake is often humming with the sounds of seaplanes taking off or landing, motorboats en route to Lac La Croix, Sand Point and Namakan lakes, and an occasional tow boat delivering canoeists to Quetico Park. By comparison, there aren't many canoes being paddled north. Near the boat landing, you may find all of the amenities that a small town can offer (including an outfitter with one of the best saunas in the north country!), and an American Customs station for American trippers returning from Canada, as well as for Canadian visitors to the United States.

Wind can be a problem right away. Both Crane Lake and Sand Point Lake are susceptible to menacing northwest winds. Normally, though, you should be off the big lakes and on the tranquil Loon River before the afternoon winds are a problem.

Canoists departing at Crane Lake

87

High Fall on the Namakan River

For those wishing to spend the night before departure at a campground, the closest U.S. Forest Service campground is at Echo Lake on the Echo Trail, just east of its junction with County Road 24.

Canadian Customs is located on an island in the southern end of Sand Point Lake. After your north-bound journey to that island, you will then veer to the southeast and follow the international border. From Little Vermilion Lake onward, the Boundary Waters Canoe Area Wilderness is on the American side of the route. Both private and Crown lands are on the Canadian side. Since you should not camp on private lands, and since there is a fee required for a camping permit on Crown lands, and since you may not know which lands are Crown and which are private, I recommend that you secure an overnight travel permit that allows camping in the BWCAW. The permit is free. If you wish to reserve the permit ahead of time, however, there is a charge for this service. (See The Boundary Waters Canoe Area Wilderness, page 32.)

DAY 1 (12 miles): **Crane Lake, King William's Narrows, Sand Point Lake, Little Vermilion Narrows, Little Vermilion Lake.** If there is a brisk wind this day, you can rest assured that it will be against you only half the time. Adjacent to Canadian Customs is a trading post that sells virtually everything — except ice cream! If souvenirs are tempting you, do yourself a favor: wait until your return; you have enough to carry already!

Plan to go no further than Little Vermilion Lake. There are three USFS campsites near its south end. There are no good campsites along the Loon River.

DAY 2 (18 miles): **Little Vermilion Lake, Loon River, Rapids, River,** p. 80 rods, **Loon Lake,** p. 50 rods, **Lac La Croix.** In spite of frequent motorized traffic, the

Loon River is an enjoyable route toward Quetico Park. Unlike many small rivers in this region, which are lined with cattails and spruce, hardwoods often prevail along its shoreline, including a stand of maples at one point.

When the water level is low, at "56 Rapids" an 11-rod portage on the U.S. side of the river may be necessary. Otherwise, you may be able to paddle right up the swift current in this short stretch.

At Loon Falls and Beatty Portage, the trails follow good uphill paths that are well-traveled. At each there is a mechanized portage system for large boats enroute to Lac La Croix. People who live at these portages transport boats overland on "railway cars." For a couple of bucks (half the price of motor boats) canoeists may have their canoe and gear transported for them. But, then, the portages are so easy, an enthusiastic canoeist will have a hard time justifying the expense.

Plan to camp just north of Snow Bay, where there are several good campsites on the U.S. side of the border.

DAY 3 (16 miles): **Lac La Croix.** This beautiful lake is indeed impressive: twenty-five island-studded miles from end to end. Even when the wind is strong, there are usually means to hide from it. Stay close to its crooked shoreline, or hop from island to island, but avoid paddling right down the middle of the vast, wind-swept northern part of the lake. Even a tail wind can be dangerous on a large lake like La Croix. In fact this big lake derives its name from a man who drowned there during a storm in 1688 — Sieur de la Croix.

As you paddle across the lake, you'll notice resorts on the Canadian side. At the source of the Namakan River, there is also a village of the Neguaguon Lake Indian Reserve. Indian members of the Lac La Croix Guides Assocation are the only people permitted to use motors (10 h.p. or less) on certain lakes in the western part of Quetico Park.

Plan to camp in the vicinity of Fish Stake Narrows, just west of the north end of Irving Island. From there it is but a short paddle to the Ranger Station the following morning.

Entry Point 41 — Threemile Lake

Daily Quota: 2
Use Level: Moderate

LOCATION: Threemile Lake is located twelve miles by air northeast of the Lac La Croix Ranger Station. To reach it by canoe, you must paddle 12 miles across Lac La Croix and then five miles north via the Namakan River. (See Entering From Lac La Croix.)

DESCRIPTION: There are two unfortunate aspects of using the Threemile Lake entry. First, because of the amount of time it takes to paddle all the way from Crane Lake, or from the Namakan bridge, to the Ranger Station and then up to Threemile (four days from Crane Lake, three days from the Namakan River bridge), canoeists with only a week's vacation should not even consider this entry point. Second, during dry years or low-water seasons, routes leading into the Quetico interior may be unnavigable, due to the fluctuating condition of Bearpelt Creek.

Similarly, for those trying to rapidly escape from the sounds of motors, this entry point offers a slow start. Lac La Croix, the Namakan River, and Threemile Lake are outside the boundaries of Quetico Park (their east shores constitute the perimeter). So there are no restrictions to motor boats in those waters (except on the U.S. side of Lac La Croix). In addition, Wolseley Lake is one of the few lakes in Quetico Park where Indians of the Lac La Croix Guides Association are permitted to use motors to a total of 10 horsepower.

Nevertheless, for the diehard canoeists who are willing to tolerate a little adversity, routes penetrating the Park's interior from Threemile Lake are exceptional. In fact, from the moment you portage north from Wolseley Lake, you will find yourself in a totally different canoeing world than that from which you just emerged. The route suggested will provide you with a high-quality wilderness experience.

Route #15: The Bearpelt Route

FROM & TO THE RANGER STATION:
5 Days, 75 Miles, 8 Lakes, 2 Rivers, 1 Creek, 18 Portages

FROM CRANE LAKE:
9 Days, 126 Miles, 15 Lakes, 3 Rivers, 1 Creek, 21 Portages

FROM NAMAKAN RIVER BRIDGE:
7 Days, 91 Miles, 10 Lakes, 2 Rivers, 1 Creek, 24 Portages

DIFFICULTY: Challenging

FISHER MAPS: F-15, F-16, F-22, F-23, F-28

HIGHLIGHTS: Historic Bearpelt Creek, Good variety, Pictograph, Namakan River falls

CAUTION: During low-water periods, Bearpelt Creek may be too low for navigation of a loaded canoe. Consult a Ranger before departure!

Introduction: This interesting loop first heads northwest from the Lac La Croix Ranger Station to Threemile Lake. From there, you will veer toward the northeast and paddle up the Bearpelt Creek flowage, through Wolseley, Cub and Omeme lakes to Badwater Lake. At the west end of Badwater Lake is the longest

Sunset over Three Mile Lake

portage of the route, a mile north to Quetico Lake. From there, the rest of the trip is downhill, as you follow the Quetico River through Beaverhouse Lake to the Namakan River. At that point, those who will be flown or towed from Lac La Croix will turn left and follow the Namakan River southeast, back to the big lake. Those who are paddling back to their cars, on the other hand, will steer in the opposite direction and float downstream on the Namakan. Those who aren't ending their trips at Lady Rapids will continue paddling to the mouth of the Namakan River, across the east end of Namakan Lake, and then south through Sand Point Lake to their origin at Crane Lake.

Airborne trippers who begin and end their journey at Lac La Croix could complete the route in five days. Those who are towed from Crane Lake to the east end of Lac La Croix could paddle all of the way back to Crane Lake in six days. But the hardcore American paddler must allow nine days for the same route.

Anglers will have plenty of opportunities to catch their favorite fish. Walleyes, northern, smallmouth bass and trout inhabit Lac La Croix, Quetico and Beaverhouse lakes. Walleyes, northern and perch are also contained in Wolseley, Omeme and Badwater lakes. Badwater also has trout.

If variety is what you are looking for, this route has it: huge lakes, tiny creeks, wide rivers and lovely lakes of smaller magnitude.

Since there are several different ways to arrive at the La Croix Ranger Station, each requiring a different amount of time, the description of this route will begin at the Ranger Station.

DAY 1 (18 miles): **Lac La Croix, Namakan River,** p. 48 rods, **River,** p. 25 rods, **River, Threemiles Lake.** Yes, this day covers quite a distance! If the wind is not a problem on La Croix, however, you should make good time to the first portage — almost fourteen miles northwest of the Ranger Station.

Omeme Lake

The Indian Village sits at the headwaters of the Namakan River, and it is visible from a considerable distance across the lake. The river provides a scenic contrast to the vast expanse of the Lac La Croix, plummeting 14 feet at Snake Falls, meandering through Ivy Channel on the east side of Douglas Island, and then cascading over Ivy Falls, en route to Threemile Lake.

If you haven't found a suitable campsite by the time you reach the mouth of Bearpelt Creek, continue paddling further northwest on Threemile Lake. There are a couple of nice island sites near the center of the lake.

DAY 2 (13 miles): **Threemile Lake, Bearpelt Creek,** p. 15 rods, **Creek, Wolseley Lake, Bearpelt Creek,** p. 12 rods. **Creek,** p. 57 rods, **Creek,** p. 25 rods, **Creek, Cub Lake, Omeme Lake.** This is the part of the route that will "make or break" the trip. If Bearpelt Creek has dried up, you might as well set up camp on Wolseley Lake and either: 1) Pray for a downpour, or 2) Fish for three days and then head for home. If the creek is "marginal," you may be able to walk your canoe through the shallowest stretches and clear the sandy bottom.

None of the four portages is difficult, although none is well-traveled, either. At each you may see evidence of the logging operations that penetrated this region fifty years ago. Sawn timbers and long spikes in dilapidated dams, rusted cable and mysterious iron parts from antique machinery offer clues to the woodland culture that has vanished from this part of the country.

There are small campsites along the north shore of Omeme Lake. For energetic anglers, this charming lake contains walleyes, nothern and perch. Save a little energy for tomorrow, though — you will need it!

DAY 3 (11 miles): **Omeme Lake,** p. 10 rods, **Bearpelt Creek,** p. 40 rods, **Creek,** beaver dam, **Creek,** p. 7 rods, **Creek, Badwater Lake,** p. 320 rods, **West Bay** (Quetico lake), p. 5 rods, **Quetico Lake, Quetico River,** p. 24 rods, **River, Beaverhouse Lake.** Don't be deceived by the "11 miles." Although this is the shortest mileage of any day thus far, it is, by no means, the easiest.

To begin with, that first 10-rod portage may stretch to 30 rods (or more) if Bearpelt Creek is low. And even after that, you may have to walk your canoe part (or much) of the way to your next portage.

The 40-rod trail follows a good, level path across a large clover meadow — a pretty setting in mid-summer, when the field is covered with sightly daisies and a select smattering of Indian paint brush. At both of these first two portages are the time-worn remains of a logging route, including traces of a cabin at the east end of the meadow.

Immediately beyond the 40-rod portage is a beaver dam across the creek, requiring a lift-over. And shortly beyond that dam is another beaver dam at the top of a small rapids, around which a 7-rod portage passes.

At the west end of Badwater Lake is the only bad portage of this entire route. Actually, when it is dry, the mile-long trail isn't too bad. But, after heavy rains or in early spring, it can be nasty. The portage follows a general uphill course for the first 195 rods. At 110 rods in, you will cross the first of two spongy spruce bogs. 50 rods over the "hump" is the first of two mud holes. The final 40 rods are downhill and relatively dry, but extremely rocky, over a path on which it is hard to walk. The landing at West Bay may be muddy. Fortunately, in 1984, portage crews covered most of the trail over the bogs with fresh "corduroy."

If you have had enough portaging for awhile, the 5-rod carry can be bypassed by paddling around the long peninsula over which it passes. The final portage cannot be avoided, but it is very easy, on a well-used downhill path. You will be hiking across a grassy meadow that was once the site of another logging operation. Beside the trail is the battered carcass of an antique automobile. The trail splits in the middle. Either branch will lead you to the base of the rapids, but the right fork is slightly shorter.

Beaverhouse Lake is the hub of traffic — by land, by sea and by air — in this part of the Park. Two Quetico entry points originate here, and a Ranger Station is located in a small bay on the southeast shoreline. A road allows visitors to drive to within 75 rods north of the lake, and seaplanes are permitted to land on the lake. As many as fourteen groups per day may enter Quetico Park from Beaverhouse Lake, though seldom do that many appear.

Plan to camp at the west end of the lake, if you wish to remove yourself from the activity around the Ranger Station. An Indian rock painting (pictograph) is located on the south shore, near .the west end of the lake — a weathered trace of another civilization that inhabited this region for hundreds of years.

DAY 4 (11 miles): **Beaverhouse Lake, Quetico River,** p. 64 rods, **River,** p. 60 rods, **River,** p. 60 rods, **River, Namakan River.** All three portages are generally downhill as you continue to follow the route used by loggers down the Quetico River. It will be a much easier day than the one before it. Plan to camp near the mouth of the river, at Wawa Island, the westernmost point of Quetico Provincial Park.

DAY 5 (8 or 13 miles): **Namakan River,** p. 10 rods, **River, Bill Lake,** p. 18 rods, **Namakan River, Little Eva Lake,** p. 146 rods, **Namakan River,** p. 50 rods, **River, Namakan Lake.** This day will be entirely outside the boundary of Quetico Park. Nevertheless, the Namakan River is as lovely as any river within the Park. One of the most magnificent waterfalls in this region, in fact, is High Falls — a matchless 20' cascade on the north side of Eva Island (18-rod portage). Motorized canoes, however, are likely to be heard along the river's course.

The 146-rod portage around Hay Rapids follows a good, level path. After rains, though, it may be muddy in several places.

Canadians who started this trip at Lady Rapids will end it at the top of the whitewater, to conclude a pleasant 8-mile day. Americans headed back to Crane Lake, on the other hand, will portage 50 rods along the north bank of the river. The first half, leading up to the bridge, is fairly well-used. But it appears that few people walk the path west of the bridge. It is overgrown and hard to see, and there are several optional landings at which to put in, which varies the length of the trail from 50 to 100 rods. Going downstream, as you are, the first landing option should be suitable. Experienced whitewater paddlers, however, may prefer to run Lady Rapids, down the straight shoot along the north bank of the river.

Namakan Lake is a giant. If a strong west wind prevails, you can probably dodge from island to island, to work your way to one of the many campsites in Voyageurs National Park, on the U.S. side of the border, northwest of Namakan Narrows. There are numerous private summer cabins and a resort on the Canadian side of the border. There are designated campsites, with fire grates and box latrines, in Voyageurs National Park. No permit is required, and there is no charge to camp there.

(**Note:** Those who intend to fly out of Lac La Croix will not follow this route. Instead, paddle up the Namakan River (opposite direction) for nine miles to Lac La Croix. Along the way, you will have three portages (4 rods, 25 rods, and 48 rods) around a small rapids and two waterfalls. The total distance is 22 miles to the Ranger Station. Although it is possible to complete the route in one day, you may want to split the journey into two easy days of paddling.)

DAY 6 (14 miles): **Namakan Lake, Namakan Narrows, Sand Point Lake, King William's Narrows, Crane Lake.** The scenic shoreline of Sand Point Lake is exceptional. So it is easy to understand why so many cabins are situated there, on both sides of the international boundary. Plan on an early start, so you can beat the wind back to your origin at the south end of Crane Lake.

Another Route Suggestion

6-DAY LOOP (From the Lac La Croix Ranger Station): Route #16 enters Quetico Park via the Maligne River and exits through Threemile Lake. By simply changing the entry points, you could reverse this route. Those who paddle back to either Crane Lake or the Namakan River bridge, however, will have to repeat a small part of the route on the Namakan River, between Lac La Croix and Threemile Lake. See Route #16 for details.

Twin Falls

Entry Point 42 —
The Maligne River

Daily Quota: 2
Use Level: Moderate

LOCATION: The Maligne River flows into the northwest corner of Lac La Croix, five and a half miles northwest of the Ranger Station. By canoe, it is 7½ miles, first north and then east, to Bell Island, the western shoreline of which denotes the boundary of Quetico Provincial Park. (See Entering From Lac La Croix.)

DESCRIPTION: The magnificent Maligne River system bisects Quetico Park into two land masses of nearly comparable dimension. Entering the Park at Cache Bay, in the southeast corner, the river flows northwest, cascading its way over no less than twelve exquisite waterfalls en route to a massive widening in its course, called Sturgeon Lake. Sturgeon marks the northernmost extension of the lakes, pools and rapids that constitute this continuous system of flowing water. From there it flows with less turbulence southwest to its final precipitous plunge into Lac La Croix at Twin Falls.

The historic river has long been used as an aquatic highway by Sioux and Chippewa Indians, French and English explorers and fur traders, and most recently by Canadian loggers. And today, it is still one of the most popular canoe routes through the interior of Quetico Provincial Park.

Since there are several different ways to arrive at the Lac La Croix Ranger Station, each requiring a different amount of time, the description of these routes will begin at the Ranger Station.

Route #16: The Historic Logging Route

FROM & TO THE RANGER STATION:
6 Days, 72 Miles, 14 Lakes, 2 Rivers, 3 Creeks, 21 Portages

FROM CRANE LAKE:
10 Days, 131 Miles, 21 Lakes, 3 Rivers, 3 Creeks, 25 Portages

FROM NAMAKAN RIVER BRIDGE:
8 Days, 100 Miles, 16 Lakes, 2 Rivers, 3 Creeks, 28 Portages

DIFFICULTY: Challenging

FISHER MAPS: F-15, F-16, F-22, F-23, F-24

HIGHLIGHTS: Extensive stream travel, many historic logging sites, Twin Falls, Namakan River falls.

CAUTION: During low-water periods, the creeks on this route may be too low for the navigation of a loaded canoe. Consult a Ranger before departure.

Introduction: This fascinating loop will take you from one of the busiest lakes in the area to one of the less-traveled parts of Quetico Provincial Park. From the northwest corner of Lac La Croix, you will paddle up the Maligne River to Sturgeon Lake. Touching only the western end of that awesome lake, you will steer now to the northwest and follow Bentpine and Trail creeks to Little Pine Lake. From there you will head north, crossing Snow, Your and Fair lakes en route to Badwater Lake. From near the center of Badwater, you will begin your journey down tiny Bearpelt Creek, through Omeme, Cub and Wolseley lakes, to the perimeter of Quetico Park at Threemile Lake. From that point, the Namakan River will carry you downstream, past magnificent High Falls, either to your starting point (for those who put in at Lady Rapids) or to Namakan Lake (for those returning to Crane Lake). A southbound course from Namakan will take you back to your origin at Crane Lake. (Those who will fly out of Lac La Croix will turn left at Threemile Lake and follow that river upstream to La Croix.)

Along the way, you will have an opportunity to experience virtually everything that a wilderness trip could possibly offer: enormous lakes like La Croix and Sturgeon, tiny creeks like the Bearpelt, majestic rivers like the Maligne and the Namakan, splendid waterfalls like Twin and High, and plenty of enticing whitewater. With a multitude of beaver dams and logging dams, this is one of the best dam trips Quetico has to offer.

Anglers, too, will have plenty to point their rods at. Walleyes and northern pike live in all of the Quetico lakes along this route. Trout fishermen may want to try their luck in the depths of Lac La Croix or Badwater Lake. And those who are partial to smallmouth bass may want to linger awhile on Sturgeon and Wolseley lakes.

Although the Maligne River, itself, offers an easy route for canoeists of all experience levels, this route penetrates a remote wilderness area that is not frequently visited. Indeed, the route may be virtually impassable if creeks dry up. Some portages are more difficult to find, if not to follow. Consequently, this route is recommended only for seasoned trippers who are most comfortable in an isolated wilderness environment.

DAY 1 (11 miles): **Lac La Croix, Wegwagum Bay** (Lac La Croix), p. 16 rods, **Maligne River.** There are enough islands, bays and peninsulas in this part of Lac La Croix so that wind should not be a serious hindrance.

Soon after entering Quetico Park, you will be greeted by an exquisite pair of waterfalls on the southeast side of Lou Island — Twin Falls. The portage is on the left (west) side of the left falls. Plan to camp in the vicinity of Twin Falls.

DAY 2 (11 miles): **Maligne River, Rapids, River,** p. 4 rods, **Tanner Lake, Maligne River, Rapids, River, Rapids, River, Rapids, River,** p. 42 rods, **River, Rapids, River,** p. 61 rods. **River,** p. 52 rods, **Sturgeon Lake.** The ease of this day will depend largely on the water level of the Maligne River. You will be paddling against the current, which may be very swift wherever the river constricts. When the water level was high, in 1984, my wife and I were able to paddle up through all of these small rapids — until we reached the last one before the 61-rod portage. Through that swift-flowing water we employed rope and a pole to line our canoe from the south bank of the river.

The 42-rod portage could stretch to a 54-rod carry, depending on where you take out, which, in turn, depends on the water level. The Maligne Portage (61 rods) may be divided into two short carries of 19 and 18 rods. The longer portage is very easy, however, and it's much quicker to unload and load your canoe only once.

There are several campsites at the southwest end of Sturgeon Lake, including a couple small island sites. Fish in this huge lake include walleyes, northern pike, smallmouth bass, sturgeon and herring.

DAY 3 (11 miles:) **Sturgeon Lake, Bentpine Creek,** p. 17 rods, **Creek,** p. 35 rods, **Creek,** p. 25 rods, **March Lake,** p. 60 rods, **Trail Lake, Trail Creek, Little Pine Lake, Rapids, Snow Lake,** p. 167 rods, **Your Lake.** (See comments for DAY 4, Route #13.)

*Logging structures
on Bentpine Creek*

98

DAY 4 (8 miles): **Your Lake,** p. 30 rods, **Creek, Fair Lake,** p. 30 rods, (**Unnamed Lake**), p. 30 rods, **Badwater Lake, Bearpelt Creek,** p. 7 rods, **Creek,** beaver dam, **Creek,** p. 40 rods, **Creek,** p. 10 rods, **Omeme Lake.** That first, little, innocent-looking portage has a tendency to be very muddy, with the kind of deep, smelly swamp ooze that graps your foot and climbs quickly up to your knee. In addition, if the water is low, you might have to extend the portage more than 30 rods — perhaps all the way to Fair Lake.

Between Fair and Badwater lakes, there are two options. Near the center of Fair Lake is a 167-rod portage extending north to Badwater Lake. There is also a route extending from the east end of Fair Lake across two short portages and a small, unnamed lake to Badwater Lake. The latter option offers an easier route, but not without obstacles. The first 30-rod trail passes over a small hill and then drops steeply down to the nameless lake. The next 30-rod path starts just above and to the right (east) of a beaver dam, crosses a creek, drops steeply downhill, and then crosses the creek again — over a crude log bridge that requires a balancing act to remain upright and dry.

After a respite from portages during your cruise over Badwater Lake, you will begin your adventure on Bearpelt Creek. The first two obstacles are beaver dams — one that requires a 7-rod carry; the other a mere liftover. After the second dam, you will barely get your paddle wet before you arrive at the 40-rod portage. The level path crosses a large meadow that was once the site of a logging outpost. At the east end of the meadow, vestiges of a building are now nearly hidden by sweet clover in mid-summer.

The creek may be very low after that portage. In 1984, my wife and I paddled a short distance, then tugged and pulled the canoe awhile, and finally uttered in exasperation: "Let's portage the rest of the way to Omeme!" So, instead of the "normal" 10-rod portage, we hiked for over 30 rods along the grassy bank of the creek. At the "normal portage" are more deteriorated remnants of the logging era, including a dam and a "retaining wall" to guide the logs down the creek.

Omeme Lake offers a lovely setting to settle for the night. There are small campsites along the north shore of the lake. Lurking nearby are walleyes, northern and perch, just waiting to strike at your lures!

DAY 5 (13 miles): **Omeme Lake, Cub Lake, Bearpelt Creek,** p. 25 rods, **Creek,** p. 57 rods, **Creek,** p. 12 rods, **Creek, Wolseley Lake, Bearpelt Creek,** p. 15 rods, **Threemile Lake.** If you have no problems caused by low water before today, this part of the creek should be fine, too. The creek may be shallowest after the second portage. Since the creek has a good, sandy bottom, however, it would not be a problem to step out and tow your canoe over the lowest sections.

None of the four portages is difficult. At each you will see more evidence of early-20th Century logging operations — sawn timbers and long spikes in crumbled dams, rusted cable and unidentifiable iron pieces from antique machinery.

DAY 6 (12 or 17 miles): **Threemile Lake, Namakan River, Rapids, River,** p. 10 rods, **River, Bill Lake,** p. 18 rods, **Namakan River, Little Eva Lake,** p. 146 rods, **Namakan River,** p. 50 rods, **River, Namakan Lake.** If you don't feel comfortable running the small rapids north of Threemile Lake, there is a 4-rod portage over the small island there. (See comments for DAY 5, Route #15.) For those returning to the Lac La Croix Ranger Station, the paddling distance is 18 miles. (See DAY 2 of the Namakan River Access.)

DAY 7 (14 miles): **Namakan Lake, Namakan Narrows, Sand Point Lake, King William's Narrows, Crane Lake.** (See comments for DAY 6, Route #14.)

Route #17: The Maligne-Jean Route

FROM & TO THE RANGER STATION:
8 Days, 94 Miles, 10 Lakes, 3 Rivers, 1 Creek, 19 Portages

FROM CRANE LAKE:
11 Days, 145 Miles, 16 Lakes, 4 Rivers, 1 Creek, 22 Portages

FROM NAMAKAN RIVER BRIDGE:
9 Days, 110 Miles, 12 Lakes, 3 Rivers, 1 Creek, 25 Portages

DIFFICULTY: Challenging

FISHER MAPS: F-15, F-16, F-22, F-23, F-28, F-29

HIGHLIGHTS: Twin Falls, Jean Creek, Pictographs, Namakan River falls, good blend of lakes and streams

Introduction: This, in my humble opinion, is one of the best routes that Quetico Park has to offer — at any time of year. Unlike Routes #15 and #16, this multifaceted loop is not as likely to be affected by fluctuations of the water levels. But you will still have an opportunity to experience small streams and placid rivers.

Like Route #16, you will first paddle up the Maligne River to big Sturgeon Lake. From its west end, however, you will plot a course straight north, following Jean Creek to Rouge and Burntside lakes. Continuing northbound, you will portage into Jean Lake and push onward to Quetico Lake. Paddling to the north shore of this scenic lake, you may enjoy viewing several displays of ancient Indian rock paintings (pictographs) before portaging west to Beaverhouse Lake. From the west end of Beaverhouse, you will glide down the Quetico River to its confluence with the Namakan River. Those who plan to fly out of Lac La Croix will steer left and paddle up the Namakan River to their origin at Lac La Croix. Others will veer to the right and follow the lovely Namakan River downstream. Canadians who put in at Lady Rapids will stop there. Americans en route to Crane Lake will continue paddling west to Namakan Lake. From the east end of that large lake, a southbound journey will take you back to your origin at the south end of Crane Lake.

Regardless of the starting and ending points, this route offers trippers an excellent blend of wilderness waters — all sizes of lakes, one enchanting creek, and at least three days of river travel.

For visitors with two weeks to spare, the entire loop from Crane Lake is exceptional. If you are short on time, don't rule it out; flying or being towed to and from Lac La Croix may be the answer.

Trout fishermen will be delighted by the deep lakes at the northeast end of the route. Jean, Burntside, Quetico and Beaverhouse lakes all contain trout, as well as walleyes, northern pike and bass. Both smallmouth and largemouth bass inhabit the waters of Quetico Lake, which is considered to be a great lake in which to catch those little fighters. In fact, avid fishermen will surely want to add an extra day or two to a canoe trip following this route. As it is, you will be averaging between twelve and thirteen miles per day, which leaves little time for trolling or casting during the days.

DAY 1 (11 miles): **Lac La Croix, Maligne River,** p. 16 rods, **River.** (See comments for DAY 1, Route #16.)

DAY 2 (11 miles): Maligne River, Rapids, River, p. 4 rods, Tanner Lake, Maligne River, Rapids, River, Rapids, River, Rapids, River, p. 42 rods, River, Rapids, River, p. 61 rods, River, p. 52 rods, Sturgeon Lake. (See comments for DAY 2, Route #16.)

DAY 3 (10 miles): Sturgeon Lake, p. 40 rods, Jean Creek, p. 21 rods, Creek, p. 18 rods, Creek, p. 9 rods, Creek, p. 22 rods, Rouge Lake, Jean Creek, Burntside Lake, p. 80 rods, Jean Lake. (See comments for DAY 4, Route #4).

DAY 4 (10 miles): Jean Lake, p. 30 rods, Conk Lake. p. 19 rods, Quetico Lake. From Conk Lake, the water cascades thirty scenic feet down to Quetico Lake, where hills rise nearly 200 feet above its eastern shoreline. It's a beautiful setting!

Quetico Lake is an entry point that allows up to twelve groups per day into Quetico Park. Seldom do that many parties enter on the same day. But I once witnessed eighteen other canoes between Conk Lake and the middle of Quetico Lake, on a warm day in July. So don't delay in finding your campsite. There is a nice site about midway down the narrow south arm of Quetico Lake, on its north shore. From that area you should have no trouble landing some of the smallmouth or largemouth bass that this lake is noted for. Quetico also contains trout, walleyes, northern and perch.

DAY 5 (16 miles): Quetico Lake, Quetico River, p. 24 rods, River, Beaverhouse Lake. At the south end of Eden Island, steer toward the northeast and follow the east shore of this large island to the north shore of Quetico Lake. This five-mile detour enables you to view several fascinating exhibits of Indian pictographs. Located along the rugged north shore, most are easy to spot from a distance, situated near the base of steep cliffs. The most interesting display, however, was inconspicuously painted under a low rock overhang. It is the easternmost exhibit of the Quetico Lake ''gallery.''

The 24-rod portage crosses a large grassy meadow that was once the site of a thriving logging operation. Beside the trail is the rusty framework of an antique automobile. The good path splits near the middle. Either branch will lead you to the bottom of the rapids, but the right one is slightly shorter.

Judging from the activity at the east end of Beaverhouse Lake, you may feel like you have left Quetico Park behind. You have not. Beaverhouse Lake is the only other lake in the Park (besides Lac La Croix) that allows seaplanes to deposit canoeists right at the door of the Ranger Station. The Ranger's cabin is located in a small bay on the south shore, near the east end of the lake. A road ends only 75 rods north of the lake, allowing easy access for canoeists using either the Quetico Lake or the Cirrus Lake entry points.

If you still have some energy left, you may want to paddle to the west end of Beaverhouse, to escape the congestion at the east end. (But that will take you more than sixteen miles this day.)

DAY 6 (14 miles); Beaverhouse Lake, Quetico River, p. 64 rods, River, p. 60 rods, River, p. 60 rods, River, Namakan River. (See comments for DAY 4, Route #15.) Another Indian pictograph is located on the south shore of Beaverhouse Lake, near its west end.

DAY 7 (8 or 13 miles): Namakan River, p. 10 rods, River, Bill Lake, p. 18 rods, Namakan River, Little Eva Lake, p. 146 rods, Namakan River, p. 50 rods, River, Namakan Lake. (See comments for DAY 5, Route #15.)

DAY 8 (14 miles): Namakan Lake, Namakan Narrows, Sand Point Lake, King William's Narrows, Crane Lake. (See comments for DAY 6, Route #15.)

Entry Point 43 — McAree Lake

Daily Quota: 2
Use Level: Moderate

LOCATION: McAree Lake is located a scant two miles (by air) east of the Lac La Croix Ranger Station. By canoe, it is three miles away, via two short portages to and from Brewer Lake. (See Entering from Lac La Croix.)

DESCRIPTION: By virtue of its proximity to the Ranger Station, McAree Lake is the most convenient of the four entry points accessible from Lac La Croix. From here, it is only three miles to Quetico's interior. Beyond is some of the most beautiful scenery in the entire Quetico-Superior region. Argo and Crooked Lakes, Curtain Falls, the Siobhan and Darky rivers and the pictographs of Darky Lake are among the splendid not-too-distant attractions.

McAree and Minn lakes are among the six lakes in Quetico Park where treaty Indians of the Lac La Croix Guides Association are permitted to use motors not to exceed a total of ten horsepower. East of these two lakes, however, the only buzzing will be that of the humming bird.

Route #18: The Crooked-Brent Route

FROM & TO THE RANGER STATION:
6 Days, 72 Miles, 13 Lakes, 3 Rivers, 1 Creek, 23 Portages

FROM CRANE LAKE:
11 Days, 154 Miles, 21 Lakes, 5 Rivers, 1 Creek, 31 Portages

FROM NAMAKAN RIVER BRIDGE:
9 Days, 119 Miles, 16 Lakes, 4 Rivers, 1 Creek, 34 Portages

DIFFICULTY: Challenging
FISHER MAPS: F-15, F-16, F-17, F-22, F-23, F-24
HIGHLIGHTS: Rebecca Falls, Curtain Falls, Twin Falls, Indian pictographs, beautiful Crooked Lake

Introduction: This outstanding loop is primarily a lake route, but there is enough river travel to add the spice of variety. After entering McAree Lake from Brewer Lake, you will paddle to the south end of McAree Lake, and then portage to Iron Lake on the international border. After viewing two of Quetico's magnificent waterfalls, you will follow the U.S. boundary across the many lovely bays of Crooked Lake to its easternmost cove. At Moose Bay, then, you will veer to the north and travel over a chain of smaller lakes en route to Brent Lake. From the scenic west end of Brent Lake, you will let the charming Darky River carry you west, through Darky Lake, to Minn. Lake. From its north shore, you will "Puddle jump" north to the Maligne River and follow it downstream to its final dazzling drop at Twin Falls. From the northwest corner of Lac La Croix, air-bound Voyageurs will paddle to their predetermined pick-up point, while water-bound trippers will follow the north shore of La Croix to the source of the Namakan River. Floating down this elegant river, past three captivating cascades and several alluring rapids, those who started their trip at the Namakan River Bridge will end their trip at Lady Rapids. Others will portage around this tempting whitewater and continue west-bound to Namakan Lake. From there, a day's paddling southward will return you to your origin at Crane Lake.

Rebecca Falls

Beaver Dam south of Malign River

Astute anglers may find trout, walleyes, northern and bass in most of the lakes along this route. Minn is the only major lake without trout.

Photographers will want plenty of film. Curtain Falls is one of the most photogenic falls in the region. The jagged chasms created by Rebecca Falls are matchless. And Twin Falls ain't too shabby, either!

Most of the route is fairly well-traveled. The busiest part will probably be along the U.S. border, for one good reason: it is one of the most attractive parts of the entire Quetico-Superior region.

The description of this route will begin at Lac La Croix. When planning your trip, be sure to include in your itinerary your means to arrive at the Ranger Station. (See Entering From Lac La Croix.)

DAY 1 (11 miles): Lac La Croix, p. 32 rods, **Brewer Lake**, p. 8 rods, **McAree Lake**, p. 50 rods, **Iron Lake**, p. 140 rods, **Crooked Lake.** This day rates high among the ''nicest first days in Quetico Park.'' The appealing stage set by Brewer and McAree rapids is brought to a fever pitch by Rebecca Falls, at the south end of McAree Lake. Yet the climax is still to come. Curtain Falls present an absolutely stunning performance where the waters of Crooked Lake tumble unashamedly thirty feet down to Iron Lake.

There are two ways to portage around Rebecca Falls. If you portage over the island, use the left path on the south side of the island; the trail on the north side is reserved for mountain goats. The 50-rod portage is safer. It begins at the shore of a small bay south of the twin falls. The trail follows a good, though overgrown, uphill path to Iron Lake.

The Curtain Falls portage follows an excellent, wide, heavily-used path that ascends gradually most of the way to Crooked Lake. Two canoe rests have been constructed beside the trail, to allow you to rest your aching shoulders — compliments of the U.S. Forest Service. You may put in at the very brink of the falls, or about 100 feet farther into Crooked Lake. The latter choice is the safest, especially for a group that might not be strong enough to paddle against the swift current above the falls. After you drop your gear above the falls, hike back down to a rock outcropping that affords a splendid view of the comely cataract.

There are several good ''designated'' campsites on the American side of the border. Unless you have a BWCAW Travel Permit in your possession, however, you are restricted to select from the smaller assortment north of the border. Plan to camp near the falls.

Crooked is traditionally a popular lake among anglers. Species there include walleyes, northern pike, smallmouth, largemouth and rock bass, trout, bluegills, perch and black crappies.

DAY 2 (15 miles): **Crooked Lake, Moose Bay** (Crooked Lake). This will be your only day off from portaging. Enjoy it!

If any lake in the north country should ever be selected for a seminar in ''reading your map and compass,'' one of the top prospects would undoubtedly be Crooked Lake. Paddling from one scenic end to the other, you must study your map religiously. It seems more like a series of small lakes joined by secret channels than the one huge lake that it is. If you become disoriented (you're not ''lost'' — just disoriented — if you haven't taken a portage and therefore know that you are still on the same lake!), don't panic. There is so much canoe traffic on the international border, you seldom find yourself out of sight of other parties — at least not for long. (If you do, then you probably ARE lost!) This may be attributed to the influx of groups using entry points for the Boundary Waters Canoe Area Wilderness — most likely NOT parties from other Quetico entry points.

At a prominent point jutting north into Wednesday Bay is a site called Table Rock. This level slab of rock outcropping has been a popular place to rest for hundreds of years. It is still a designated campsite for visitors to the BWCAW.

Continue paddling beyond Table Rock to the mouth of Moose Bay. At the south end of the bay is a magnificent campsite on a high ridge overlooking the lake. At the landing is a nice sand beach for the kids to enjoy.

DAY 3 (13 miles): **Moose Bay** (Crooked Lake), **Tuck River**, p. 43 rods, **River, Rapids, River, Rapids, River, Robinson Lake**, p. 18 rods, **(Unnamed Lake)**, p. 77 rods, **Cecil Lake**, p. 42 rods, **Deer Lake**, p. 10 rods, **McIntyre Lake**, p. 4 rods, **(Unnamed Lake)**, p. 18 rods, **Brent Lake.** You will be paddling upstream on the shallow Tuck River. The portages are well-traveled and follow good paths. There are no portages around two small rapids, but you may be able to paddle up both. If the current is too swift or too shallow, simply walk or line your canoe through the riffle. Plan to camp at the east end of Brent Lake. Anglers may want to explore the waters for the walleyes, northern, trout and largemouth bass that inhabit the lake.

DAY 4 (10 miles): **Brent Lake**, p. 18 rods, **Darky River**, p. 182 rods, **River**, p. 15 rods, **Darky Lake.** The narrow, twisting channels of Brent Lake create a fascinating environment in which to paddle. Near its west end, high bluffs rise from the water's edge and, beyond them, hills tower more than 200 feet above the lake.

The Darky River begins as a series of small pools and interconnecting rapids that all add up to one short portage followed by the longest carry of the trip. Although it is downhill most of the way, the 182-rod trail follows a fairly rugged (but well-used) path over sharp rocks, frequent roots, and a potentially muddy spot near the middle. When the river is low, you may have to walk five rods farther, to put in at a more suitable access. Those who prefer to break up the big portage into two segments may do so by putting into a small pool after 56 rods, paddling 18 rods, and then portaging an additional 108 rods to the end.

There are three excellent campsites at the north end of Darky Lake. Plan to stop early, so that you will have time to paddle to the south end of the lake to view two of the Park's finest displays of Indian pictographs.

While making this four-mile round-trip, anglers may want to bring along their gear. Darky Lake is home for trout, walleyes, northern, smallmouth and rock bass, black crappies and perch.

DAY 5 (12 miles): **Darky Lake, Darky River**, beaver dam, **River**, p. 45 rods, **River**, p. 33 rods, **River, Rapids, River, Rapids, River**, p. 11 rods, **River**, p. 55 rods, **River, Rapids, River, Rapids, Minn Lake, Rapids, Darky River**, p. 90 rods, **River, Maligne Creek**, beaver dam, **Creek**, p. 6 rods, **Creek**, p. 13 rods, **Creek**, p. 9 rods, **Creek, Maligne River.** You won't travel a great distance this day, but it may seem like you did. There is a log jam at that first beaver dam, requiring a 1-rod "slide-over." Within sight of the dam is the first portage, where the trail climbs steeply before descending gradually to the bottom of a ravine. If the water level is high, you may be able to paddle past the first access to the next portage and shorten your carry to only 11 rods. That trail, too, climbs steeply and drops down just as quickly.

You should have no difficulty gliding through the small riffle below the 33-rod portage, or at the one just after the river's confluence with Andrew's Creek. The 55-rod portage allows you to bypass another small riffle and a barracade of fallen trees above a major rapids. You can shorten that carry to just 25 rods by running through the riffle and picking your way through the trees.

Judging from the wear on the portage trails (or rather, lack of wear), it seems that few people travel north from Minn Lake to Maligne River. In fact, it is difficult to even find the portages! The 90-rod trail is the roughest — overgrown and with several windfalls obstructing the path in 1984.

The next three short portages are the hardest to find. Your map may not be much help, so pay attention. The problem is seeing the trails from the water. During the summer, the entrances at both ends of all three portages are so overgrown, it is impossible to recognize them until you are standing on the paths — and sometimes, even then, you may not be **certain.**

Paddle into the mouth of the creek, located about a half mile west of the 90-rod portage. An old beaver dam will necessitate a liftover before you continue across the small pond. The 6-rod portage begins on the right (east) side of a small, rocky rapids. After paddling through another small pond, you will find the 13-rod portage on the **left** side of another rapids. Soon after putting in again, you will have to lift over a low rock ''dam'' that spans the pond. Thereafter, stay to the left and follow the creek to the **right** side of the last rapids, which drains the Maligne River.

There are two nice island campsites on the Maligne River. One is nearly half a mile upstream from Twin Falls. A larger site is next to the falls.

DAY 6 (16 miles): **Maligne River,** p. 16 rods, **Wegwagum Bay** (Lac La Croix), **Lac La Croix, Namakan River,** p. 48 rods, **River,** p. 25 rods, **River, Threemile Lake.** All three portages bypass scenic waterfalls. The 16-rod trail begins on the right (west) side of the right channel of spectacular Twin Falls. (See comments for DAY 1, Route #15.)

If you are planning to fly from the Ranger Station, you have only one portage and 11 miles of paddling from Twin Falls — an easy last day, if south winds are not gale-force.

DAY 7 (12 or 17 miles): **Threemile Lake, Namakan River, Rapids, River,** p. 10 rods, **River, Bill Lake,** p. 18 rods, **Namakan River, Little Eva Lake,** p. 146 rods, **Namakan River,** p. 50 rods, **River, Namakan Lake.** If you don't feel comfortable running the small rapids north of Threemile Lake, there is a 4-rod portage over the small island there. (See comments for DAY 5, Route #15.)

DAY 8 (14 miles): **Namakan Lake, Namakan Narrows, Sand Point Lake, King William's Narrows, Crane Lake.** (See comments for DAY 6, Route #15.)

A Shorter Route Suggestion

4-DAY Loop (From the Ranger Station): This very pleasing loop includes most of the highlights enjoyed on Route #18, but with two days less traveling. Following the same route to the west end of Crooked Lake, you will then steer a northeasterly course and follow Route #19 along the Siobhan River to beautiful Argo Lake. After portaging north to Darky Lake, you will follow the Darky River northwest to the Maligne River, and then paddle back to Lac La Croix. It is an excellent route for those with less time to spare, or for those who would rather spend more time fishing. The shorter route does not sacrifice beautiful scenery, and it includes a stop at the Darky Lake pictographs. (For details, see DAY 1 of Route #18, and DAYS 2-4 of Route #19.)

Curtain Falls

Entry Point 44 — Bottle River

Daily Quota: 1

Use Level: Moderate

LOCATION: The tiny Bottle River flows into the southeast end of Lac La Croix 3½ miles (by air) south of the Lac La Croix Ranger Station. By canoe, it is a 4½-mile paddle to the Bottle Portage, which bypasses the turbulent lower part of the river and gives access to Quetico Park.

DESCRIPTION: The Bottle River, a short segment of the Canadian-American boundary, leads canoeists to a beautiful chain of lakes, rivers, falls and rapids that is very popular among paddlers from the United States visiting the Boundary Waters Canoe Area Wilderness.

Before January 1, 1984, motors had been allowed on the American side of the border, on Crooked Lake and the Basswood River. But now they are banned on both sides of the border.

Many wilderness purists thumb their collective noses at the "crowded" BWCAW and the border lakes. Nevertheless, some of the most beautiful scenery in Quetico Park, including some of the most spectacular waterfalls and rapids, is found along this southwestern perimeter of the Park.

Because this Quetico entry point is so close to several BWCAW entry points along the Echo Trail (Moose River, Portage River, Stuart River, and others), Americans entering Quetico Park here may want to consider shuttling their cars to a convenient BWCAW entry point and plot a one-way route from their origin at Crane Lake. (See Entering From Lac La Croix.)

Route #19: The Bottle and Darky Rivers Loop

FROM & TO THE RANGER STATION:
4 Days, 43 Miles, 10 Lakes, 4 Rivers, 1 Creek, 16 Portages

FROM CRANE LAKE:
9 Days, 125 Miles, 18 Lakes, 6 Rivers, 1 Creek, 24 Portages

FROM NAMAKAN RIVER BRIDGE:
7 Days, 90 Miles, 13 Lakes, 5 Rivers, 1 Creek, 27 Portages

DIFFICULTY: Challenging

FISHER MAPS: F-15, F-16, F-17, F-22, F-23, F-24

HIGHLIGHTS: Rebecca Falls, Curtain Falls, Twin Falls, Warrior Hill, Indian pictographs, Argo Lake.

Introduction: On this four-day swing through the western part of Quetico Park, you will spend only two full days in the interior and two days on the perimeter of the Park. During those four days, however, you will see more outstanding scenery than many canoeists do in a full week elsewhere. From the southeast end of Lac La Croix, you will follow the American border east to Crooked Lake. Already you will have viewed two dazzling waterfalls, a fascinating display of Indian rock paintings, and the incredible panorama from atop Warrior Hill. From the west end of Crooked Lake, you will follow the Siobhan River northeast to lovely Argo Lake and then portage north to Darky Lake. After studying another intriguing pictograph exhibit at the south end of Darky Lake, you will paddle to the lake's north end and begin your journey down the Darky River, through Minn Lake, to the Maligne River. From magnificent Twin Falls, you will then enter the northeast end of Lac La Croix. Those flying out will paddle to their predetermined pick-up point, while water-bound trippers will journey west to the source of the Namakan River. While floating down this resplendent river, you will pass three more exquisite waterfalls and several alluring rapids en route to the Namakan River bridge at Lady Rapids. That is the route's end for some. Others will continue west-bound to Namakan Lake and then paddle south to their origin at Crane Lake.

Anglers may find walleyes and northern pike in most of the lakes along this route. Trout and smallmouth bass also inhabit Lac La Croix, Crooked and Darky lakes. Argo contains trout, walleyes and northern, while Minn shelters virtually all species except trout.

The description of this route begins at the Ranger Station. Be sure to add your route to Lac La Croix, when planning your itinerary.

DAY 1 (10 miles): **Lac La Croix**, p. 80 rods, **Bottle Lake, Bottle River, Iron Lake**, p. 140 rods, **Crooked Lake.** You will not have to paddle far before your first stop. On the west side of Irving Island, just around the bend from the Ranger Station, is the largest and best display of Indian pictographs in all of Quetico Park. Allow plenty of time to study the symbolic figures at the base of the granite cliffs. Two small paintings are located around the corner from the main site. (See the map for precise locations.)

Paddling further south, you will soon come to Warrior Hill. Legends tell of Indian braves racing to the pinnacle of this steep slope. A climb to the summit will be rewarded by a splendid panorama across Lac La Croix.

On your way across Iron Lake, take a side-trip to its northern end. Rebecca Falls plunges 23 feet from Iron Lake through two narrow, jagged chasms to McAree Lake below. Use caution as you approach the falls. The only good vantage point is from the island that splits the falls. You must land on the island between the two falls and hike along the island's perimeter to view the spectacle. If you have arrived here in late July or early August, you may find a blue-speckled patch of tasty blueberries on the sunny side of the island.

When you have had your fill of berries, continue on to the 140-rod portage, which follows a good, wide path along the American bank of the turbulent whitewater. Near the top of the trail is Curtain Falls, a captivating 30-foot cascade that drains Crooked Lake. An excellent vantage point for lunch or photographs is found about midway up the torrent on a granite outcropping just below the primary falls.

Plan to camp near the west end of Crooked Lake, where the dull roar of the falls will lull you to sleep. For the fishermen in your group, Crooked Lake produces walleyes, northern pike, smallmouth bass, largemouth bass, trout, bluegills, perch and black crappies.

DAY 2 (10 miles); **Crooked Lake**, p. 40 rods, **Siobhan River, Little Roland Lake**, p. 5 rods, **Middle Roland Lake**, p. 42 rods, **Roland Lake**, p. 10 rods, **Siobhan River, Argo Lake**, p. 126 rods, **Darky Lake.** All of the portages along the Siobhan River system follow fairly good paths that receive moderate use. When the water level is high enough, paddle into the mouth of the Siobhan River to the take-out point thirty-three rods up the river. During low-water periods, however, you will have to begin the carry at Crooked Lake on the west side of the river's mouth, stretching the portage to 73 rods. The trail connecting Middle Roland and Roland lakes climbs steeply uphill, but follows a good path.

Argo must be one of the the clearest and loveliest lakes in the world! Paddling over its sparkling, vivid-green water is a precious wilderness experience. Even though the Darky portage and the Siobhan River are both at the northwest end of Argo, take a side-trip to the center of this exquisite lake, before continuing on to Darky Lake. The extra time and effort spent is well worth it.

The portage to Darky Lake, except for the first fifteen muddy rods, follows an excellent path over a large hill. The trail begins to drop steeply forty rods from Darky Lake.

At the south end of Darky Lake are two excellent displays of Indian rock paintings. The exhibit includes a moose cow and calf, several canoes, a man with a gun and its projectile, two small moose, hand smears, a maymayguishi and other small abstractions. (See the map for the locations of these two sites.)

Three superb campsites are located at the north end of Darky Lake. The northernmost is large enough for a group of any size. Anglers will find trout, walleyes, northern pike, smallmouth bass, rock bass, perch and black crappies in Darky Lake.

DAY 3 (12 miles): **Darky Lake, Darky River,** beaver dam, **River,** p. 45 rods, **River,** p. 33 rods, **River, Rapids, River, Rapids, River,** p. 11 rods. **River,** p. 55 rods, **River, Rapids, River, Rapids, Minn Lake, Rapids, Darky River,** p. 90 rods, **River, Maligne Creek,** beaver dam, **Creek,** p. 6 rods, **Creek,** p. 13 rods, **Creek,** p. 9 rods, **Creek, Maligne River.** (See comments for DAY 5, Route #18.)

DAY 4 (16 miles): **Maligne River,** p. 16 rods, **Wegwagum Bay** (Lac La Croix), **Lac La Croix, Namakan River,** p. 48 rods, **River,** p. 25 rods, **River, Threemile Lake.** (See comments for DAY 6, Route #18.)

DAY 5 (12 or 17 miles): **Threemile Lake, Namakan River, Rapids, River,** p. 10 rods, **River, Bill Lake,** p. 18 rods, **Namakan River, Little Eva Lake,** p. 146 rods, **Namakan River,** p. 50 rods, **River, Namakan Lake.** (See comments for DAY 7, Route #18.)

DAY 6 (14 miles): **Namakan Lake, Namakan Narrows, Sand Point Lake, King William's Narrows, Crane Lake.** (See comments for DAY 6, Route #15.)

Extended Route Suggestion

6-DAY Loop (from the Ranger Station): After the first day, this loop follows the same trail as Route #18. From the Ranger Station, you will first paddle south to the Bottle Portage, cross the portage, and then proceed in an easterly direction, past Rebecca and Curtain falls to Crooked Lake. You will continue to follow the U.S. boundary across the many lovely bays of Crooked Lake to its easternmost cove. At Moose Bay, then, you will veer to the north and travel over a chain of smaller lakes en route to Brent Lake. From the scenic west end of Brent Lake, you will let the charming Darky River carry you west to Darky Lake and then northwest to Minn Lake. From its north shore, you will cross a series of small ponds en route to the Maligne River. From the northwest corner of Lac La Croix, you will return to your origin, either at the Ranger Station (to fly or be towed out), the Namakan River bridge or Crane Lake. (For details, see DAY 1 for Route #19 and DAYS 2-6 for Route #18.)

CHAPTER 5: Entry From Prairie Portage
– The Southern Region

Five entry points in the south-central part of Quetico Provincial Park are controlled by the Prairie Portage Ranger Station, located at the south end of Basswood Lake's Inlet Bay: Basswood River (#51), Sarah Lake (#52), Kahshahpiwi Lake (#53), Agnes Lake (#61) and Carp Lake (#62). For all, a maximum of fifteen groups per day may enter Quetico Park at Prairie Portage. About twenty rods west of the Ranger's cabin is the Canadian Customs office. Until recently, another station was operating on a small island south of Ottawa Island in south-central Basswood Lake, controlling entry points 51-53.

Even before "Cabin 16" ceased operations, Prairie Portage was usually a busy place. With all traffic from the Ely region now routed through this portage, it is bustling now more than ever before. Almost any time of the summer, it is not unusual to experience congestion at the small boat landings on the Sucker Lake side of the portage. In addition, it is not at all unusual to have to wait in line to see the Ranger.

Not all of the congestion is headed for Quetico Park, however. This trail is shared by visitors to the Boundary Waters Canoe Area Wilderness, who flock to Basswood Lake and its environs. On the west side of the rapids is a truck portage, where motor boats are transported to and from Basswood. Motors of 25 horsepower or less are allowed on the American side of Basswood Lake (except the area north of Jackfish Bay and Washington Island, as well as on the Moose Chain of lakes leading to it.

The best access to Prairie Portage is from Moose Lake, which is 6½ miles southwest to the public landing. It is located nineteen miles northeast of Ely, Minnesota, via Highway 169 (which turns into the Fernberg Road) and the Moose Lake Road. Moose Lake is the busiest of all entry points for the BWCAW. With many resorts, outfitters and private cabins situated at the southwest end of the lake, don't expect wilderness solitude — not until you portage north from Basswood Lake.

Serving the needs of canoeists in this part of the Quetico-Superior region is the modern community of Ely. If Atikokan is the "Canoeing Capital of Canada," then Ely must certainly deserve to be called the "Canoeing Capital of America," if not the world! There is surely no other community in the world with more canoe trip outfitters per capita than Ely. All of them cater to Quetico Park visitors, although not all are located on Moose Lake. Ely is bustling with canoeists and fishermen during the summer months. Supermarkets, motels, restaurants, laundromats, service stations and a variety of specialty and department stores serve the tourist industry. Tourist information is available at the Chamber of Commerce log cabin near the east end of town. A very nice airport is located about five miles south of town.

The closest public campground to Moose Lake, for those wishing to camp the night prior to their trips, is at Fall Lake, about five miles northeast of Ely, just north of the Fernberg Road. Outfitters will provide showers for their own customers. Some will also sell showers to the public.

Prairie Portage Ranger Station

Sunset over Bayley Bay

Entry Point 51 — Basswood River

Daily Quota: 2
Use Level: Moderate

LOCATION: The Basswood River drains the northwest corner of Basswood Lake, ten miles (by air) northwest of the Prairie Portage Ranger Station. Canoeists must paddle the entire length of this enormous lake — fifteen miles from end to end. (See Entry From Prairie Portage.)

DESCRIPTION: Although only two groups per day are allowed to enter Quetico Park via this entry point, don't be fooled into thinking that few people invade the region through which the river flows. On the contrary, the Basswood River is used extensively by visitors to the Boundary Waters Canoe Area Wilderness. No less than five BWCAW entry points direct visitors toward Basswood Lake and the Basswood River, allowing as many as 84 overnight GROUPS per day to camp in this region. During the peak season (late July and the whole month of August), it is not unusual to see literally dozens of other parties between Moose Lake and the Basswood River.

Because of the one-mile portage at the turbulent headwaters of the Basswood River, however, most of the crowd on Basswood Lake is content to go no further than Basswood Falls. So your route down the river will not be nearly as populated as your route to the river.

The flowage of the Basswood River, from Basswood Lake essentially to Lac La Croix, provides us with some of the most splendid scenery to be found anywhere in the North Woods. It is a series of bewitching waterfalls, rushing rapids and lovely lakes. It is a river steeped in history — the Voyageurs' Highway to the hinterlands.

Route #20: The Crooked-Brent Route
8 Days, 85 Miles, 16 Lakes, 2 Rivers, 3 Creeks, 27 Portages

DIFFICULTY: Challenging
FISHER MAPS: F-10, F-17, F-18
HIGHLIGHTS: Basswood River falls, Indian pictographs, beautiful Crooked Lake, big Basswood Lake

Introduction: This pleasing route will take you through some of the loveliest scenery in Quetico Park. And, with only a few nasty portages, it is not all that difficult.

After paddling from Moose Lake to Prairie Portage, you will steer a westerly course across Big Basswood Lake to Basswood Falls at the source of the Basswood River. A full day of traveling along the American border will take you to the center of Crooked Lake, where you will portage north to Argo Lake. From that stunning lake, you will portage north to Darky Lake. After viewing two outstanding displays of Indian rock paintings, then, you will point east and begin your homeward journey up the Darky River to Brent Lake. At the east end of that narrow, winding lake, you will veer toward the southeast and paddle across McIntyre Lake to Sarah Lake, and then across a chain of tiny lakes to Basswood Lake. A shortcut through Burke Lake to Bayley Bay will lead you back to Prairie Portage. From there you must backtrack through the Boundary Waters Canoe Area Wilderness to your origin at Moose Lake.

Below Wheelbarrow Falls

Along the way, you will witness three fascinating exhibits of ancient Indian pictographs, three dazzling waterfalls and some of the prettiest lakes in Ontario. Although much of the American border waters will likely be heavily traveled in mid-summer, the part of the route within the interior of the Park receives only moderate use.

Since you will be camping along the international border the first three nights of this trip, you may want to have a BWCAW Overnight Travel Permit, so that you may legally choose from the selection of campsites on both sides of the border.

DAY 1 (8 miles): **Moose Lake, Newfound Lake, Sucker Lake,** p. 20 rods, **Inlet Bay** (Basswood Lake), **Bayley Bay** (Basswood Lake). Of all the entries to Quetico Provincial Park, this one may be the most disappointing to adventurers in search of wilderness solitude. Motorboats (up to 25 horsepower) are allowed on the Moose chain of lakes and on the American side of Basswood Lake (south and east of Washington Island only). On one busy Monday in July, I once passed over 100 canoes between Moose Lake and Prairie Portage. That number includes neither the many canoes paddling in my direction nor the many motor boats used by fishermen scattered over the area. Nevertheless, for most people, just being on a clear North Woods lake, with warm sun on their backs and a light breeze against their faces, is enough cause for excitement — and knowing that they are finally on their way to that isolated wilderness haven they have been dreaming of all winter.

The first day is a short one. Since Bayley Bay is often plagued by high winds and huge waves, you might as well just plan to take it easy this day and camp at one of the many campsites at the east end of the bay. If Bayley Bay is calm, however, by all means keep paddling! Who knows what tomorrow will bring? The wise paddler will take advantage of calm waters. The farther you can paddle today, the less likely you will find yourself wind-bound tomorrow.

DAY 2 (13 miles): **Bayley Bay** (Basswood Lake), **Basswood Lake.** You can pack away your portage boots this morning. The whole day will be spent paddling across this mammoth lake. Plan to get an early start. If the wind prevails from the southwest, as it often does in mid-summer, the worst stretch will be across the southern part of the lake. If you can make it to Ottawa Island before the wind picks up, you will not have much difficulty until you reach King's Point. But, then, that is close to where you should be camping this evening, anyway.

If you are a vacationing desk jockey who cannot find a tan line with a magnifying glass anywhere on your tender body, **beware of sunburn.** Remember, you will have eight full days to achieve your prize-winning tan; don't try to do it all at once! On a leisurely day of continuous paddling across a long expanse of water, it is very easy to roast your back and shoulders. With a one-mile portage coming up tomorrow, a bad burn could end your trip at the top of Basswood Falls. Don't let this happen to you!

DAY 3 (10 miles): **Basswood Lake,** p. 340 rods, **Basswood River,** p. 30 rods, **River,** p. 32 rods, **River,** p. 32 rods, **River, Crooked Lake.** On this day you will paddle through one of the most scenic parts of Quetico Park — and one of the most dangerous. These turbulent waters drop more than fifty feet from Basswood Lake down to Crooked Lake. The most prominent cascades are at Basswood Falls ((340-rod portage), Wheelbarrow Falls (32 rods) and Lower Basswood Falls (32 rods). In addition, there are several smaller rapids along the route.

Except for its exhausting length, the first portage is relatively easy, following an excellent path that is either level or downhill most of the distance. Potentially muddy spots have been well-maintained with log ''bridges,'' and the U.S. Forest Service has constructed five canoe rests along the trail. To bypass all of the whitewater, bear left at all

Lower Basswood Falls

intersections in the trail. This is definitely the safest way to go. Those who prefer to flirt with the tempting whitewater, however, may split the portage into as many as five shorter portages and paddle the river between them. Many people have drowned in the Basswood River, so use extreme caution!

Just below the long portage is another small rapids. If the water level is suitable and your skills are sufficient, this whitewater may be safely run, eliminating the 30-rod portage. This is the only portage that you can safely eliminate. But if there are doubts in your mind, use the easy portage.

There are portages on both sides of the river at both Wheelbarrow and Lower Basswood falls. I prefer the Canadian trails, which both follow well-beaten downhill paths.

About a mile below Lower Basswood Falls is an interesting display of Indian rock paintings — the red-brown remnants of a woodland culture that once thrived on these waters. This is the second largest display in the Quetico Park region (though just outside the park itself). There you will see two horned figures, a sturgeon in a net, two pelicans, a bull moose, elk, heron, bear, canoe and several abstract symbols.

Three miles north of the pictographs is a low, flat rock called Table Rock. It has been a popular campsite for hundreds of years. Legends say that the Sioux and Ojibwa used Table Rock as a meeting place after one of their wars. No doubt, the Voyageurs may have repaired many a canoe damaged in the Basswood River at this site.

Plan to camp in the vicinity of Wednesday Bay. Crooked Lake has always been popular with fishermen. Walleyes, northern pike, smallmouth and largemouth bass, trout, rock bass, bluegill, perch and black crappies all lurk somewhere beneath its surface.

DAY 4 (10 miles) Crooked Lake, p. 225 rods, **Argo Lake**. Keep your map and compass right in front of you today. You may need them both. Crooked Lake is a challenge to even a seasoned orienteering buff. Because of the many separated bays and winding channels throughout this sprawling lake, you are not likely to see many other canoeists, even though some are undoubtedly nearby.

The long portage to Argo Lake follows the edge of a swamp the first half. During wet conditions, you may have to take alternative trails to higher ground to avoid sinking. The last half of the trail surmounts a long hill. Over the final 50 rods, the path levels off and then descends gently to a sand beach on Argo Lake.

Argo is one of the most stunning lakes in the park. Its water is among the clearest I have ever seen, and definitely the greenest. There aren't many good campsites from which to choose, but two excellent sites are located on small islands in the middle of the lake.

DAY 5 (12 miles): **Argo Lake**, p. 126 rods, **Darky Lake**, p. 15 rods, **Darky River**, p. 182 rods, **River**, p. 18 rods, **Brent Lake**. Except for the first 15 muddy rods, the first portage follows an excellent path over a large hill, dropping steeply down to Darky Lake the final 40 rods. Just beyond the portage are two superb displays of Indian pictographs — one on the left (west) shore, and one further up the right (east) shoreline. These groups of paintings include depictions of a moose cow and calf, several canoes, a man with a gun and its projectile, two small moose, a maymayguishi and hand smears.

The long Darky River portage bypasses a series of small pools and interconnecting rapids. It is an uphill trek on a rugged path over sharp rocks, frequent roots and a potentially muddy section near the middle. When the river is low, or when the current is too swift, you may have to put in five rods sooner at a more suitable access. Those who prefer to break up the long carry into two segments may do so by putting into a small pool after 108 rods, paddling 18 rods, and then portaging the final 56 rods to the end.

Near the west end of Brent Lake, bluffs rise from the water's edge and beyond them hills tower more than 200 feet above the lake. The narrow, twisting channels create a fascinating environment in which to paddle. Plan to camp near the east end of the lake. For the anglers in your group, Brent Lake produces walleyes, northern pike, trout and largemouth bass.

DAY 6 (10 miles): **Brent Lake**, p. 18 rods. (**Unnamed Lake**), p. 4 rods, **McIntyre Lake**, p. 24 rods, **Sarah Lake**. The 24-rod portage to Sarah Lake drops very steeply after 16 rods. Watch your step on this treacherous trail!

The scenery throughout this day is pleasant. But the sheer cliffs and tall hills bordering them make the north end of Sarah Lake exceptional! Amidst this exquisite backdrop is one of the nicest campsites in Quetico Park. Inhabiting Sarah Lake are trout, walleyes, northern pike, smallmouth bass and largemouth bass.

DAY 7 (11 miles): **Sarah Lake**, p. 21 rods, **Side Creek**, p. 22 rods, **Creek**, p. 7 rods, **Side Lake**, p. 94 rods, (**Unnamed Lake**), p. 37 rods, (**Unnamed Lake**). p. 50 rods, **Point Lake**, p. 165 rods, **Nest Lake**, p. 10 rods, **Creek**, p. 18 rods, **Basswood Lake**, **North Bay** (Basswood Lake), p. 11 rods, **Burke Creek**, p. 9 rods, **Creek**, p. 16 rods, **Burke Lake**. With up to twelve portages possible, this is a rugged day. At the east end of Sarah Lake, you will have a choice between a creek route to Side Lake, with three short portages, or one portage of 112 rods over a steep hill. Normally, I prefer one long hike instead of three short ones, BUT this particular portage is ''affectionately'' referred to as ''heart-stop hill.'' Need I say more? Besides, the creek is very scenic. The creek route starts at a 27-rod portage over a small hill. Paddle up the creek to the northeast until you reach a junction in the creek. Then bear to the right and paddle toward the southeast until you arrive at the uphill, 22-rod portage. At the end of this trail, you

Argo Lake

may either put in and paddle 18 rods to a final short portage of 7 rods, or continue hiking along the right side of the creek all the way to Side Lake — a total carry of 47 rods. When the water level is low, your only choice may be the 47-rod portage.

You will be faced with yet another choice at the south end of Side Lake. The portage trail there splits after the first 15 rods, each trail leading to a different unnamed lake. The left branch is the better route, although you may not think so at first. It climbs abruptly for the next 20 rods — suitable only for mountain goats with strong hearts. After reaching the summit, however, the remaining 60 rods are no problem.

On the next lake, follow the right shoreline toward the southeast. The portage at the end of the lake is downhill, descending steeply over a smooth rock face to another nameless lake. When wet, this can be very slippery!

The north half of the 50-rod trail to Point Lake is over a muddy bog. At the midway point, however, it climbs out of the bog and ascends on a drier trail to Point Lake.

The half-mile portage follows an excellent path most of the way to Nest Lake. Near the beginning, however, the trail crosses over a bog and may be muddy. Near the midpoint, the path climbs over a low rock ridge before descending to Nest Lake.

The creek connecting Nest Lake with Basswood Lake may be a problem late in the summer or during a dry year. At best, it is very shallow. Instead of two short downhill portages, you may have to walk all the way from Nest to Basswood Lake.

Your final choice comes at the south end of North Bay. There are two ways to enter Burke Creek, at the creek's two outlets. The westernmost outlet has two short portages of 11 and 9 rods. Or, you may portage 30 rods from the mouth of the east outlet.

There are a couple of nice island campsites at the south end of Burke Lake. If you still have ambition to fish, Burke Lake is home for trout, walleyes, northern pike, and smallmouth, largemouth and rock bass.

DAY 8 (11 miles): **Burke Lake**, p. 84 rods, **Bayley Bay** (Basswood Lake), **Inlet Bay** (Basswood Lake), p. 20 rods, **Sucker Lake, Newfound Lake, Moose Lake**. After that first easy portage, you will be back on the same route on which you started eight days ago.

A Shorter Route Suggestion

5-DAY Loop: To enjoy a very pleasant route via the Tuck River, you may simply reverse Route #21. Like DAYS 1-3 of Route #20, you will first paddle across the entire length of Basswood Lake and then travel down the Basswood River to Crooked Lake. At Moose Bay, however, you will leave the American border and veer north, up the Tuck River to Robinson Lake. From Robinson, you will then plot a northeasterly course through Tuck Lake to Sarah Lake. A chain of small lakes and tiny creeks will lead you southeast to Basswood Lake. From there you will backtrack to your origin at Moose Lake.

(See Route #21 for details.)

Entry Point 52 — Sarah Lake

Daily Quota: 2
Use Level: Moderate

LOCATION: Sarah Lake is located 11 miles by air northwest of Prairie Portage. By canoe, one must paddle and portage 15 miles from the Ranger Station (22 miles from the origin at Moose Lake). (See Entry from Prairie Portage.)

DESCRIPTION: With at least 10 portages, the 2-day route to Sarah Lake is one of the more difficult ways to penetrate Quetico's interior. It shares the route with its neighboring entry point, Kahshahpiwi Lake. Each allows two groups per day to enter; so the route is not as deserted as you might think. Nevertheless, you are not likely to encounter "crowds" once you portage north from Basswood Lake.

The region northwest and west of Sarah Lake contains some of the loveliest lakes and streams in Quetico Park. Also, there are some of the most interesting Indian pictographs, several magnificent waterfalls and a host of resplendent rushing rapids. Either of the two suggested routes will provide you with a high-quality wilderness excursion.

Route #21: The Tuck River Route

5 Days, 53 Miles, 16 Lakes, 2 Rivers, 3 Creeks, 22 Portages

DIFFICULTY: Challenging
FISHER MAPS: F-10, F-17, F-18
HIGHLIGHTS: Basswood River falls, pictographs, big Basswood Lake

Introduction: This medium-sized loop provides a hearty taste of virtually every flavor Quetico Park has to offer: lakes of all sizes, several small streams, portages of all difficulties, and one of the prettiest rivers in the North Woods.

Eighteen of the twenty-two portages are squeezed into the middle three days, including a one-mile carry. So, in spite of a relatively easy start and finish, this route is recommended for only those who are in good physical condition.

From Prairie Portage, you will first cross wind-swept Bayley Bay en route to Burke Lake. From the north end of Burke, you will then cross an even bigger bay of Basswood Lake. At the north end of North Bay, you will begin a route through a chain of creeks and small lakes north and west to Sarah Lake. From the southwest end of scenic Sarah Lake, you will paddle west through Tuck Lake to Robinson Lake and then veer south on the Tuck River to Crooked Lake and the Basswood River. Portaging around three delightful waterfalls, you will follow the Basswood River upstream, back to mammoth Basswood Lake. From Wind Bay, at the south end of Basswood, a short-cut across Wind Lake will deliver you back to your origin on Moose Lake.

The first and last two days of this route will be along the U.S. border, adjacent to the most heavily used part of the Boundary Waters Canoe Area Wilderness. Your two days in the Quetico Park interior, however, will probably not be shared with too many other canoeists.

DAY 1 (11 miles): **Moose Lake, Newfound Lake, Sucker Lake**, p. 20 rods, **Inlet Bay** (Basswood Lake), **Bayley Bay** (Basswood Lake), p. 84 rods, **Burke Lake.** Expeditioners in search of wilderness solitude may wonder if they took a wrong turn

Indian Pictos on Basswood River

somewhere. Heavy canoe and motor boat traffic will likely be encountered most of this day. Motors of 25 horsepower or less are allowed in all of these U.S waters, and most of them are headed for Basswood Lake (a truck portage on the U.S. side of Prairie Portage makes the route attractive).

If you can make it all the way to Burke Lake, however, most of the noisy traffic will be left behind. Bayley Bay may challenge your desire to achieve the Burke Lake goal. The bay is infamous for its white-capped waves and rolling swells created by a strong west wind whipping unimpeded across the six-mile open expanse of Basswood Lake. If the wind is just too strong to attempt a crossing of the bay, you may consider two options: 1) Hold up at one of the many campsites in the vicinity of Green Island and wait for the evening calm; or 2) Sneak around the corner to Sunday Bay and portage into a Sunday Lake detour. The detour will necessitate a much rougher carry at North Portage, followed by an easy trek over Singing Brook Portage.

There are a couple of nice island campsites near the center of Burke Lake, as well as an appealing site at Singing Brook Portage. Anglers may find trout, walleyes, northern, smallmouth, largemouth and rock bass in Burke Lake. Wind bound fishermen on Bayley Bay will also find all of these species in Basswood Lake, as well as crappies, bluegills and perch.

DAY 2 (11 miles): **Burke Lake**, p. 16 rods, **Burke Creek, Rapids, Creek**, p. 11 rods, **North Bay (Basswood Lake), Creek**, p. 6 rods, **(Unnamed Lake), Isabella Creek**, p. 5 rods, **Isabella Lake**, p. 30 rods, **(Unnamed Lake)**, p. 37 rods, **(Unnamed Lake)**, p. 94 rods, **Side Lake**, p. 7 rods, **Side Creek**, p. 22 rods, **Creek**, p. 21 rods, **Sarah Lake**. With ten portages (at least), this is not an easy day. Depending on the water level, it could be even worse. If Burke Creek is deep enough, you may be able to run a small rapids (around which a 9-rod portage is available). Soon thereafter, the stream splits and the left branch leads to an 11-rod portage to North Bay. If the creek is too low for this route, your best bet is to use a 30-rod portage from just above the small rapids to the mouth of the creek's right (east) channel. This will put you on North Bay further east than the first option, behind a large island.

Isabella Creek will probably be blocked by several beaver dams that slow your progress. If the creek appears to be too dry for navigation of a loaded canoe, you can bypass it entirely by portaging a quarter mile north to an unnamed lake and again to Isabella Lake. The portages between Isabella and Side lakes contain some steep sections. Be on the alert for slick rocks. At the bottom of a steep descent in the 94-rod portage, the trail joins another portage path from another lake. Keep right.

From the west side of Side Lake, you may either follow Side Creek, with its three short portages, or you may hike directly from Side Lake to Sarah Lake on a steep 112-rod path "affectionately" referred to as "heart-stop hill." The creek may be slower, but your heart will thank you!

There are a couple of campsites on an island in the southeast end of Sarah Lake. If there is any angling ambition left in your group, the potential prizes are trout, walleyes, northern, and smallmouth and largemouth bass.

DAY 3 (11 miles): **Sarah Lake,** p. 20 rods, **Tuck Lake,** p. 14 rods, (**Unnamed Lake**), p. 18 rods, **Robinson Lake, Tuck River, Rapids, River, Rapids, River,** p. 43 rods, **River, Moose Bay** (Crooked Lake), **Basswood River.** Compared to the day prior, this is a very easy day. The portages are well-traveled and should be no problem. If the water level is not too low on the Tuck River, the two small rapids can be easily and safely run, lined or walked down.

On the American side of the Basswood River, about a mile south of Moose Bay, there are several Indian paintings scattered along the rock cliffs, just above the water level.

South of Moose Bay, and for the remainder of this route, you will be paddling the waters of the international border, shared by the Boundary Waters Canoe Area Wilderness. Three popular BWCAW entry points provide access to the region just south of the Basswood River. So find your campsite early, and don't expect too much privacy this evening.

DAY 4 (12 miles): **Basswood River,** p. 32 rods, **River,** p. 32 rods, **River,** p. 30 rods, **River,** p. 340 rods, **Basswood Lake.** In spite of the long portage, and in spite of the many people who visit this area, you are bound to enjoy this day along the beautiful Basswood River. Three of the four portages bypass scenic waterfalls; Lower Basswood Falls (32 rods), Wheelbarrow Falls (32 rods) and Basswood Falls (340 rods). Since you're heading upstream, all of the portages, obviously, are uphill; but none is difficult. Even the mile-long trail follows an excellent path that is nearly level much of the way. The U.S. Forest Service has constructed five canoe rests along the side of the trail, where you can rest your aching shoulders without having to lower the canoe. The long trail can be divided into shorter segments, if you wish, by paddling upstream between rapids. If you'd rather get it all over in one trip, however, keep right at all intersections.

Plan to camp in the vicinity of Canadian Point, near the center of Basswood Lake.

DAY 5 (8 miles): **Basswood Lake,** p. 170 rods, **Wind Lake,** p. 170 rods, **Moose Lake.** You don't have far to go this day, but two challenging portages await you. The first will lead you uphill to Wind Lake, and the second will drop back down to Moose Lake. If you prefer paddling over portaging, you may want to follow the international border back to Prairie Portage and then backtrack along the Moose Chain to your origin — a total distance of 14 miles, but only one 20-rod portage.

Side Creek

Route #22: The Route of Five Falls

9 Days, 101 Miles, 21 Lakes, 3 Rivers, 3 Creeks, 32 Portages

DIFFICULTY: Challenging

FISHER MAPS: F-10, F-18, F-17, F-16

HIGHLIGHTS: 5 waterfalls, 5 displays of pictographs, Warrior Hill, beautiful Crooked Lake, big Basswood Lake

Introduction: This multifaceted loop covers much of the southwestern corner of Quetico Provincial Park. Like Route #21, you will first head north and west, across Bayley and North bays of Basswood Lake, and then along a chain of small lakes and creeks to Sarah Lake. From the northwest end of Sarah, then, you will enter McIntyre Lake and continue paddling north to Brent Lake. After paddling all the way to the west end of Brent Lake, you will then follow the Darky River northwest to Minn Lake. Through McAree Lake to Lac La Croix, you will then turn the corner and begin your return trip along the international boundary, past two spectacular waterfalls, through the winding channels of Crooked Lake, and finally up the Basswood River to Basswood Lake. From the south end of Basswood Lake, you will portage to Wind Lake and then to Moose Lake, a short paddle from your origin at the public landing.

Along the way, you'll enjoy the opportunity to experience the grandeur of huge lakes, the serenity of tiny creeks, the magnificence of five dazzling waterfalls, the mystery of several Indian pictographs, and the loveliness of the lakes in this part of Quetico Park. With 28 portages during the seven middle days of the trip, including a one-mile trek and three trails over a half-mile in length, only canoeists in good shape should consider this loop.

DAY 1 (11 miles): **Moose Lake, Newfound Lake, Sucker Lake,** p. 20 rods, **Inlet Bay** (Basswood Lake), **Bayley Bay** (Basswood Lake), p. 84 rods, **Burke Lake.** (See comments for DAY 1, Route #21.)

DAY 2 (11 miles): **Burke Lake,** p. 16 rods, **Burke Creek, Rapids, Creek,** p. 11 rods, **North Bay** (Basswood Lake), **Creek,** p. 6 rods, **(Unnamed Lake), Isabella**

Sarah Lake

124

Creek, p. 5 rods, **Isabella Lake**, p. 30 rods, **(Unnamed Lake)**, p. 37 rods, **(Unnamed Lake)**, p. 94 rods, **Side Lake**, p. 7 rods, **Side Creek**, p. 22 rods, **Creek**, p. 21 rods, **Sarah Lake**. (See comments for DAY 2, Route #21.)

DAY 3 (14 miles): **Sarah Lake**, p. 24 rods, **McIntyre Lake**, p. 4 rods, **(Unnamed Lake)**, p. 18 rods, **Brent Lake**. The first 8 rods of that 24-rod carry climb steeply, but the rest of the day is downhill. Plan to camp toward the west end of Brent Lake. There you will find several nice island campsites facing scenic bluffs along the lake's edge, with nearby hills rising more than 200 feet above the water. It is a splendid setting in which to cast your line. Walleyes, trout, northern and largemouth bass inhabit the lake.

DAY 4 (12 miles): **Brent Lake**, p. 18 rods, **Darky River**, p, 182 rods, **River**, p. 15 rods, **Darky Lake, Darky River**, beaver dam, **River**, p. 45 rods, **River**, p. 33 rods, **River, Rapids, River, Rapids, River**, p. 11 rods, **River**, p. 55 rods, **River, Rapids, River, Rapids, Minn Lake**. The Darky River begins as a series of small pools and interconnecting rapids that all add up to one short portage and the second-longest carry of the whole trip. Although it is downhill, the 182-rod trail follows a fairly rugged (but well-traveled) path over sharp rocks, frequent roots and a potentially muddy spot near the middle. When the river is low, you may have to walk five rods farther to put in at a more suitable access. Those who prefer to break up the portage into two segments may do so by putting into a small pool after 56 rods, paddling 18 rods, and then portaging an additional 108 rods to the end.

If there is plenty of sunlight left in the day, you may want to take a 4-mile side-trip to the south end of Darky Lake, where you will find two excellent displays of Indian pictographs.

Your first obstacle northwest of Darky Lake is a log jam at a beaver dam, requiring a 1-rod balancing act. Within sight of the dam is the first actual portage, where the trail climbs steeply before descending gradually to the bottom of a ravine.

If the water level is high, you may be able to paddle past the first access to the next portage and shorten your carry to only 11 rods. That trail, too, climbs steeply and then drops down just as quickly.

You should have no difficulty gliding through the small riffle below the 33-rod portage; nor at the one just after the river's confluence with Andrew's Creek. The 55-rod carry allows you to bypass another small riffle and a barracade of fallen trees above a major rapids. You can shorten that portage to just 25 rods by running through the riffle and picking your way through the trees.

Minn is one of six lakes in Quetico Park on which treaty Indians of the Lac La Croix Guides Association are permitted to use motors of 10 horsepower or less. So don't be shocked if you see or hear small motor boats. They are attracted by the northern, smallmouth bass, walleyes, perch and rock bass that inhabit Minn Lake.

There is a nice island campsite near the south shore of the lake.

DAY 5 (11 miles): **Minn Lake**, p. 14 rods, **McAree Lake**, p. 66 rods, **Lac La Croix**. You deserve an easy day, so here it is. Two easy portages separate you from the scenic southeast end of Lac La Croix. Since Lac La Croix falls outside of the Park's boundaries, there are no restrictions to the use of motors on the Canadian side of that beautiful lake. Resorts and an Indian village are located along the north shore. Two popular BWCAW entry points allow canoeists quick access to the border region. What this all adds up to is: you are now back in a busy part of the wilderness.

On the west side of Irving Island, just around the bend from the La Croix Ranger Station, is the largest and best display of Indian pictographs in all of Quetico Park. Take time to study the symbolic figures at the bases of the granite cliffs. Around the corner from the main site are two more smaller paintings. (See the map for the precise locations.) South of the rock painting is Warrior Hill, where legends tell of Indian braves racing to the pinnacle of this steep slope. A climb to the summit will be rewarded by a spendid panorama.

Plan to camp just south of Warrior Hill. Fishermen should be able to catch any species they desire. Lurking beneath the surface of this enormous lake are trout, walleyes, northerns, smallmouth bass, perch, sturgeon, rock bass and black crappies. Don't forget: Crown Land Camping Permits are required for ''non-residents'' camping on Lac La Croix.

DAY 6 (12 miles): **Lac La Croix**, p. 80 rods, **Bottle Lake, Bottle River, Iron Lake**, p. 140 rods, **Crooked Lake.** On your way across Iron Lake, take a side trip to its northern end. Rebecca Falls plunges 23 feet from Iron Lake through two narrow chasms to McAree Lake below. Use caution as you approach the top of the falls. The only vantage point is from the island which splits the falls. You must land on the island between the two falls and hike along its perimeter to view the spectacle. If you have arrived here in late July or early August, you may find a huge patch of tasty blueberries on the sunny side of the island.

When you have had your fill of berries, continue on to the 140-rod portage. Near the top of this good, wide, well-traveled portage, is Curtain Falls, a captivating 30-foot cascade that drains Crooked Lake. An excellent vantage point for lunch or photographers is found on a granite outcropping below the primary falls. You may enter Crooked Lake at the very brink of the falls, or about 100 feet farther along the shoreline. The latter choice is the safest for a group that may not be strong enough to paddle against the swift current at the top of the falls.

Plan to camp near the mouth of Friday Bay. There are several good ''designated'' campsites on the American side of the border. Unless you have a BWCAW Travel Permit in your possession, however, you are restricted to select from a smaller assortment north of the border.

Crooked is traditionally a good lake for anglers. Its species include walleyes, northern, smallmouth, largemouth and rock bass, trout, bluegills, perch and black crappies.

DAY 7 (10 miles): **Crooked Lake, Basswood River.** This is your only day of the whole trip without a single portage. So pray for sunshine and warm temperatures! (See comments for DAY 2, Route #18.)

On the American side of the Basswood River, about a mile south of Moose Bay, are several more Indian rock paintings scattered along the rock cliffs, just above the water level.

Try to find a campsite early, and don't expect too much privacy this evening. Three popular BWCAW entry points provide access to the region just south of Basswood River.

DAY 8 (12 miles): **Basswood River**, p. 32 rods, **River**, p. 32 rods, **River**, p. 30 rods, **River**, p. 340 rods, **Basswood Lake.** (See comments for DAY 4, Route #21.)

DAY 9 (8 miles): **Basswood Lake**, p. 170 rods, **Wind Lake**, p. 170 rods, **Moose Lake.** (See comments for DAY 5, Route #21.)

Another Route Suggestion

8-DAY Loop: By simply changing your entry point from 51 — Basswood River to 52 — Sarah Lake, you could reverse Route #20. This excellent route has many of the same highlights as does Route #22. It also includes one of the loveliest lakes in Quetico Park — Argo Lake. See Route #20 for details.

Entry Point 53 — Kahshahpiwi Lake

Daily Quota: 2
Use Level: Heavy

LOCATION: Kahshahpiwi Lake is located 15 miles due north of the Moose Lake landing, 12 miles northwest of Prairie Portage. By canoe, however, it is a challenging 23 miles, across 11 lakes and 11 portages, from the parking lot to Kahshahpiwi Lake.

DESCRIPTION: Kahshahpiwi is a very pretty lake, bordered by rocky cliffs and hills that tower more than 250 feet above the water's edge. It is also the source of Kahshahpiwi Creek, which connects a series of lovely lakes leading northeast to Kawnipi Lake and the central flowage of the Maligne River — a route that nearly bisects Hunter's Island.

The last manned Ranger Station in the interior of Quetico Park was situated on the west shore of Kahshahpiwi Lake, adjacent to a fire lookout tower. That cabin was abandoned a few years ago, and now there are no Rangers permanently stationed in the Park's interior.

In spite of the fact that this is the most difficult entry point to arrive at, and in spite of the fact that only two groups per day are allowed to enter here, the Kahshahpiwi chain is one of the most heavily used routes in Quetico Park. The entry point gets "booked up" early in the season. If you are planning a trip through Kahshahpiwi Lake during the peak weeks of late July and the month of August, you would be wise to make your reservation as soon as you possibly can!

Route #23: The Kahshahpiwi — Agnes Lake Loop

7 Days, 80 Miles, 21 Lakes, 1 River, 3 Creeks, 24 Portages

DIFFICULTY: Challenging
FISHER MAPS: F-10, F-18, F-25, F-11
HIGHLIGHTS: Kahshahpiwi Creek, Indian pictographs Louisa Falls, the Meadows portages, only four portages longer than 100 rods

Introduction: This popular route slices right up the middle of Quetico Provincial Park. From Prairie Portage, you will steer a northwesterly course, across Inlet and Bayley bays, Burke Lake and North Bay to the northeast end of big Basswood Lake. From there, the setting changes considerably, as you enter a world of smaller lakes and meandering creeks that lead first west, through Isabella Lake, and then north, through Side Lake, to the end of beautiful Kahshahpiwi Lake. For the next day and a half, you will follow Kahshahpiwi Creek along its straight northeasterly course to the northwest end of Kawnipi Lake. After twisting your way through the scenic, narrow channels leading to Kasie Island, you will then paddle south, through Keewatin Lake, to Agnes Lake. Fourteen miles of uninterrupted paddling will push you to the south end of that incredible lake. There you will take time to soak in the bathtub at Louisa Falls and to enjoy the panorama from atop that exquisite cascade. At the south end of

Agnes, then, you will forge across the Meadows portages to Sunday Lake, and then portage back to Basswood Lake. You will backtrack the final nine miles to your origin at Moose Lake.

Were it not for the second and sixth days of this trip, the route would surely be labeled "easy." Nine of the 24 portages will be encountered during the second day of travel. That leaves an average of only two carries per day for the rest of the route. But two of the roughest are back-to-back portages leading to and from Meadows Lake. Nevertheless, only four portages along this entire route are in excess of 100 rods. If you can make it through the second day without too many aches and battle scars, you are sure to enjoy the rest of the trip!

For the anglers in your group, this route offers something for everyone. Virtually all of the waters contain walleyes and northern pike. Trout also live in most of the larger lakes, and smallmouth bass are found in several.

DAY 1 (11 miles): **Moose Lake, Newfound Lake, Sucker Lake,** p. 20 rods, **Inlet Bay** (Basswood Lake), **Bayley Bay** (Basswood Lake), p. 84 rods, **Burke Lake.** (See comments for DAY 1, Route #21.)

DAY 2 (13 miles): **Burke Lake,** p. 16 rods, **Burke Creek, Rapids, Creek,** p. 11 rods, **North Bay** (Basswood Lake), **Creek,** p. 6 rods, (Unnamed Lake), **Isabella Creek,** p. 5 rods, **Isabella Lake,** p. 30 rods, (Unnamed Lake), p. 37 rods, (Unnamed Lake), p. 94 rods, **Side Lake,** p. 35 rods, (Unnamed Lake), p. 182 rods, **Kahshahpiwi Lake.** (See first two paragraphs of comments for DAY 2, Route #21.) If you don't think you can make it all the way to Kahshahpiwi Lake, there are a couple campsites on Side Lake that you might want to consider.

Half of the canoe traffic headed this way has Sarah Lake as its destination. That entry point also allows two groups per day. Side Lake is the junction of the two routes.

Indian rock paintings are at the south end of Kahshahpiwi Lake. They depict a turtle, a salamander and several abstractions. An eagle nest, also, has been sighted a short distance north of the portage. Plan to camp at one of the campsites near the south end of the lake. For the anglers in your group, Kahshahpiwi contains trout, walleyes, northern and smallmouth bass.

DAY 3 (12 miles): **Kahshahpiwi Lake,** p. 27 rods, **Keefer Lake,** p. 76 rods, **Sark Lake, Kahshahpiwi Creek,** p. 84 rods, **Cairn Lake.** Compared to what you have already been through, this day is a "breeze." And, if the breeze is out of the south, you can literally sail most of the way to Cairn Lake. This part of your route is a scenic series of lakes separated by rapids and connected by easy portages.

There are a couple of island campsites on Cairn Lake. You should be able to make camp early. Then cast a line for one of the walleyes, northern or rock bass that inhabits this lovely lake.

DAY 4 (12 miles): **Cairn Lake,** p. 20 rods, **Kahshahpiwi Creek,** p. 40 rods, **Creek,** p. 10 rods, **Kawnipi Lake.** Depending on the water level in the creek, you may be able to run, line or walk your canoe down that first set of gentle rapids north of Cairn Lake. Kahshahpiwi Creek enters the Maligne River just below a set of twin rapids that pass on both sides of a small island. You will be going upstream this time, so you will have to either portage or walk your canoe up the stream.

For the remainder of this day, you will be paddling on the historic and ever-popular Hunter's Island Route. Traffic may be heavy, so be sure to look both ways before crossing the river . . .

Plan to camp in the vicinity of Rose Island, at the southwest end of Kawnipi Lake. Walleyes, northern and perch inhabit this big, sprawling lake.

DAY 5 (12 miles): **Kawnipi Lake,** p. 84 rods, **Keewatin Lake,** p. 80 rods, (Unnamed Lake), p. 76 rods, **Agnes Lake.** After three quick quarter-mile portages, you'll have clear sailing down the fifteen-mile stretch of big, beautiful Agnes Lake. Or, if there is a strong south wind opposing you, you may have another adjective to describe the monster.

Regardless, this day is devoted to the historians in your group. You will pass three different displays of Indian rock paintings on this south-bound journey: one on the west shore of Keewatin Lake, one on the west shore of Agnes Lake, and one island site near the middle of Agnes. (Before you leave Agnes, you'll have an opportunity to search for one more exhibit at the lakes south end.)

And for the ornithologist in the group, he or she will want to be alert for ospreys in the area. Two nests have been reported in the north end of Agnes Lake.

Plan to camp five or six miles from the south end of the lake. That should allow plenty of time for the anglers in your group to test their collective luck. Trout, walleyes, northern pike, smallmouth bass, perch and rock bass all share the waters of Agnes Lake.

DAY 6 (8 miles): **Agnes Lake,** p. 140 rods, **Meadows Lake,** p. 212 rods, **Sunday Lake.** With only eight miles to travel, there will be plenty of time to enjoy Louisa Falls, at the south end of Agnes Lake. (See About Louisa Falls, pp. 135.)

It is unfortunate that you won't be able to enjoy the Louisa massage **after** the two "Meadow portages." That's when you'll need it. Either of the back-to-back portages, by itself, is a challenge. Together, well, it's not a pretty sight . . .

Nevertheless, you should be able to make camp early. That's important, since Sunday Lake is a popular resting spot. Ambitious anglers will attract trout, walleyes, northern, smallmouth, rock and largemouth bass, and black crappies.

DAY 7 (12 miles): **Sunday Lake,** p. 134 rods, **Sunday Bay (Basswood Lake),** **Bayley Bay (Basswood Lake), Inlet Bay (Basswood Lake),** p. 20 rods, **Sucker Lake, Newfound Lake, Moose Lake.** North Portage is not an easy carry, by any means. By now, however, the food pack is light (or completely empty?), your muscles are strong, and your shoulders are callous. Once on Bayley Bay, you'll backtrack the busy route to Moose Lake.

Route #24: The Old Pines Loop
4 Days, 47 Miles, 22 Lakes, 3 Creeks, 23 Portages

DIFFICULTY: Challenging
FISHER MAPS: F-10, F-18, F-17
HIGHLIGHTS: Pictographs, moose habitat, giant virgin pines

Introduction: This delightful route will take you through the best stand of virgin red and white pines in all of Quetico Provincial Park. En route, you will have an opportunity to explore a vast variety of interesting waterways, ranging in character from big Basswood Lake to the tiny creeks and tranquil ponds lying north of that awesome expanse. From Moose Lake, you will first follow the Moose chain northeast to the Canadian-American border. From Prairie Portage you will steer a northwesterly course to Burke Lake, where your first campsite awaits. At the north end of Burke, you will portage to Burke Creek and then let it carry you on to North Bay of Basswood Lake. From the northeast corner of the bay, you will then enter a world of small, peaceful lakes and streams that will transport you further north, through Shade, Grey and Yum Yum lakes to your destination at McNiece Lake. From McNiece, you will begin your southwest-bound journey, first across the south end of Kahshahpiwi Lake, and then across a chain of smaller lakes leading to Ranger Bay of Basswood Lake. Your last day will require only two portages, as you paddle south, across the length of Basswood Lake to Wind Bay. From there you will portage into and out of Wind Lake, en route to your origin at Moose Lake.

When the route is complete, you will have enjoyed four challenging days in Quetico Park. You will have crossed nineteen portages during your second and third days — a feat that should be undertaken only by canoeists in excellent physical condition. Though none of the portages is exceptionally difficult, the cumulative sum takes its toll!

It is highly unlikely that any of this route will be void of any other people, unless taken in early summer or fall. The second day, however, will probably exhibit the greatest solitude. By returning via Wind Lake, you will miss most of the crowd on the Moose chain of lakes and at Prairie Portage.

Anglers will have an opportunity to catch virtually any species of fish known to Quetico Park. Many of the lakes on this route contain trout, walleyes, northern and bass, and some contain perch, crappies and assorted pan fish. Those who plan to fish a great deal should allow at least five days, and perhaps six, for this loop. In four days, there is only enough time to stop for pictures, except on the lakes where you will camp.

DAY 1 (11 miles): **Moose Lake, Newfound Lake, Sucker Lake,** p. 20 rods, **Inlet Bay** (Basswood Lake), **Bayley Bay** (Basswood Lake), p. 84 rods, **Burke Lake.** (See comments for DAY 1, Route #21.)

DAY 2 (12 miles): **Burke Lake,** p. 16 rods, **Burke Creek, Rapids, Creek,** p. 11 rods, **North Bay** (Basswood Lake), **Creek,** p. 14 rods, **South Lake,** p. 12 rods, **West Lake,** p. 9 rods, **Pond, Creek,** p. 4 rods, **Shade Lake,** p. 80 rods, (Unnamed **Lake**), p. 128 rods, **Grey Lake,** p. 96 rods, **Yum Yum Lake,** p. 20 rods, (Unnamed **Lake**), p. 27 rods, **McNiece Lake.** Your route from Burke Lake to North Bay will depend, in part, upon the water level of Burke Creek. When the level is high, you should have no difficulty running down a short rapids. Afterwards, when the creek splits, follow the left fork to the 11-rod portage that leads to North Bay. Should the water level be too low to run the small rapids, you may wish to take an alternative 30-rod portage to North Bay. It begins on the right (east) bank of the creek, just above the rapids. If the wind is anything else but northerly, you should have no problem crossing North Bay.

The creeks and small lakes northeast of the bay are good places to observe moose. In 1984, my wife and I witnessed five moose between Burke Creek and South Lake. Keep a watchful eye!

A short side-trip on Shade Lake will enable you to see an ancient Indian rock painting. Located about half a mile northeast of the portage leading to the next unnamed lake, the pictograph contains two abstract Thunderbird symbols.

At Yum Yum Lake, if you have the temptation to take a short-cut across Yum Yum Portage to Kahshahpiwi Lake, RESIST IT. In the first place, you would miss the impressive stand of virgin pines around McNiece Lake and the unnamed lake east of McNiece. In the second place, Yum Yum Portage hardly qualifies as a "short-cut." Short-cuts should be easier than the original route. It is not!

If the anglers in your group have any energy left at the end of this exhausting day, they may find trout and northern pike in McNiece Lake.

DAY 3 (11 miles): **McNiece Lake,** p. 164 rods, **Kahshahpiwi Lake,** p. 182 rods, (Unnamed **Lake**), p. 35 rods, **Side Lake,** p. 94 rods, (Unnamed **Lake**), p. 37 rods, (Unnamed **Lake**), p. 50 rods, **Point Lake,** p. 165 rods, **Nest Lake,** p. 90 rods, **Ranger Bay** (Basswood Lake). If you thought the day before was rugged, brace yourself! Among the eight portages to be crossed this day, three are longer than half a mile (each). All are challenges, but none is exceptionally difficult. The 94-rod portage at the south end of Side Lake hides another challenge. After walking 15 rods, you will come to a split in the trail. Following the left trail, you must climb steeply for twenty rods, before leveling off and then beginning a gradual descent to the lovely unnamed lake. The first half of the 50-rod portage to Point Lake crosses a bog, and the path may be very muddy during wet seasons.

Basswood Lake offers a variety of fishing opportunities. It contains trout, walleyes, northern, smallmouth and largemouth bass, perch, crappies, rock bass, bluegills and pumpkinseed.

DAY 4 (13 miles): **Ranger Bay** (Basswood Lake), **Basswood Lake, Wind Bay** (Basswood Lake), p. 170 rods, **Wind Lake**, p. 170 rods, **Moose Lake**. Get an early start, before the winds pick up. If there is a strong wind, you might as well stay where you are and enjoy a relaxing layover day.

Extended Route Suggestion

11-DAY Loop: This appealing route follows the same northbound trail as Route #23 for the first three days. At the confluence of Kahshahpiwi Creek with the Maligne River, however, you will continue paddling north to Shelley Lake. From that point on, you will be following the last 8 days of the Hunter's Island route. Essentially, you will paddle downstream on the Maligne River flowage to Lac La Croix, and then follow the U.S. border all the way back to Prairie Portage. It's an excellent route for those with plenty of traveling time. (See DAYS 1-3 of Route #23 and DAYS 6-13 of Route #27.)

Louisa Falls

Entry Point 61 — Agnes Lake

Daily Quota: 7
Use Level: Heavy

LOCATION: Agnes Lake is located 6 miles, by air, northeast of Prairie Portage. By canoe, the shortest route to the lake is by way of Sunday Lake, a total distance of 15 miles from the Moose Lake landing.

DESCRIPTION: Agnes Lake is an entry point that requires reservations long in advance. Even though seven groups per day may enter Quetico Park at this point, the quota is often filled throughout the summer. Fifteen miles long, with a rocky shoreline and occasional dramatic cliffs, three known exhibits of ancient Indian rock paintings and spectacular Louisa Falls splashing into its south end — it's no wonder that so many canoeists are drawn to that alluring lake.

For many, Agnes Lake offers quick access to the remote interior of Quetico Park. For others, this elegant lake may be the destination. Regardless, there are three good routes by which one can arrive there.

Route #25: The Louisa Falls Loop
4 Days, 41 Miles, 12 Lakes, 2 Creeks, 14 Portages

DIFFICULTY: Easy to Challenging
FISHER MAPS: F-10, F-18, F-11
HIGHLIGHTS: Moose, pictographs, Louisa Falls, the Meadows portages

Introduction: This short and varied loop takes you over the least used route to Agnes Lake. From Prairie Portage, you will paddle across Inlet and Bayley bays and then portage to Burke Lake. From the north end of Burke Lake, you will follow Burke Creek north to North Bay of Basswood Lake. At the east side of North Bay, you will enter a different world of small lakes and tiny creeks that will carry you eastward to Agnes Lake. Having paddled to the south end of Agnes Lake, you will take time to enjoy the "bathtub" at Louisa Falls, before continuing on your journey across the rugged "Meadows portages" to Sunday Lake. From the southwest end of Sunday Lake, you must cross one more rugged portage en route to Basswood Lake, and then you will backtrack to your origin at Moose Lake.

Though most of the route is well-traveled, your second day in the region between North Bay and Agnes Lake will likely be spent alone. There you should have an excellent chance to view a magnificent moose browsing along the bank of a tiny creek or along the shore of one of those isolated lakes. This will be your only respite from the "crowds" that visit Louisa Falls.

Most of the portages are short and should pose no problem. Unfortunately, the only three long and difficult carries fall on the same day — your third. Save your energy for that day!

DAY 1 (11 miles): **Moose Lake, Newfound Lake, Sucker Lake,** p. 20 rods, **Inlet Bay** (Basswood Lake), **Bayley Bay** (Basswood Lake), p. 84 rods, **Burke Lake.** (See comments for DAY 1, Route #21.)

DAY 2 (11 miles): **Burke Lake,** p. 16 rods, **Burke Creek, Rapids, Creek,** p. 11 rods, **North Bay** (Basswood Lake), p. 14 rods, **South Lake,** p. 12 rods, **West Lake, Jeff Creek,** p. 24 rods, **(Unnamed Lake),** p. 8 rods, **Jeff Lake,** p. 41 rods, **East Lake.** As you are paddling north on Burke Creek, you will see the beginning of a

132

(30-rod) portage on the right side of the creek, just above a set of small rapids. If the water level is too low to run down the rapids, you might as well take that portage. Otherwise, continue on down the rapids. Then, when the creek splits, follow the left fork to an 11-rod portage that leads to North Bay.

As you might expect, the wind certainly can be a problem on North Bay. If it's a prevailing southwesterly, however, it might just blow you all the way to the narrow outlet at the east side of the bay. From that point until you reach Agnes Lake, you are not likely to see many other canoes.

If you are quiet and watchful, however, you just may see moose, instead. While silently paddling this route in June of 1984, my wife and I observed a cow and two calves browsing along the shore of South Lake. A young bull was also seen above the eastern shoreline of the narrow outlet leading north from the bay.

The shallow creek extending from the southeast end of West Lake is plenty deep for navigation — at first. When you reach the intersection of two creeks, bear left on the branch that leads east and then northeast. After that junction, even during a wet time of the year, the creek becomes so shallow and so narrow, you may have to walk your canoe much of the way to the next portage. And that portage is not easy to find! When the creek becomes so narrow that you can barely turn your canoe around the tight bends, and when you have rounded a major bend in the creek to the sight of an apparent "dead end" looming ahead of you, STOP. Don't proceed any further. Instead, look to the left bank for signs of the portage: a slight parting of the bushes, a ribbon or other remnant from explorers who have gone this way before you. If you make it all the way to the rapids, you have gone about 20 rods too far. Believe me, this little portage is not easy to find. Twice, I have missed it and had to "bushwhack" up along the steep and overgrown side of the rapids. The portage is much easier!

The 41-rod trail to East Lake begins at the very tip of the northeast end of Jeff Lake. Don't be fooled by another lightly used path on the right shore as you approach the true portage.

A large, beautiful campsite is located on the north shore of East Lake. Walleyes and smallmouth bass inhabit the lake.

DAY 3 (8 miles): **East Lake**, p. 39 rods, **Agnes Lake**, p. 140 rods, **Meadows Lake**, p. 212 rods, **Sunday Lake.** This day is planned to be shorter than the others, so that you may have plenty of time to enjoy Louisa Falls. Before you arrive there, however, you may want to paddle past a faded Indian rock painting on the east side of an island about 2½ miles north of the falls. (See comments for DAY 6, Route #23.)

DAY 4 (11 miles): **Sunday Lake**, p. 134 rods, **Sunday Bay** (Basswood Lake), **Bayley Bay** (Basswood Lake), **Inlet Bay** (Basswood Lake), p. 20 rods, **Sucker Lake, Newfound Lake, Moose Lake.** North Portage is almost as rough as Part II of the Meadows portages. If you prefer two easy portages and a couple extra miles of paddling, rather than negotiate North Portage, you could portage to Burke Lake and then to Bayley Bay. Once on Basswood Lake, you will backtrack the busy route to Moose Lake.

Route #26: The "S" Chain
5 Days, 55 Miles, 18 Lakes, 1 Creek, 19 Portages

DIFFICULTY: Challenging
FISHER MAPS: F-10, F-11, F-18
HIGHLIGHTS: big Basswood Lake, 3 pictographs, Louisa Falls, the Meadows portages

Introduction: Like Route #25, this interesting loop also takes you to popular Louisa Falls, but it takes a day longer to get you there. From Prairie Portage, you will follow the international boundary across much of mammoth Basswood Lake. From its north end, you will portage into Nest Lake and then begin a northeasterly course through Point and Isabella lakes, and a chain of smaller, nameless ponds, en route to the "S" Chain: Shade, Summer, Sultry and Silence lakes (Noon Lake should have been Six or Seven, to fit the theme!). From the east end of Silence Lake, you will portage to Agnes Lake and then paddle eight miles to its south end. After splashing in the bathtub of Louisa Falls, you will then proceed across the rugged, back-to-back Meadows portages to Sunday Lake. From Sunday, it is another rough carry across North Portage to Basswood Lake. Nine miles of backtracking will return you to your origin at Moose Lake.

With Louisa Falls as the ultimate destination, this loop follows a much more challenging route than does Route #25. Thirteen of the nineteen portages will be crossed on the second and third days. But most carries are very short. Only four of the nineteen portages exceed 100 rods in length. Fortunately, the longest and most rugged carries will be near the end of the loop. Only two short segments of this route are questionable when the water level is down. Both can be bypassed, if necessary.

Anglers will surely enjoy the fishing opportunities throughout the route. Virtually every North Woods species is represented. Walleye, northern, trout and smallmouth bass inhabit most of the lakes. Largemouth bass also live in many of the lakes.

DAY 1 (9 miles): **Moose Lake, Newfound Lake, Sucker Lake,** p. 20 rods, **Inlet Bay** (Basswood Lake), **Bayley Bay** (Basswood Lake). (See DAY 1, Route #20.)

DAY 2 (13 miles): **Bayley Bay** (Basswood Lake), **Basswood Lake,** p. 18 rods, **Creek,** p. 10 rods, **Nest Lake,** p. 165 rods, **Point Lake,** p. 24 rods, **Isabella Lake.** That first short portage (18 rods) climbs rather abruptly to a shallow creek that may be a problem during late summer or during an abnormally dry year. The bottom is too muddy to permit walking your canoe. If you can't pole through the muck, your only alternative is to portage around the whole mess — a distance of approximately eighty bushwhacking rods, without a discernible trail on which to walk.

The half-mile portage from the north end of Nest Lake follows a good path, but it climbs up and over a rocky ridge near the center of the trail. Near the end, the path crosses a bog. Otherwise, the trail is ''clean.''

Isabella is a very pretty lake, its long, narrow shape resembling a river with high, scenic banks. A nice campsite is elevated above the south shoreline. Take extra precautions here for bears. In 1984, a ''problem bear'' was harassing campers at the north end of North Bay. Isabella Lake is well within the cruising range of that bear, if it is still around. (See Making Your Camp Bear-able.)

If you already have a craving for fish, you are camped on a good lake. Isabella contains walleyes, northern, smallmouth bass, largemouth bass and perch.

DAY 3 (10 miles): **Isabella Lake,** p. 5 rods, **Isabella Creek,** (**Unnamed Lake**), p. 80 rods, **West Lake,** p. 9 rods, **pond, Creek,** p. 4 rods, **Shade Lake,** p. 20 rods, **Noon Lake,** p. 15 rods, **Summer Lake,** p. 16 rods, **Sultry Lakes,** p. 40 rods, **Silence Lake.** Days, like this, with frequent short portages, are no problem for canoeists who can carry all their gear in one trip. None of the trails exceed a quarter mile in length, and all nine combined add up to only 195 rods — 6/10 of a mile. If it takes you two trips to carry the gear, however, you are in for a long day — 1.8 miles of hiking!

Isabella Creek is likely to blockaded by occasional beaver dams. If the creek appears to be too low for navigation, you can bypass it entirely by portaging 110 rods from Isabella Lake to an unnamed lake north of the creek, and then another 67 rods back to the original route.

The recommended mileage this day includes a one-mile side-trip to a display of Indian pictographs near the north end of a bay in Shade Lake. (See the map for exact location.) There you will see the faded remnants of two abstract thunderbird symbols. To the Indians, a thunderbird was an enormous, supernatural bird that could produce thunder, lightning and rain. Keep your raincoats handy . . .

For the fishermen in your group, Silence Lake is another good location at which to camp. Walleyes, northern, trout, smallmouth, largemouth and rock bass, and perch all share its waters.

DAY 4 (9 miles): **Silence Lake,** p. 8 rods, **Agnes Lake.** The historians in your group will, no doubt, want to paddle out of their way, a bit, to view two more pictographs on Agnes Lake. One display is just north of the small bay into which you will portage from Silence Lake. The other is on an island 1½ miles northeast of the portage. These rock paintings include representations of rabbits, a bear, a canoe, hand smears and two maymayguishi standing in a canoe.

With only nine miles to travel, you should be able to make camp early at the south end of Agnes Lake. From there it is short distance across the lake to Louisa Falls.

About Louisa Falls

Louisa Creek plummets nearly one hundred feet in two stages from Louisa Lake to Agnes Lake. Most of that precipitous plunge is at Louisa Falls — a dazzling spectacle, but far more than just another pretty rock face. Were it not for a unique feature, it is doubtful that canoeists would flock here from every direction. Louisa may be the only major falls in all of the Quetico-Superior region that welcomes ''participation.'' Midway up the falls is a natural bowl that has been carved out of the solid rock formation — a wilderness jacuzzi, of sorts. You may safely soak in the swirling ''bathtub,'' lean against the vertical rock cliff, and enjoy the pulsating pressure of the cascading creek upon your back and shoulders. ''Kids'' of all ages love this place! The bathtub is most easily accessible from the portage trail on the south (right) side of the falls. At the top of the falls is a lovely location that affords a panoramic view of the south end of Agnes Lake. Use caution when climbing this steep path. It is extremely treacherous when wet, and not easy when dry.

There may be many nights during July and August when all of the available campsites in the immediate vicinity of Louisa Falls are occupied. To avoid the congestion, you may want to camp at a nice site one mile north of the falls, on the east side of the lake. The flat, grassy campsite at the base of the falls has been closed because of excessive use over the years.

Trout, walleyes, northern, smallmouth bass, perch and rock bass inhabit Agnes Lake.

DAY 5 (6 miles): **Agnes Lake,** p. 140 rods, **Meadows Lake,** p. 212 rods, **Sunday Lake,** p. 134 rods, **Sunday Bay** (Basswood Lake), **Bayley Bay** (Basswood Lake). It is, indeed, unfortunate that you will not be able to enjoy Louisa's massage at the end of **this** day. That's when you will really need it! The back-to-back "Meadows portages" are rugged. After a brief respite on Sunday Lake, North Portage is almost as rough as the carry at the other end of Sunday Lake. If you cannot carry all of your gear in one trip, you have 4½ miles of walking in store for you this day. If you would rather avoid North Portage, you may detour through Burke Lake, crossing two easy portages en route to Bayley Bay.

DAY 6 (9 miles): **Bayley Bay** (Basswood Lake), **Inlet Bay** (Basswood Lake), p. 20 rods, **Sucker Lake, Newfound Lake, Moose Lake.** This whole day is the reverse of your first. You are back on the busy motor route, so be sure to look both ways before crossing the lake . . .

Extended Route Suggestion

7-DAY Loop: Route #23, a splendid 80-mile loop that slices through the heart of Quetico Park, may be reversed for an equally nice route. You will enter the south end of Agnes Lake and paddle north to Kawnipi Lake. From the northwestern tip of Kawnipi, then, you will follow the Kahshahpiwi Creek flowage south to beautiful Kahshahpiwi Lake. After crossing a chain of small lakes and creeks, leading to the north end of Basswood Lake, you will paddle back to Prairie Portage and on to your origin at Moose Lake. (See Route #23 for details.)

Louisa Falls provides a delightful bathtub

Entry Point 62 — Carp Lake

Daily Quota: 2
Use Level: Heavy

LOCATION: Carp Lake is five miles east of Prairie Portage. By canoe, it is just one long lake and a short portage from the Ranger Station.

DESCRIPTION: Carp Lake is, by far, the most easily accessible entry point in the southern part of Quetico Provincial Park. Because it provides direct access to the scenic "border lakes" and to the popular "Man Chain," it is another entry point that requires reservations long in advance, especially if you are planning a trip in July or August.

Canoe traffic leading to Carp is usually very heavy — at almost any time of year — because the border route is shared by visitors to the Boundary Waters Canoe Area and served by the busiest entry point in all of the BWCAW. The only way to avoid the congestion is to paddle north from the U.S. border toward the less-traveled (but still very popular) "Man Chain."

Route #27 describes the historic Hunter's Island Route, which first follows the border lakes northeast to Cache Bay. Route #28 first follows the popular border lakes northeast to Silver Falls, and then returns via the beautiful Man Chain.

Route #27: Hunter's Island Loop
13 Days, 148 Miles, 25 Lakes, 4 Rivers, 29 Portages

DIFFICULTY: Easy to Challenging
FISHER MAPS: F-10, F-11, F-16, F-17, F-18, F-19, F-23, F-24, F-25, F-26
HIGHLIGHTS: Dorothy Molter, 18 waterfalls, 6 displays of Indian pictographs, Warrior Hill, serveral rapids to run

Introduction: This magnificent loop has it all. Period. For canoeists with two full weeks to spend on the water, I cannot recommend a more scenic, more historic, or more varied route. It is a fascinating blend of awesome, large lakes and charming small ones, resplendent rivers and exquisite waterfalls. Throughout the loop are historic sites where Indians, prospectors, settlers and loggers left their marks on this beautiful country.

The lakes and rivers that constitute this loop were part of the Voyageurs' Highway — the route of the fur traders between Lake Superior and Rainy Lake. The border lakes, from Saganaga Lake west to Lac La Croix, comprised the "customary" waterway for most Voyageurs during the Eighteenth Century. Originally, and again during the Nineteenth Century, the most common route crossed Quetico Park from Pickerel Lake to Sturgeon Lake, and down the Maligne River to Lac La Croix. The area between these two historic routes, adjacent to their confluence, was known as Hunter's Island.

Technically, the land mass contained therein is an island, at least in the sense that waterways of lakes and rivers completely encircle it. The waters flowing out of Saganaga Lake split at Cache Bay, half flowing northwest to the Maligne River system, and half flowing southwest through the Knife and Basswood river systems. Eventually, the two waterways join at Lac La Croix, after flowing around the perimeter of Hunter's Island.

Counter-clockwise is the best direction to paddle the loop, allowing you to take advantage of the Maligne River's occasional swift current. Any trip of this length should include a scheduled "layover day." By allowing at least fourteen days to complete the route, you won't have to worry about the possibility of becoming wind-bound somewhere in the loop (most likely Sturgeon Lake!).

HINT: If you have decided on this route, but you are unable to acquire a permit for entry at Carp Lake, perhaps you can reserve a permit for entry at the Falls Chain, for two days later. If so, you will need to secure a BWCAW Overnight Travel Permit, to allow your passage up the border lakes on the U.S. side, until you reach Cache Bay. And you must camp only in the U.S. the first two nights.

DAY 1 (12 miles): **Moose Lake, Newfound Lake, Sucker Lake, Birch Lake,** p. 40 rods, **Carp Lake.** Don't forget to paddle a short distance out of your way to report at the Prairie Portage Ranger Station (and Americans at Customs).

Once you paddle through the narrow channel from Sucker Lake to Birch Lake, you will leave the noisy motorboats behind. Since January 1, 1984, motors are no longer allowed on the U.S. side of Birch and Knife lakes. Most of the BWCAW canoe traffic will head northwest from Sucker Lake to Basswood Lake or east from Newfound Lake to Ensign Lake. A good deal of traffic, however, will continue along the border route to Carp Lake and up the Knife River to Knife Lake.

A nice campsite is located next to the base of the rapids, where the Knife River flows into Carp Lake. Carp Lake contains trout, northern, perch, smallmouth bass and walleyes.

DAY 2 (14 miles): **Carp Lake,** p. 16 rods, **Knife River,** p. 15 rods, **Seed Lake** p. 15 rods, **Knife River,** p. 75 rods, **Knife Lake,** p. 5 rods, **Ottertrack Lake.** Depending on the water's depth, most of the gentle rapids of the Knife River can be walked or lined up without too much difficulty. Only twice must you lift your canoe and gear — once around a low falls, and then over a small dam. This time-worn logging dam was built just after the turn of the century. Now there is little remaining. If "oldtimers" are correct, there may have been other dams along the Knife River at one time, between Seed and Carp lakes and between Carp and Birch lakes.

Near the southwest end of Knife Lake, on three small islands in U.S. waters lives the "rootbeer lady." Dorothy Molter has lived at her "Isle of Pines" alone for most of her 77 years. But she is seldom alone during the summer months, when literally thousands of admiring canoeists drop by to meet the legendary woman who makes and sells homemade rootbeer (ice-cold!) for thirsty canoeists. By exemption from federal law, she is now the only person allowed to dwell in the BWCA Wilderness. Stop by and say "Hello."

At the junction of the South Arm with the main part of Knife Lake is a hill on the U.S. peninsula known as Thunder Point. An 80-rod climb to the summit will be rewarded by a splendid panorama of the international boundary from over 150 feet above the lake.

Ottertrack Lake is a beautiful, long and slender lake, bordered by majestic cliffs and a rocky shoreline. According to Indian legend, the tracks of an otter are embedded in the rock face of one of the cliffs.

Just before the lake splits into two arms, you may see a grassy clearing on the American shoreline. Benny Ambrose lived there for sixty years until his death in 1982. Ambrose came to the North Woods in 1921, prospecting for gold. He spent a lifetime searching, spurred on by the belief that an Ojibwa chief named Blackstone knew the whereabouts of a mine that was rich with gold ore, somewhere in the vicinity of Ottertrack Lake, in Quetico's greenstone belt. After Ambrose's death, at age 84, the U.S. Forest Service demolished his cabins. The stone foundations are all that remain.

For those who would prefer to camp away from the busy border route, a nice camp-site is on a point near the north end of the north arm of Ottertrack Lake. For those anglers in your group, northern pike, walleyes, smallmouth bass and trout are patiently waiting to strike at your lures.

DAY 3 (10 miles): **Ottertrack Lake**, p. 80 rods, **Swamp Lake**, p. 3 rods, **Saganaga Lake, Cache Bay** (Saganaga Lake), p. 130 rods, **Saganagons Lake.** Don't worry: Monument Portage is not named for its height or excessive difficulty. There is a large steel international boundary marker in the middle of the trail. Nothing to fret about! Nor is the portage around Silver Falls (when you're going in this direction!). It is a rocky trail that descends nearly all of the way from Cache Bay to Saganagons Lake. 50 rods down the path, a spur trail branches off to the west and descends 10 rods down to the river. Since that access will put you into the river above the final set of rapids, the condition of which is not apparent from the end of the portage, you should **not** consider this to be a safe shortcut. Continue to the end of the 130-rod path.

Before reaching Silver Falls, you may want to paddle past an exhibit of Indian rock paintings that are tucked away in the sheltered west end of Cache Bay. There you will see a distinct group of three human-like figures (probably maymayguishi), two canoes and tally marks.

In the narrow canyon between Cache Bay and Saganagons Lake is the site of a reputed Indian massacre. Legends tell how a Cree war party set out to attack an Ojibwa village in present Quetico Park. The Ojibwa braves, alerted to the impending onslaught, evacuated their village. Finding the village empty, the Cree warriors turned homeward and passed through the narrow canyon, where the Ojibwa tribe waited to ambush them. The Cree were nearly annihilated. Nearby, on the shore of Cache Bay, Ojibwa women took refuge in caves during the massacre. If you hear terrifying cries of pain and anguish above the roar of the falls during the night, don't be alarmed. They are still echoing from the ancient slaughter. Sleep well!

Silver Falls is one of the most spectacular cascades in Quetico Park. The best view is from a short spur trail near the beginning of the portage.

Plan to camp a short distance below the falls. Saganagons Lake contains walleyes, northern and trout.

DAY 4 (10 miles): **Saganagons Lake**, p. 75 rods, **Saganagons Lake, Maligne River**, p. 50 rods, **River**, p. 17 rods, **River**, p. 7 rods, **River**, p. 32 rods, **River**, p. 56 rods, **River**, p. 48 rods, **Kenny Lake**, p. 4 rods, **Kawnipi Lake.** The first portage is an easy overland shortcut that eliminates about six miles of paddling around Boundary Point. In the northern part of the lake, keep your compass handy. A plethora of islands makes navigation confusing through this region that was burned over in the late 1960's.

In the short span of only four airline miles between Saganagons Lake and Kawnipi Lake — the upper flowage of the Maligne River — are eight lovely waterfalls that plummet nearly 100 feet in all. This is aptly called the Falls Chain. Some of the portages are hard to see, and the current may be swift; so it is very important — no, it's IMPERATIVE — that you approach each falls on the correct side of the river. Between the first and second nameless falls, in particular, the current is swift where the channel constricts on both sides of a small island. The next portage (17 rods) is on the left (south) side of the twin falls. As you glide through the narrow channel, keep to the left of the small island and hug the left bank until you reach the portage. This is no place to play in the current. Be careful!

In case your map is not clearly marked, here is a summary of the portage locations. The first and second portages are on the **left.** The third passes over a smooth rock out-cropping on the **right.** Little Falls is portaged on the **right.** One rough portage bypasses Koko Falls and an unnamed falls on the **left.** Canyon Falls has a 48-rod portage on the

Splitrock Falls

Chatterton Falls

left. But there is also a beautiful portage trail over an island dividing the two shoots of Canyon Falls. Beginning near the top of the large right shoot, the trail is very scenic and much shorter and easier than the 48-rod path. **CAUTION,** however, must be exercised in getting to this island portage. The current is swift and may be treacherous. When the water is unusually high, in fact, you would be wise to stick with the 48-rod portage. Kennebas Falls is also portaged on the **left.**

There is a nice campsite in the narrow channel of Kawnipi Lake, just beyond Kennebas Falls. Anglers will find walleyes, nothern pike and perch in the lake.

DAY 5 (12 miles): **Kawnipi Lake.** Pack away your boots this morning. This is the first of two days on this trip when you will not have a single portage. After yesterday, you deserve it!

Kawnipi Lake is one of the best places in Quetico Park to view a majestic bald eagle. According to Shan Walshe, Park Naturalist, both the south end and Kawa Bay are especially good locations. At least two nests have been sited. In August of 1984, my wife and I were captivated by the sight of an eagle soaring effortlessly high above Kawnipi Lake. In contrast, but equally as thrilling, seven herons, flying in loose formation at a much lower altitude, were also observed. Their huge wings seemed to be laboring with a great deal of effort, while the eagle seemed to hover like a hot air ballon, unaffected by the gravitational force that afflicts the herons.

There are two displays of Indian pictographs on Kawnipi Lake — two of the less impressive exhibits in the Park. One depicts two maymayguishi in a canoe; the other has two shaded figures. If you don't find them, don't worry; there are much better displays further along in this route.

Plan to camp at the far northwestern end of Kawnipi Lake, where it finally constricts into the continuation of the Maligne River.

DAY 6 (10 miles): **Kawnipi Lake,** p. 10 rods, **Maligne River, Rapids, River,** p. 11 rods, **Shelley Lake,** p. 60 rods, **Keats Lake,** p. 72 rods, **Chatterton Lake,** p. 76 rods, **Russell Lake.** (See comments for DAY 4, Route #2.)

DAY 7 (13 miles): **Russell Lake, Maligne River,** p. 6 rods, **River, Sturgeon Lake, Sturgeon Narrows, Sturgeon Lake.** Depending on the water level, that first short portage will probably not be necessary. The swift current drops no more than a foot from Russell to Sturgeon Lake.

Sturgeon Lake was a veritable highway during the 1800's. The Dawson Trail extended across Sturgeon Lake and down the Maligne River to Lac La Croix, en route to Manitoba. Steam barges plied the waters then. The long island southwest of Scripture Island is the reputed site of Dawson's wood yard. It is likely that wood was cut there to power the steam engines. At the southwest end of the lake, close to the portage, a boiler was discovered submerged in the water. It can be mistaken for a large, flat rock. But, when the light is right, the door gives it away. It was one of Dawson's boilers that burned the wood to generate steam in a barge on Sturgeon Lake.

The island west of Dawson's wood yard is said to be the site of McLaren's Post, an old Northwest Company trading post. All that remains is a low, but discernible, mound where the trading post once stood.

The size, shape and direction of Sturgeon Lake make it highly susceptible to the efforts of wind. Plan to get an early start. If you become wind-bound at the east end of the largest part of the lake, you will see a beautiful sand beach at which to hold up until the wind subsides. This spectacular campsite is on a point on the lake's south shore.

Otherwise, plan to camp near the southwest end of Sturgeon. Fishermen will have a large assortment of fish species at which to cast their lines. This huge lake contains walleyes, northern pike, sturgeon, smallmouth bass, herring and others.

DAY 8 (11 miles): **Sturgeon Lake,** p. 52 rods, **Maligne River,** p. 61 rods, **River, Rapids, River,** p. 42 rods, **River, Rapids, River, Rapids, River, Rapids, River, Tanner Lake,** p. 4 rods, **Maligne River, Rapids, River.** The five "rapids" mentioned are nothing more than swift and shallow currents where the river constricts. They pose no problems for canoeists paddling downstream, as you are.

Most of the larger rapids are basically "blind." It is difficult, or impossible, to see from the top whether the whitewater is safe to run. WHEN IN DOUBT, ALWAYS PORTAGE!

There are two known sites of old logging camps along the Maligne River. Shelvin Clark logged there in 1937 and 1938. It was was also reported once that Indian burial mounds exist somewhere along the river, between Tanner Lake and Lac La Croix.

Tanner Lake is named after John Tanner, a white boy who was captured by and adopted into an Ojibwa family at age ten and who lived with the Indians for thirty years. In 1823, he was shot by an Indian (who was "hired" by his Indian wife) and left to die in Tanner Rapids. Found by men of the Hudson's Bay Company, he was cared for and taken to Rainy Lake. His fascinating story is told in a book called **John Tanner — Thirty Years' Captivity in the Indian Country** (Ross and Hanes, Minneapolis, 1956).

Tanner Lake and the Maligne River to Lac La Croix is a waterway where treaty Indians of the Lac La Croix Guides Association are permitted to use motors up to ten horsepower.

Plan to camp in the vicinity of Twin Falls, at the mouth of the Maligne River.

DAY 9 (14 miles): **Maligne River,** p. 16 rods, **Wegwagum Bay** (Lac La Croix), **Lac La Croix.** Twin Falls is an exquisite pair of waterfalls on the southeast side of Lou Island. Island Portage, located on the right (west) side of the right falls, has been known by that name ever since the Voyageurs plied these waters. (See comments for DAY 5, Route #22.)

DAY 10 (12 miles): **Lac La Croix,** p. 80 rods, **Bottle Lake, Bottle River, Iron Lake,** p. 140 rods, **Crooked Lake.** (See comments for DAY 6, Route #22.)

DAY 11 (12 miles): **Basswood River,** p. 32 rods, **River,** p. 32 rods, **River,** p. 30 rods, **River,** p. 340 rods, **Basswood Lake.** (See comments for DAY 4, Route #21.)

DAY 13 (8 miles): **Basswood Lake,** p. 170 rods, **Wind Lake,** p. 170 rods, **Moose Lake.** (See comments for DAY 5, Route #21.)

Maligne River

Route #28: The Jasper-Lilypad Loop

6 Days, 62 Miles, 22 Lakes, 2 Rivers, 1 Creek, 24 Portages

DIFFICULTY: Challenging

FISHER MAPS: F-10, F-11, F-18, F-19

HIGHLIGHTS: The Rootbeer Lady, Silver Falls, scenic lakes

Introduction: The route will take you across some of the loveliest lakes and lead you to one of the most magnificent waterfalls in all of Quetico Park. From Prairie Portage, you will first follow the popular border lakes — Birch, Knife, and Ottertrack lakes — northeast to beautiful Jasper Lake. From Jasper, you will portage north to Lilypad Lake and then east to the base of Silver Falls. After pausing to view that dazzling spectacle, you will paddle to the west end of Saganagons Lake to begin your return trip by steering a southwesterly course across Slate, Fran and Bell lakes to the scenic Man Chain lakes: Other Man, This Man, No Man and That Man. Continuing through Sheridan Lake to Carp Lake, you will then retrace your path back to your origin at Moose Lake.

The route starts and ends with two very easy days. Twenty-one portages are squeezed into the middle four days, however, averaging five or six carries per day. Only five of the portages exceed 50 rods, though, and only two are longer than 100 rods. For trippers in good physical condition, it is basically an easy route.

(For additonal information about the Man Chain, see the Description for Entry Point 72 — Man Chain Lakes.)

DAY 1 (12 miles): **Moose Lake, Newfound Lake, Sucker Lake, Birch Lake,** p. 40 rods, **Carp Lake.** (See comments for DAY 1, Route #27.)

DAY 2 (14 miles): **Carp Lake,** p. 16 rods, **Knife River,** p. 15 rods, **Seed Lake,** p. 15 rods, **Knife River,** p. 75 rods, **Knife Lake,** p. 5 rods, **Ottertrack Lake.** (See comments for DAY 2, Route #27.)

DAY 3 (10 miles): **Ottertrack Lake,** p. 100 rods, **Jasper Lake,** p. 40 rods, **Lilypad Lake,** p. 26 rods, **Silver Falls River,** p. 24 rods, **Saganagons Lake,** p. 8 rods, **Slate Lake, Creek,** p. 5 rods, **Fran Lake,** p. 74 rods, **(Unnamed Lake),** p. 18 rods, **Bell Lake.** With a side-trip to Silver Falls, this is a very full day! All of the portages between Ottertrack and Saganagons lakes are rough, rocky, occasionally swampy, and may have windfalls. It is not a well-traveled waterway. And that is one reason why it is a good area to see moose, deer and other wildlife.

An old steam engine is found along the shore of Lilypad Lake. It was used in the early 1920's to drill for iron ore.

The two short portages between Lilypad and Saganagons lakes are seldom used by human beings (though there is plenty of evidence that other critters walk the trails), and they are likely to be plagued by windfalls in early summer and nearly overgrown by mid-summer. Another 83-rod portage will also lead you to Saganagons from Lilypad, but then you will have to paddle an extra couple miles to see Silver Falls. Regardless of how you get to Saganagons Lake, be sure to paddle over to the base of the Silver Falls portage and hike up to this exquisite cascade. The best vantage point is from a short spur trail near the Cache Bay end of the portage.

When you paddle northwest from the Silver Falls portage, be alert for a tiny channel that offers a shortcut to your next portage. This passage saves about a mile of paddling on Saganagons Lake. Near that channel is the site of a small mining operation that drilled back in 1920. A cabin was built next to the lake, and the mine was reported to be ten-minute walk back into the woods. Equipment was brought in from the Gunflint

Trail. Drill bits, however, would not cut through the rock, so the rig was abandoned at the end of the year. Nothing remains now where the cabin once stood.

The creek between Slate and Fran lakes should be navigable almost all of the way to Fran Lake. A short rapids and a beaver dam, however, necessitate either a 5-rod "liftover," or wet feet from walking your canoe through the trickle.

The portage out of Fran Lake climbs steeply for the first 52-rods, before descending to an unnamed lake. The short carry into Bell Lake, too, is steep at the beginning.

There are several small campsites on Bell Lake. The only large, and very nice, site is located just south of the 18-rod portage. The lake offers only black crappies and sunfish for the anglers in your group.

DAY 4 (10 miles): **Bell Lake**, p. 21 rods, **(Unnamed Lake)**, p. 4 rods, **(Unnamed Lake)**, p. 39 rods, **Other Man Lake**, p. 49 rods, **This Man Lake**, p. 32 rods, **No Man Lake**, p. 101 rods, **That Man Lake.** The Man Chain lakes are bordered on the northwest by ridges that tower as much as 150 feet above the lakes. During our long journey down This Man Lake, in June of 1984, my wife and I observed a cow moose and her calf swimming across the lake. Other moose sightings have also been reported in this area.

The 4-rod "liftover" is steeply uphill, and so are the first three rods of the 39-rod trail to Other Man Lake. There are two portages between This Man and No Man lakes. The one on the left (south side of the creek) is best and shortest, descending rather steeply to No Man Lake. The other trail begins on the north side of the creek, climbs for a few rods, and then descends more gradually to No Man Lake, for a total distance of 60 rods.

The 101-rod portage, you're longest to date, should be no problem. It is mostly level, with only a couple of muddy spots along the way.

There is a gorgeous, large campsite on the west end of the first small island at the east end of the lake. Trout, walleyes, northern, smallmouth bass and black crappies are yours for the catching in this pretty lake.

On a prominent point along the north shore of the lake, across from this island campsite, there was once a mining camp with five buildings. Drilling was done in 1949-51, and fragments of core samples may still be found scattered about the site.

DAY 5 (9 miles): **That Man Lake**, p. 136 rods, **Sheridan Lake**, p. 15 rods, **Carp Lake**, p. 40 rods, **Birch Lake.** Your longest portage of this trip (136 rods) has its ups and downs, but, overall, it is not too difficult. It bypasses a small scenic waterfall near That Man Lake. A deep prospector's hole is located beside the trail.

There is a very nice Canadian campsite on a small island about midway across Birch Lake. You are back on the busy border route, but most of the canoeists will be camped on the American side of the border. For your last big fish fry, anglers will find trout and northern pike in Birch Lake.

DAY 6 (7 miles): **Birch Lake**, p. 5 rods, **Sucker Lake, Newfound Lake, Moose Lake.** The portage is a shortcut that eliminates two miles of paddling. From that point on, you will be back-tracking the route of your first day.

That Man Falls

Portage into Jasper Lake

CHAPTER 6: Entry From Cache Bay — The Southeastern Region

Four entry points in the southeastern part of Quetico Provincial Park are controlled by the Cache Bay Ranger Station, located at the west end of Saganaga Lake: Knife Lake (#71), Man Chain Lakes (#72), the Falls Chain (#73), and Boundary Point (#74). Through all of them, a maximum of seven groups per day may enter the park.

Americans entering Canada from Saganaga Lake must first paddle to the Customs office. It is located five miles straight north of the public boat landing at the south end of the lake, almost seven miles northeast of the Ranger Station.

Saganaga Lake is the second busiest entry point for the Boundary Waters Canoe Area Wilderness (U.S.). Motors not exceeding 25 horsepower are permitted on the American side, except west of American Point. On the Canadian side, there are no motor restrictions outside of Quetico Park. Several private cabins, lodges and canoe trip outfitters are located along the southernmost shore of the lake.

Saganaga is at the northwest end of the historic Gunflint Trail (now Cook County Road 12). This scenic drive begins at the small town of Grand Marais, on the shore of Lake Superior. All but the last mile of this 56-mile road is on a good, black-topped surface.

A good place to camp the night prior to a trip from Saganaga Lake is at Trail's End Campground, located 2½ miles west of the Saganaga Lake turn-off (County Road 11), at the very end of the Gunflint Trail. There is a campsite fee of $5/night, and there are many campsites to accommodate the heavy traffic in this area.

Grand Marais, Minnesota, serves visitors to this part of the Quetico-Superior region. It is a bustling village that thrives on tourism. Like Ely and Atikokan, the accommodations there include motels, restaurants, supermarkets, service stations, a laundromat and a variety of other stores. A municipal campground is located near the center of the town. Adjacent to the campground is a municipal indoor swimming pool where grimy canoe trippers may purchase inexpensive showers and saunas. An airport is located northeast of town.

Entry Point 71 — Knife Lake

Daily Quota: 2
Use Level: Heavy

LOCATION: Knife Lake is seven miles (by air) southwest of the Cache Bay Ranger Station, and twelve miles west of the Gunflint Trail. By canoe, it may be reached by paddling sixteen miles across Saganaga, Swamp and Ottertrack lakes to the Little Knife Portage at the northeast end of Knife Lake.

DESCRIPTION: Knife Lake receives a great deal of canoe traffic from several directions. Extending more than ten miles along the Canadian-American border, most of the visitors to this beautiful lake are Americans using the Boundary Waters Canoe Area Wilderness, on the south side of the border.

Knife Lake probably received its name because of the presence there of a very hard, dark, sharp-edged rock, called felsite. The Indians made weapons and shaped tools from it.

Saganagons Lake

Knife Lake has one feature that makes it unique among all other lakes in the Quetico-Superior wilderness area. Near the southwest end of the lake, on three small islands in U.S. waters, lives the "rootbeer lady." Dorothy Molter has lived at her "Isles of Pines" alone for most of her 77 years. But she is seldom alone during the summer months, when literally thousands of admiring canoeists drop by to meet the legendary woman who makes and sells homemade rootbeer (ice-cold!) for thirsty canoeists. By exemption from federal law, she is now the only person allowed to dwell in the BWCA Wilderness.

Route #29: The Knife - McEwen Lakes Loop
8 Days, 88 Miles, 24 Lakes, 2 Rivers, 2 Creeks, 33 Portages

DIFFICULTY: Challenging

FISHER MAPS: F-19, F-18, F-11, F-10, F-26

HIGHLIGHTS: The Rootbeer Lady, Louisa Falls, Indian pictographs, the Falls Chain, Silver Falls

Introduction: This superb loop begins and ends on two of the busiest routes in Quetico Park, but it also follows one of the least-traveled waterways in this part of the Park. From Saganaga Lake, you will first paddle southwest, following the international boundary waters, through Ottertrack, Knife and Birch lakes, to Basswood Lake. At Bayley Bay, you will portage north to Sunday Lake and then plot a northeasterly course to Louisa Lake. A chain of small lakes and creeks will carry you further northeast to McEwen Lake, and then to Wet Lake. After crossing Wet Lake, you will enter the Falls Chain and paddle up the Maligne

River to Saganagons Lake. From the southwest end of Saganagons Lake, you will portage around beautiful Silver Falls to Cache Bay. Finally, weaving between a host of islands, you will paddle across Saganaga Lake to your origin at the lakes's south end.

Along the way, you will have an opportunity to view five stunning waterfalls, soak your tired muscles in Louisa's bathtub, drink ice-cold rootbeer on Knife Lake, run several small rapids in the Knife River, and paddle across some of the prettiest lakes in all of God's Country.

For the ambitious angler looking for trout, six of the seven nights will be camped on trout lakes. Nearly all of the waters along this route contain northern pike, and walleyes are in most of the lakes.

DAY 1 (14 miles): **Saganaga Lake, Cache Bay, Saganaga Lake.** West of American Point motorboats are not allowed on either side of the border — the only motorless refuge on this enormous lake. Plan to camp in the sheltered southwest end of the lake, a couple miles beyond the entrance to Cache Bay. There are several small campsites on both sides of the border, and one large site on a Canadian peninsula near the Swamp Lake portage.

Anglers may find trout, northern pike and walleyes in Saganaga Lake and Cache Bay.

DAY 2 (13 miles): **Saganaga Lake, p. 3 rods, Swamp Lake, p. 80 rods, Ottertrack Lake, p. 5 rods, Knife Lake.** Monument Portage is not the challenge that its name might imply. There are three bronze international boundary markers in the middle of the trail. Nevertheless, the trail does have some fairly steep grades, and you must cross a swamp (over logs) at the east end.

Ottertrack Lake is a beautiful, long and slender lake, bordered by majestic cliffs and a rocky shoreline. According to Indian legend, the tracks of an otter are embedded in the rock face of one of the cliffs.

Just after the two arms of the lake join together, you may see a grassy clearing on the American shoreline. Benny Ambrose lived there for sixty years until his death in 1982. Ambrose came to the North Woods in 1921, prospecting for gold. He spent a lifetime searching, spurred by the belief that an Ojibwa chief, named Blackstone, knew the whereabouts of a mine that was rich with gold ore, somewhere in the vicinity of Ottertrack Lake, in Quetico's greenstone belt. After Ambrose's death, at age 84, the U.S. Forest Service demolished his cabins. The stone foundations are all that remain.

Plan to camp near Thunder Point, at the junction of the South Arm with the main part of Knife Lake. At the point of that peninsula is an 80-rod trail that leads to the summit of a 150-foot hill. The panoramic view from the top is well worth the effort.

For the anglers in your group, Knife Lake contains trout, smallmouth bass, northern and walleyes. The sparkling water is so clear you can see them swimming.

DAY 3 (12 miles): **Knife Lake, p. 75 rods, Knife River, p. 15 rods, Seed Lake, p. 15 rods, Knife River, p. 16 rods, Carp Lake, p. 40 rods, Birch Lake, Sucker Lake, p. 20 rods, Inlet Bay** (Basswood Lake), **Bayley Bay** (Basswood Lake). You will pass Dorothy Molter's place near the southwest end of Knife Lake, just barely on the U.S. side of the boundary.

The remnants of an old logging dam are found at the source of the Knife River. Built sometime in the early years of this century, there is now little remaining.

An adventuresome group of whitewater fanatics may eliminate most of the portages along the Knife River, if the water level is sufficient to run the rapids. Only at the dam, and again at a low falls, must you lift your canoe and gear. The final rapids into Carp Lake, however, is "blind." Be sure to scout it before attempting a run. And if there is any doubt in your mind — any at all — don't try it!

149

After you paddle through the narrow channel from Birch Lake to Sucker Lake, you will be on a busy motor route. Fed by the Moose Lake entry point, by far the busiest of all the entry points for the Boundary Waters Canoe Area Wilderness, this waterway is often buzzing with the sound of motor boats (up to 25 horsepower) traveling to and from Basswood Lake.

Prairie Portage is the site of both a Canadian Customs and a Quetico Ranger Station. On the American side of the rapids is a truck portage, that carries the big motorboats from Sucker to Basswood Lake, and later back again. The Prairie Portage dam was originally built in 1901 and 1902 for sluicing logs from Sucker, Knife, Newfound and Moose lakes. It was abandoned by lumber companies in 1915, after which it was maintained by the U.S. Forest Service. After it went out in 1968, the Forest Service rebuilt it.

Bayley Bay is well known for its rough water on windy days. Plan to camp at its east end, where several sites are available, so that you can cross it early in the morning. Trout, walleyes, northern, smallmouth bass, perch, largemouth bass, black crappies and other pan fish inhabit these waters.

DAY 4 (10 miles): **Bayley Bay** (Basswood Lake), **Sunday Bay** (Basswood Lake), p. 134 rods, **Sunday Lake**, p. 212 rods, **Meadows Lake**, p. 140 rods, **Agnes Lake**, p. 15 rods, **Louisa Creek**, p. 15 rods, **Louisa Lake.** This is, by far, your toughest day of portaging. North Portage (134 rods) and the two back-to-back ''Meadows portages'' (212 and 140 rods) are the three longest carries — and the most rugged — of the entire route. If you cannot carry all of your gear in one trip, you'll have to walk 4½ miles across these three trails!

Save some energy for those two short carries between Agnes and Louisa lakes. Those two trails climb nearly a hundred feet over a walking distance of only thirty rods. Most of that ascent is at Louisa Falls (the first portage), where you must scramble up a near-vertical ledge on the right (south) side of the falls. The path is treacherous, even when dry. Lighten your loads, and make as many trips as you have to, to ensure safety. Unless you're highly adept at carrying a canoe, it wouldn't be a bad idea to team up at this portage.

After you have completed the rugged portage, take time out to enjoy Louisa Falls. (See About Louisa Falls pp. 135.) At the other end of Louisa Creek is another portage of equal length, but not nearly as steep. It climbs around a rapids draining Louisa Lake.

There is a large island campsite midway up the lake. A terrific wind toppled many of the huge Norway pines there. Prior to that happening, it must have been a stately sight.

If you have any angling ambition left after this rugged day, you may find trout, northern pike and perch in Louisa Lake.

DAY 5 (9 miles): **Louisa Lake**, p. 96 rods, **Arp Lake**, p. 25 rods, **Star Lake,** p. 52 rods, **Fauquier Lake**, p. 72 rods, **Dumas Lake, McEwen Creek**, p. 8 rods, **Creek, Rod Lake, McEwen Creek**, p. 16 rods, **Edge Lake**, p. 8 rods, (**Unnamed Lake**), p. 16 rods, **Turn Lake**, p. 15 rods, **McEwen Creek**, p. 23 rods, **Glacier Lake.** With ten portages, this is another challenging day. Don't let the relatively short lengths of the portages fool you; all of them are tricky, and some are downright treacherous! Most are very rocky, with sharp, jagged rocks that are extremely slippery when wet. Windfalls are not uncommon.

The first, and longest, carry of the day climbs uphill, gradually, to Arp Lake. As you paddle toward the end of Arp Lake, watch carefully for your next portage in a small bay on the left (north) side of the lake. It **appears** that the portage should be at the very **end** of the lake, just to the left of the creek. In fact, there **is** the beginning of a trail there — one left by other Voyageurs who missed the correct portage. Although the portage is merely 25 rods, it is not easy — steep up, and then steep down. From that point on, all of the carries are generally downhill, following the flowage of McEwen Creek.

If you wish, you may replace the 52-rod downhill path to Fauquier Lake by portaging 23 rods down a much steeper hill to a creek that flows into Fauquier. You will have at least one beaver dam to lift over, but it is a scenic entry to the south end of Fauquier Lake.

The most difficult and treacherous portage of the day — perhaps the entire trip, rivalled only in treachery by the Louisa Falls climb — is the 72-rod portage connecting Fauquier and Dumas lakes. It is situated precariously on the left (northwest) bank of the creek, and it requires careful attention to one's foot placement. A careless step might result in a "refreshing" swim in the creek.

In spite of the difficulties encountered, this stretch between Louisa and McEwen lakes is one of my favorites. The scenery is pleasant, and you are not likely to encounter many (if any) other persons along this isolated interior route.

The only two decent campsites along this entire route are at the north end of Glacier Lake. The best site is a bit out of the way, located on the east bank of the lake, hidden from view by a peninsula. Trout, smallmouth bass and walleyes inhabit the lake.

DAY 6 (11 miles): **Glacier Lake,** p. 25 rods, **McEwen Creek, Rapids, Creek, McEwen Lake,** p. 24 rods, **Wet Lake, Rapids, Maligne River.** The first portage will get your blood stirring! It climbs steeply at the beginning, before dropping downhill to the creek. In 1984 there were a couple windfalls across the path.

McEwen Creek is a lovely stream. Under normal conditions, a small rapids just beyond the 25-rod portage can be easily negotiated, without using the 8-rod portage trail there. The same is true in the channel connecting Wet Lake with the Maligne River.

Once on McEwen Lake, you are more likely to encounter other campers who entered Quetico Park via the Falls Chain (Entry Point 73). The Maligne River is part of the popular Hunter's Island Route, and it receives heavy canoe traffic during July and August. Even in June (1984), I counted ten strangers, in two groups, on McEwen Lake alone. More groups were passed on the Maligne River.

This part of the Maligne River is known as the Falls Chain. Aptly named, it includes eight dazzling waterfalls that plunge a total of nearly 100 feet — all in a span of only four miles. You will be entering the chain in the middle, missing the lower five falls. Paddling upstream, you won't need to worry so much about the potential danger of the falls. Instead, you may feel the frustration of paddling against the swift current that often characterizes this stretch of the river.

There are several campsites located between Wet Lake and the first falls. One of my favorites has long been the site on the south side of that lovely 12' cascade. If you plan to enjoy a "layover" on this trip, this is a splendid location, enabling you time to explore the five falls that are not included in this route. For the fishermen in your group, walleyes and northern pike abound in this area, including Wet Lake. You may want to take extra precautions at this site for the possibility of bear trouble. This is on the outer fringe of the territory frequented by the "Wet Lake bears" — two "cubs" trained by an expert mamma to harrass campers. They are very persistent youngsters, but, fortunately, the mother hasn't been seen for a couple of years. In 1984, the Ranger at Cache Bay was warning campers to avoid the Wet Lake area.

DAY 7 (8 miles): **Maligne River,** p. 7 rods, **River,** p. 17 rods, **River,** p. 50 rods, **River, Saganagons Lake,** p. 75 rods, **Saganagons Lake,** p. 130 rods, **Cache Bay** (Saganaga Lake). There is a narrow channel between the second and third portages where the Maligne River may be very swift — perhaps too swift to paddle a canoe through it. A new 12-rod portage on the right (south) bank was recently cut there, to assist canoeists past this stretch. Unfortunately, the trail is so steep over a rocky ridge, it is virtually impossible to carry a canoe over it. Apparently designed for mountain goats, it literally requires ''all fours'' to descend to the river above the fast water. Consequently, I recommend that you simply line your canoe along the bank of the river. If the rocks aren't wet, this shouldn't be too difficult. If they ARE wet, be vary careful; this is no place to swim!

The level, easy 75-rod portage eliminates about six miles of paddling around Boundary Point. It's a bit tricky finding this trail. Many islands in the northern half of Saganagons Lake make navigation confusing. Not far southwest of that portage is an eagle nest, on a large island.

Silver Falls is one of the most spectacular cascades in Quetico Park. The ''new'' beginning of the portage trail around it climbs during the first 40 rods (though not nearly as steeply as the old trail did). The remainder of the trail ascends more gently, but there are some steep, rocky sections. At least the path is well-maintained and frequently used.

Plan to camp in the sheltered northwestern part of Cache Bay, just above the falls. Nearby is the site of a reputed Indian massacre.

Silver Falls

DAY 8 (11 miles): Cache Bay (Saganaga Lake), **Saganaga Lake.** Eleven miles without a single portage: a nice way to end your trip. Unfortunately, most of the distance must be shared with motorboats, now that you are back in the "real world."

Before leaving Cache Bay, you may enjoy a side-trip to the sheltered southwest end of the bay. There you will find a display of ancient Indian rock paintings — a distinct group of three human-like figures (probably maymayguishi), two canoes and tally marks.

Usually, even on a windy day, the many islands in the southern part of Saganaga Lake provide enough shelter to allow the safe crossing of this mammoth lake.

A Shorter Route Suggestion

6-DAY Loop: By simply reversing Route #30, you can enjoy a delightful journey through the Man Chain of Lakes. From the Cache Bay Ranger Station, instead of heading northwest, you will paddle southwest, following the international border through Swamp, Ottertrack and Knife lakes to the Knife River. After negotiating the gentle rapids of the Knife River, you will veer to the northeast at Carp Lake. Across Carp and Sheridan lakes, you will then follow the Man Chain (That Man, No Man, This Man and Other Man lakes) northeast to Saganagons Lake. After portaging around magnificent Silver Falls, you will paddle across big Cache Bay and then return to your origin at the south end of Saganaga Lake. This is an excellent "first challenging trip" into Quetico Park, since the portages are not too difficult (nor too frequent), it is well-traveled, and there is plenty of beautiful scenery along the way. (See Route #30 for details.)

Entry Point 72 — Man Chain Lakes

Daily Quota: 2
Use Level: Moderate

LOCATION: Other Man, the northeastern-most "man" in the chain, is located six miles straight west of the Cache Bay Ranger Station, twelve miles northwest of the Saganaga Lake access road. To paddlers, this interprets as an eighteen-mile journey across eight lakes and eight portages.

DESCRIPTION: The beginning of the whole "chain" is actually at Slate Lake, a short portage west of Saganagons Lake. It is there that you begin your expedition down the beautiful series of cliff-lined lakes that follows a northeast-to-southwest pattern created by a geological fault. Steep hills, towering more than 150 feet above the water's edge, line the lakes.

Geologically, unlike most of Quetico Park, this slender strip of the Park is underlain with greenstone. More easily eroded than the granite that underlies 70% of Quetico Park, this volcanic rock is less acidic and provides more abundant nutrients to support a more diversified ecosystem. According to Shan Walsh, Park Naturalist, the less acidic, more nutrient-rich soil of the greenstone belt is likely to be responsible for the dominance of trembling aspen, largetooth aspen and white birch in the early stages of upland forest succession, rather than the jackpine and black spruce that characterize the granitic areas. Extensive stands of white cedar support a fairly abundant white-tailed deer population in this region, which is also unique to the greenstone belt.

To anglers, these deep lakes mean lake trout. Many of the lakes contain trout, and, of course, most contain walleyes and northern pike.

This Man Chain is a popular route. Unlike Knife Lake (Entry Point 71), however, the Man Chain lakes are wholly within the interior of Quetico Park. Consequently, there is much less canoe traffic here than along the busy border route, which is shared with visitors to the Boundary Waters Canoe Area Wilderness.

Route #30: The Man Chain — Border Lakes Route

6 Days, 67 Miles, 18 Lakes, 1 River, 1 Creek, 20 Portages

DIFFICULTY: Challenging to Easy
FISHER MAPS: F-19, F-18, F-11
HIGHLIGHTS: Indian pictographs, Silver Falls, the Rootbeer Lady, outstanding scenery

Introduction: This beautiful route is an excellent first trip into Quetico Park. The scenery is splendid, and the portages are not too difficult. Good campsites are plentiful. And, important to an inexperienced group, the route is fairly well-traveled. In the event of a problem, help would not be far away.

From the Cache Bay Ranger Station, you will paddle northwest and portage around Silver Falls to Saganagons Lake. From Saganagons Lake, you will then steer a southwesterly course across Slate, Fran and Bell lakes to the Man Chain: Other Man, This Man, No Man and That Man lakes. Continuing on to Carp Lake, you will then veer back to the northeast and follow the Knife River up to Knife Lake. The busy border lakes of Knife, Ottertrack and Swamp lakes will carry you back to Saganaga Lake. From its west end, it is a long paddle back to your origin at the southern tip of that big, beautiful lake.

With twenty portages squeezed into the middle four days of the trip, the route will be challenging at times. On the first and last days, however, there are no portages at all. Only six of the twenty carries exceed 50 rods, including only three that are longer than 100 rods.

Trout fishermen will have plenty of time to pursue their sport. All five nights will be camped on lakes containing trout. Northern pike, walleyes, smallmouth bass and black crappies are also available for the catching.

DAY 1 (13 miles): **Saganaga Lake, Cache Bay** (Saganaga Lake). The necessity for Americans to stop at Canada Customs results in the addition of three more miles to your paddling distance across this mammoth lake. When the wind is strong out of the south or west, paddlers can usually shelter themselves by dodging from island to island or staying close to the mainland. Beyond American Point, there will be no more motorboats on either side of the border.

Plan to camp at the north end of Cache Bay. If you don't think you will have enough time to paddle all the way to Cache Bay, because of a late start, make certain that your Interior Camping Permit is reserved for the NEXT DAY. Anglers will find trout, northern pike and walleyes in the depths of Cache Bay.

After supper, when the winds have calmed and the bay is smooth as glass, you might enjoy a side-trip to the sheltered west end of the bay, where a display of Indian pictographs may be seen. A distinct group of three human-like figures (probably maymayguishi), two canoes and some tally marks were painted on the rocks there.

DAY 2 (9 miles): **Cache Bay** (Saganaga Lake), p. 130 rods, **Saganagons Lake**, p. 8 rods, **Slate Lake, Creek**, p. 5 rods, **Fran Lake**, p. 74 rods, **(Unnamed Lake)**, p. 18 rods, **Bell Lake**, p. 21 rods, **(Unnamed Lake)**, p. 4 rods, **(Unnamed Lake)**, p. 39 rods, **Other Man Lake**. Silver Falls is one of the most spectacular waterfalls in the Park. Take time to view it before crossing the portage. The best vantage point is from a short spur trail near the beginning of the portage. The portage, itself, follows a rocky trail that descends nearly all of the way from Cache Bay to Saganagons Lake, dropping most steeply at the end.

In the narrow canyon between Cache Bay and Saganagons Lake is the site of a reputed Indian massacre. Legends tell how a Cree war party set out to attack an Ojibwa village in present Quetico Park. The Ojibwa braves, alerted to the impending attack, evacuated their village. Finding the village empty, the Cree warriors turned homeward and passed through the narrow canyon, where the Ojibwa tribe waited to ambush them. The Cree were nearly annihilated. Nearby, on the shore of Cache Bay, Ojibwa women took refuge in caves during the massacre.

As you paddle northwest from the Silver Falls portage, be alert for a tiny channel that offers a shortcut to your next portage. This passage saves about a mile of paddling on Saganagons Lake. Near that channel is the site of a small mining operation that drilled back in 1920. A cabin was built next to the lake, and the mine was reported to be a ten-minute walk back into the woods. Equipment was brought in from the Gunflint Trail. Drill bits, however, would not cut through the rock, so the rig was abandoned at the end of the year. Nothing remains where the cabin once stood.

The creek between Slate and Fran lakes should be navigable almost all of the way to Fran. A short rapids and a beaver dam, however, necessitate either a 5-rod ''liftover,'' or wet feet from walking your canoe up through the trickle.

The portage out of Fran Lake climbs steeply for the first 52 rods, before descending

Rapids below Silver Falls

to an unnamed lake. The following trail, too, is steep at the beginning. The 4-rod "lift-over" is steeply uphill, and so is the first three rods of the 39-rod trail to Other Man Lake.

Benny Ambrose, a gold prospector who lived on Ottertrack Lake until his death in 1982, once reported seeing two huge copper kettles next to Bell Lake. At that time, they were covered with big sheets of birch bark. The Indians apparently used the kettles to make maple syrup, having brought them in by dog sled from Grand Portage.

There is a nice, large campsite just around the bend from the portage to Other Man Lake. Walleyes, northern pike and trout inhabit the lake. A Great Blue Heron colony, with eight nests, has been reported on a small island there.

DAY 3 (10 miles): **Other Man Lake**, p. 49 rods, **This Man Lake**, p. 32 rods, **No Man Lake**, p. 101 rods, **That Man Lake**, p. 136 rods, **Sheridan Lake.** This Man and That Man lakes are bordered on the northwest by ridges that tower as much as 150 feet above the lakes. During our long journey down This Man Lake, in June of 1984, my wife and I observed a cow moose and her calf swimming across the lake. Others have also reported moose sightings in this area.

There are two portages between This Man and No Man lakes. The one on the left (south side of the creek) is best and shortest, descending rather steeply to No Man Lake. The other trail begins on the north side of the creek, climbs for a few rods, and then descends to No Man for a total distance of 60 rods. Neither the 101-rod portage nor the 136-rod portage is difficult, though the latter has its slight ups and downs. It bypasses a scenic waterfall near the southwest end of That Man Lake.

A nice, large campsite is located on a point near the end of the 136-rod portage trail. It's what I call a "double bungalow — a two-decker campsite, with two tent sites on each level (great for parties in which half the group snores!). Sheridan Lake contains trout and northern pike.

DAY 4 (8 miles): **Sheridan Lake**, p. 15 rods, **Carp Lake**, p. 16 rods, **Knife River**, p. 15 rods, **Seed Lake**, p. 15 rods, **Knife River**, p. 75 rods, **Knife Lake.** After a steep drop down to Carp Lake from Sheridan, the rest of the portages are uphill, around rapids in the Knife River. Depending on the water's depth, most of the gentle rapids can be walked or lined up without too much difficulty. Only twice must you lift your canoe and gear — once around a low falls, and later over a small dam. This time-worn logging dam, at the top of the last rapids, was built just after the turn of the century. Now there is little remaining. If "old-timers" are correct, there may have been other dams along the Knife River at one time, between Seed and Carp lakes and between Carp and Birch lakes.

Near the southwest end of Knife Lake, on three small islands in U.S. waters lives the "rootbeer lady." Dorothy Molter has lived at her "Isle of Pines" alone for most of her 77 years. But she is seldom alone during the summer months, when literally thousands of admiring canoeists drop by to meet the legendary woman who makes and sells homemade rootbeer (ice-cold!) for thirsty canoeists. By exemption from federal law, she is the only person allowed to live in the Bouundary Waters Canoe Area Wilderness.

At the junction of the South Arm with the main part of Knife Lake is a hill on the U.S. peninsula known as Thunder Point. An 80-rod climb to the summit will be rewarded by a splendid panorama of the international boundary waters from over 150 feet above the lake. Plan to camp in the vicinity of Thunder Point.

This crystal-clear lake is home for trout, smallmouth bass, northern pike and walleyes.

DAY 5 (13 miles): **Knife Lake**, p. 5 rods, **Ottertrack Lake**, p. 80 rods, **Swamp Lake**, p. 3 rods, **Saganaga Lake.** Ottertrack Lake is a beautiful, long and slender lake, bordered by majestic cliffs and hills towering more than 200 feet above the lake. According to Indian legend, the tracks of an otter are embedded in the rock face of one of the cliffs.

Monument Portage is not named for its height or excessive difficulty. There is a large steel international boundary marker in the middle of the trail.

Plan to camp in the sheltered southwest end of Saganaga Lake, just beyond the short portage from Swamp Lake. There are several campsites in the vicinity, including one large site on the tip of the second peninsula east of the portage.

DAY 6 (14 miles): **Saganaga Lake.** With no portages this day, you should have no difficulty making it back to the landing in good time.

"2nd falls" in Falls Chain

Entry Point 73 — Falls Chain

Daily Quota: 2
Use Level: Heavy

LOCATION: The Falls Chain begins at the northwest corner of Saganagons Lake, seven miles (by air) north of the Cache Bay Ranger Station. For canoeists, it is an eighteen-mile journey across two large lakes and two portages, from the Saganaga Lake access road.

DESCRIPTION: In the short span of only four airline miles between Saganagons Lake and Kawnipi Lake are eight lovely waterfalls that, together, plunge nearly 100 feet. Aptly called the Falls Chain, these turbulent waters constitute the upper flowage of the Maligne River, which eventually flows all of the way to Lac La Croix on the west edge of Quetico Park. A system of large and small lakes, winding channels, serene pools and thunderous whitewater, this continuous waterway forms the northern perimeter of Hunter's Island. Originally called the "Back Trail", it is an historic route, used first by Sioux and Chippewa Indians, then by French and English explorers and fur traders, and most recently by Canadian loggers. Today, it is still one of the most popular canoe routes through the interior of Quetico Provincial Park.

Accordingly, if you plan to take a canoe trip using this entry point, make your reservation early. With only two groups allowed to enter each day, the Falls Chain "books up" early.

Route #31: The K-K-K Loop
(Kawnipi-Kahshahpiwi-Knife)

8 Days, 105 Miles, 26 Lakes, 2 Rivers, 3 Creeks, 37 Portages

DIFFICULTY: Challenging
FISHER MAPS: F-19, F-26, F-25, F-18, F-10, F-11
HIGHLIGHTS: Silver Falls, Indian pictographs, 8 waterfalls, virgin stands of red and white pine, rootbeer lady

Introduction: This scenic route might also be called the "not-much-time-to-fish loop." Completed in only eight days, you will have averaged between thirteen and fourteen miles per day. Any group will enjoy this big loop, but not every group can paddle 105 miles comfortably in just eight days. If you cannot portage all your gear in just one trip, if you want to fish extensively along the way, or if you are not a particularly strong paddler, you would be wise to add one or two days to your itinerary. Ten miles per day is a much more practical schedule for many trippers. For a good, strong, experienced group of paddlers, however, this route may be just what the doctor ordered.

From the Cache Bay Ranger Station, you will first paddle to the northeast end of Cache Bay. After viewing spectacular Silver Falls at your first portage, you will paddle to the north end of Saganagons Lake, where you will begin your journey down the Falls Chain to Kawnipi Lake. After paddling the entire length of Kawnipi Lake, to its northwest end, you will then steer a southerly course and follow the Kahshahpiwi Creek flowage, through Cairn, Sark and Keefer lakes, all the way to Kahshahpiwi Lake. From the east shore of Kahshahpiwi Lake, you will then climb over your most difficult portage to McNiece Lake. A chain of smaller lakes and streams will lead you south to big Basswood Lake. From Basswood's easternmost bay, you will paddle northeast on a scenic series of international border lakes back to your origin at Saganaga Lake.

Most of the thirty-seven portages are squeezed into just five days, averaging seven portages per day. If you are not in top physical condition, that's a rugged itinerary! Fortunately, though, only two of the portages are longer than 100 rods; most are less than fifty rods.

DAY 1 (13 miles): **Saganaga Lake, Cache Bay** (Saganaga Lake). (See comments for DAY 1, Route #30.)

DAY 2 (13 miles): **Cache Bay** (Saganaga Lake), p. 130 rods, **Saganagons Lake**, p. 75 rods, **Saganagons Lake, Maligne River**, p. 50 rods, **River**, p. 17 rods, **River**, p. 7 rods, **River**, p. 32 rods, **River**, p. 56 rods, **River**, p. 48 rods, **Kenny Lake**, p. 4 rods, **Kawnipi Lake**. (See paragraphs 2-4 of comments for DAY 3, Route #27, and comments for DAY 4, Route #27.)

DAY 3 (13 miles): **Kawnipi Lake**. (See comments for DAY 5, Route #27.)

DAY 4 (13 miles): **Kawnipi Lake**, p. 10 rods, **Kahshahpiwi Creek**, p. 4 rods, **Creek**, p. 40 rods, **Creek**, p. 20 rods, **Cairn Lake**, p. 84 rods, **Kahshahpiwi Creek, Sark Lake**, p. 76 rods, **Keefer Lake**, p. 27 rods, **Kahshahpiwi Lake**. If you are a whitewater enthusiast, that first 10-rod portage may not be necessary. It bypasses a short set of rapids that can usually be easily run, when the water conditions are suitable. Be sure to scout it first!

You will be going upstream after that. Nevertheless, you may be able to walk or line your canoe up the small rapids draining Cairn Lake (20-rod portage).

Nowhere else in Quetico Park is there a route as straight as that of Kahshahpiwi Creek and the lakes it connects. Steep ridges border Keefer and Kahshahpiwi lakes, where adjacent hills tower more than 200 feet above the waterway.

Plan to camp at the north end of Kahshahpiwi Lake, in it, anglers will find trout, walleyes, northern pike and smallmouth bass.

DAY 5 (12 miles): **Kahshahpiwi Lake**, p. 164 rods, **McNiece Lake**, p. 27 rods, **(Unnamed Lake)**, p. 20 rods, **Yum Yum Lake, Creek, Armin Lake**, p. 55 ords, **Grey Lake**, p. 128 rods, **(Unnamed Lake)**, p. 80 rods, **Shade Lake**, p. 4 rods, **Creek, Pond**, p. 9 rods, **West Lake**, p. 12 rods, **South Lake**, p. 14 rods, **North Bay** (Basswood Lake). By anybody's standards, this is one rough day! Starting off the parade of eleven portages is the longest and roughest carry of the whole route. From Kahshahpiwi Lake the trail climbs steeply at first, surmounting a 200-foot ridge en route to McNiece Lake. From that point on, nothing will seem too difficult.

Your efforts will soon be rewarded. According to Shan Walsh, Park Naturalist, the best stand of virgin red and white pines in all of Quetico Park is found around McNiece Lake and the nameless lake just east of McNiece.

Near the north end of a bay in Shade Lake is another display of Indian rock paintings. (See the map for the exact location.) There you will see the faded remnants of two abstract thunderbird symbols. To the Indians, a thunderbird was an enormous, supernatural bird that could produce thunder, lightning and rain. Keep your raincoat handy . . .

Plan to camp on one of the island campsites at the northeast end of North Bay. Even on an island, be sure to take precautions to avoid bear problems. In 1984, there was a pesky bear making a nuisance of himself in this area. (See Making Your Camp Bear-able.)

Anglers will have plenty of fish to cast a line at in North Bay. Basswood Lake contains trout, walleyes, northern pike, smallmouth and largemouth bass, black crappies, perch and assorted pan fish.

DAY 6 (13 miles): **North Bay** (Basswood Lake), p. 30 rods, **Burke Creek,** p. 16 rods, **Burke Lake,** p. 84 rods, **Bayley Bay** (Basswood Lake), **Inlet Bay** (Basswood Lake), p. 20 rods, **Sucker Lake, Birch Lake,** p. 30 rods, **Carp Lake.** There are two routes available between North Bay and Burke Creek. If you pass to the east side of the large island at the south end of North Bay, the first portage you will come to is 30 rods in length, following the east branch of the creek. If, on the other hand, you proceed further west in North Bay, past a small peninsula (across from a small island that is southwest of the large island), you will find an 11-rod portage to the west branch of the same creek. If you take this route, however, there will be another short portage (9 rods) just above the junction of the creek's two branches. The 30-rod trail bypasses all of this, allowing you to put in just above the second set of rapids.

After the portage to Bayley Bay, you will be on a busy route where motorboats (up to 25 horsepower) are allowed on the U.S. side of the international boundary. Moose Lake, located only three lakes south of Prairie Portage, is the most popular entry point in all of the Boundary Waters Canoe Area Wilderness (U.S.) Once you paddle through the narrow channel from Sucker Lake to Birch Lake, however, you will leave the noisy motorboats behind. Since January 1, 1984, motors are no longer allowed on the U.S. side of Birch and Knife lakes. Most of the BWCAW canoe traffic will head northwest from Sucker Lake to Basswood Lake or east from Newfound Lake to Ensign Lake. A good deal of traffic, however, will continue along the border route to Carp Lake and up the Knife River to Knife Lake.

A nice campsite is located next to the base of the rapids, where the Knife River flows into Carp Lake. Carp Lake contains trout, northern, perch, smallmouth bass and walleyes.

DAY 7 (14 miles): **Carp Lake,** p. 16 rods, **Knife River,** p. 15 rods, **Seed Lake,** p. 15 rods, **Knife River,** p. 75 rods, **Knife Lake,** p. 5 rods, **Ottertrack Lake.** (See comments for DAY 2, Route #27.)

DAY 8 (14 miles): **Ottertrack Lake,** p. 80 rods, **Swamp Lake,** p. 3 rods, **Saganaga Lake.** Fortunately, Monument Portage is not named for its height or excessive difficulty. There are three bronze international boundary markers in the middle of the trail. But the portage does have some fairly steep grades, and a swamp at the east end must be crossed via a log ''bridge.''

Another Route Suggestion

8-DAY Loop: By reversing Route #29, you may enjoy the superb 88-mile loop through one of the least-traveled waterways in this part of Quetico Park. Starting out in the same direction as Route #31, you will first paddle to the northwest end of Saganagons Lake and begin your journey down the Falls Chain. Before you reach Little Falls, however, you will leave the Maligne River and paddle across Wet Lake to McEwen Lake. At the south end of McEwen, then, you will follow McEwen Creek and a chain of small, lightly-traveled lakes southwest to Louisa Lake. At the base of Louisa Lake, you will portage around lovely Louisa Falls, and then proceed to the Meadows Portages, which lead to Sunday Lake. From Sunday Lake, you will portage to Basswood Lake. From that point, you will follow the popular border lakes northeast, all of the way back to your origin at Saganaga Lake. It is a splendid route that covers less mileage than Route #31, but includes many of the same highlights. (See Route #29 for details.)

APPENDIX

Routes Categorized by Duration

Duration*	Route #	Entry Point Name (and #)
3 Days	# 1	Baptism Creek (11)
3 Days	# 5	Batchewaung Lake (21)
3 Days	# 8	Lerome Lake (22)
4 Days	# 3	Pickerel Lake (12)
4 Days	#10	Cirrus Lake (31)
4 Days	#12	Quetico Lake (32)
4 Days	#19	Bottle River (44)
4 Days	#24	Kahshahpiwi Lake (53)
4 Days	#25	Agnes Lake (61)
5 Days	# 6	Batchewaung Lake (21)
5 Days	#13	Quetico Lake (32)
5 Days	#14	Quetico Lake (32)
5 Days	#21	Sarah Lake (52)
5 Days	#26	Agnes Lake (61)
6 Days	# 2	Baptism Creek (11)
6 Days	# 7	Batchewaung Lake (21)
6 Days	#11	Cirrus Lake (31)
6 Days	#15	Threemile Lake (41)
6 Days	#16	Maligne River (42)
6 Days	#18	McAree Lake (43)
6 Days	#28	Carp Lake (62)
6 Days	#30	Man Chain Lakes (72)
7 Days	# 4	Pickerel Lake (12)
7 Days	# 9	Lerome Lake (22)
7 Days	#15	Threemile Lake (41)
7 Days	#19	Bottle River (44)
7 Days	#23	Kahshahpiwi Lake (53)
8 Days	#16	Maligne River (42)
8 Days	#17	Maligne River (42)
8 Days	#20	Basswood River (51)
8 Days	#29	Knife Lake (71)
8 Days	#31	Falls Chain (73)
9 Days	#15	Threemile Lake (41)
9 Days	#17	Maligne River (42)
9 Days	#18	McAree Lake (43)
9 Days	#19	Bottle River (44)
9 Days	#22	Sarah Lake (52)

10 Days	#16	Maligne River (42)
11 Days	#17	Maligne River (42)
11 Days	#18	McAree Lake (43)
13 Days	#27	Carp Lake (62)

---

*Note: Durations of the trips listed are without layover days, side trips, or extensive "leisure" time for fishing. They are the actual number of days (minimum) required to complete their respective routes. Plan accordingly!

The "Garden Walk"

INDEX

INDEX (continued)

INDEX (continued)

Basswood Lake Pictographs

Horse Portage, Basswood Lake